EXECUTIVE SECRETS

EXECUTIVE SECRETS

COVERT ACTION AND THE PRESIDENCY

WILLIAM J. DAUGHERTY

Foreword by
MARK BOWDEN

THE UNIVERSITY PRESS OF KENTUCKY

Publication of this volume was made possible in part by a grant
from the National Endowment for the Humanities.

Scholarly publisher for the Commonwealth,
serving Bellarmine University, Berea College, Centre
College of Kentucky, Eastern Kentucky University,
The Filson Historical Society, Georgetown College,
Kentucky Historical Society, Kentucky State University,
Morehead State University, Murray State University,
Northern Kentucky University, Transylvania University,
University of Kentucky, University of Louisville,
and Western Kentucky University.

Editorial and Sales Offices: The University Press of Kentucky
663 South Limestone Street, Lexington, Kentucky 40508-4008
www.kentuckypress.com

The Library of Congress has cataloged the hardcover edition as follows:

Daugherty, William J., 1947–
Executive secrets : covert action and the presidency / William J. Daugherty.
p. cm.
Includes bibliographical references and index.
ISBN 0-8131-2334-8 (hardcover : alk. paper)
1. United States. Central Intelligence Agency. 2. Intelligence service—United
States—History—20th century. 3. Presidents—United States—History—20th century.
4. United States—Foreign relations—1945–1989. 5. United States—Foreign
relations—1989– 6. Espionage—United States—History—20th century. I. Title.
JK468.I6D38 2004
327.1273—dc22
2004006073

Paper ISBN-10: 0-8131-9161-0
Paper ISBN-13: 978-0-8131-9161-4

This book is printed on acid-free recycled paper meeting
the requirements of the American National Standard
for Permanence in Paper for Printed Library Materials.

Manufactured in the United States of America.

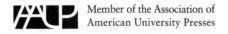

Member of the Association of
American University Presses

FOR SUSAN

CONTENTS

FOREWORD

Those of us who have lived long enough ought to be able to summon a sense of humor regarding the country's current impatience with the quality of its Central Intelligence Agency. Ever since the Islamo-fascist attacks on the United States on September 11, 2001, the nation's attitude toward its intelligence community has been one of disappointment, if not scorn. Why didn't we know? Why hadn't we acted more aggressively to prevent the attacks? Why were we so unprepared to respond? Why did we lack the language skills, contacts, influence, and ability to infiltrate the deadly cells of our enemy? Just yesterday (as I write this in April 2004) George Tenet, the current besieged CIA director, provoked gasps of disbelief by stating that it will take five years for the Agency to build a global human intelligence network suitable for combating ongoing terrorist threats.

I can remember a time when the idea of expanding the CIA's reach and power would have provoked outrage. In the wake of Vietnam and Watergate and the revelations that various presidents have spied on the American people, a venerable posse was formed that damn near lynched the entire intelligence community. The very idea of spying and acting covertly became disreputable. Conspiratorialists found evidence of CIA meddling under every rock. For most of my adult life, any mention of the spy Agency has prompted suspicion of unlawful meddling, dirty tricks, scandal, and a kind of bullet-headed redneck American approach to foreign policy.

Foreword

At its height, hatred and distrust of the CIA is wildly illogical. Critics at once assault the CIA for incompetence and omnipotence. It is an Agency made up of fools who somehow manage to deviously manipulate events in every corner of the globe. You would think that it would be one or the other. I recently interviewed a fundamentalist "scholar" in Tehran who argued—with a straight face and a strong voice—that the CIA was responsible for installing and preserving the Shah, for engineering his overthrow and secretly planning his return, for propping up the provisional government that followed the coup, and for fomenting the national unrest that ultimately undermined and toppled it. And, oh yes, it was the CIA that secretly engineered the takeover of the American embassy in Tehran in 1979, which resulted in fifty-two Americans being held hostage for more than a year.

"Aren't some of these things mutually contradictory?" I asked. "For instance, why would the CIA wish to foment trouble for a provisional government it was secretly supporting?"

The scholar smiled sweetly. It was necessary, he said, to view the world through the clear lens of Islam to see the logic of these things.

"The CIA, they just enjoy making trouble for us," he explained.

William Daugherty has more than a passing interest in that last story in particular. As a CIA officer, he was one of those held hostage in Iran during those fourteen months. Before and after that difficult period, his one reluctant turn in the national spotlight, he served a long and distinguished career in the Agency. With this book, he has done us all a tremendous service by attempting to rescue the Agency from the myths, both well-meaning and malevolent, that shape our understanding of it. The CIA is neither an all-seeing, omnipotent secret force, nor is it the blundering "rogue elephant" that was once deplored by the late senator Frank Church.

The CIA is an extremely useful, necessary tool of foreign policy and national defense in a very complex and dangerous world. The collapse of the Soviet Union and end of the cold war, by eliminating the risk of all-out nuclear war, has greatly diminished the level of danger we all face in our lives. But the resulting complexity of world affairs and the unleashing of unpredictable forces constrained by that half-century standoff have made the world *feel* a lot more dangerous and have made defending ourselves, in some ways, more difficult. National defense no longer rests on a cornerstone of Intercontinental Ballistic Missiles (ICBM) and nuclear warheads; it rests on our ability to know, to understand, to predict, and—when the moment is right—to act. In the twenty-first century, intelligence needs to become as high a priority as our nuclear arsenal used to be. We are fighting enemies without a state, without an army or physical infrastructure, without even a clearly defined hierarchy of command. We need the best global human intelligence network ever created, and we need it yesterday. We need the capability of acting in the world with an artful subtlety that matches our unparalleled brute force. Now more than ever, we need a healthy, effective CIA.

America has always had mixed feelings about covert action. It runs counter to our national ideals of openness and democracy. But from the first years of our nation, from George Washington forward, we have recognized that survival in a dangerous world requires it. Every president in our history has benefited from the ability to exert influence quietly, to throw the weight of American interest on the scale without announcing it. There are times when open American involvement can defeat a very worthy goal. Daugherty's book provides examples of successful covert operations in the recent past. It is a useful primer to the quiet side of modern American history, from efforts to undermine the growing influence of communist political parties in Western Europe to the quiet support for the Solidarity movement in Poland.

The CIA has made mistakes, but not so many as its critics allege. Some of the most famous "sins" of the Agency are commonly presented with selective hindsight and vigorous supposition. Every action taken has consequences that cannot be foreseen—toppling Mossadeq in Iran led eventually to the Ayatollah Khomeini, and arming the mujahadeen in Afghanistan lead to Al Qaeda. But as Daugherty points out, "Presidents are not clairvoyant . . . they act on what they perceive to be the best interests for the country and the world at that time and are only able to hope that history will prove them wise." Leaving Mossadeq alone in 1953 might have led to the flowering of democracy in Iran, or it might also have led to a growing communist influence, to the loss of sensitive monitoring bases along the Iran-Soviet border (needed to enforce SALT II), to a Soviet invasion, or even to a world war. Such possibilities, easily dismissed today but feared at the time, may have been more catastrophic than the Mullah-ocracy that has smothered freedom in Iran for a quarter of a century. Likewise, failing to help Islamic fighters against the Soviet invasion of Afghanistan in 1979 might have stunted the growth of Islamo-fascist terrorism, but it might also have prolonged the power and influence of the Soviet state. I'll take the threat of an occasional terrorist attack over the threat of an all-out nuclear exchange any time.

The truth is, no one can see into the future, and no one can say how history would have turned out if our nation had acted differently. In the majority of cases, as Daugherty points out, covert action has been undramatic, successful, and clearly aligned with our national values. These are not the kind of stories that make headlines, and even the stories that are newsworthy are rarely discovered and told. This book ought to dispel some of the fog that obscures our understanding of the CIA and that prompts the gigantic mood swings in our attitude toward intelligence gathering and covert actions.

We Americans are exceptionally vulnerable to spying and terrorism, but we are also exceptionally capable of swimming in those waters. We are an amalgam of every culture, every language, every religion, and every race on the planet. We are masters of telecommunications. We are rich, smart, ingenious, and brave. We are a nation founded on universal ideals that continue to inspire most of humanity. We ought to be able to penetrate, eavesdrop, analyze, and sway any state or group on this planet. Let's get to it.

Mark Bowden
Author of *Black Hawk Down:*
A Story of Modern War

PREFACE

In discharging his constitutional responsibility for the conduct of foreign relations and for ensuring the security of the United States, the President may find it necessary that activities conducted in support of national foreign policy objectives abroad be planned and executed so that the role of the United States government is not apparent or acknowledged publicly.

National Security Decision Directive-286 (1987)[1]

Before an author writes yet another book on a subject that has already seen numerous works in print, there ought to be some justification for it. What new perspective will be explored? What new information will be shared with the reader? If the answer is little or none, pen should probably not be put to paper in the first place. Books on the Central Intelligence Agency (CIA) in general, as well as exposés of the Agency's controversial covert action programs in particular, are numerous and readily available to interested readers. Why, then, this volume?

The primary objective is to show definitively that covert action programs managed by the CIA since its inception in 1947 have been done so at the express direction of the presidents of the United States. Many Americans are reluctant to believe that operations they may personally find objectionable for whatever reason were in fact explicit presidential policy. These skeptics would much rather cling to the myth that the CIA runs a rogue foreign policy beyond the ken and control of the man elected to be a moral, as well as political, leader of the nation. The reluctance to accept the truth may also lie partly in the unease that citizens in liberal democracies feel over hidden policies and governmental action, preferring instead to see "overt influences" as the engine of foreign policy. Regardless of motive, willful disregard of the truth produces a distorted history of our country's role in the world, a situation that all concerned Americans should deplore.[2]

It certainly isn't as though the nature of presidential authority over the CIA and covert action programs is so obscure or hidden in secrecy that the truth is unknowable. The multiple congressional investigations of the 1970s and 1980s "should have dispelled any notion that there was no [presidential] control over covert action, but they did not."[3] Indeed, these investigations have conclusively proven that the CIA acted well within the general guidelines established by the president and the National Security Council (NSC), particularly with the most controversial activities and reversals of foreign governments—even with regard to assassination plots. Additionally, a sizeable body of declassified materials and other documentary evidence now available in open sources both confirms and reinforces the results of the congressional investigations. But there still remain not only skeptics but unrelenting critics who continue to assert—harshly, without equivocation, and despite the objective evidence—that the CIA is a body independent of the president's control, inevitably acting in ways inimical to the interests of the United States.

Why should the unceasing harping and misrepresentations, deliberate or otherwise, put forth by critics matter? They matter greatly because the continual repetition of erroneous or misleading material, when treated as immutable fact, precludes honest answers and a fulsome understanding about how and why signal events in our nation's life occurred, and what these events meant to our national interest.[4]

They matter, too, because the Soviet Union and its foreign intelligence service, the Komitet Gozudarstevennoye Bezopasnosti (KGB), waged for four decades a relentless disinformation program against the United States and the West to undermine democratic ideals and the United States's credibility as the leader of the Free World; to discredit democratic institutions; and to promote the ideology and objectives of Communism—a decadent political system responsible for the cruel deaths of perhaps as many as one hundred million people worldwide, wherever it took root, between 1917 and 1991. The most successful of these programs (called "active measures" by the Soviets) include fabricated assertions that the CIA participated in John F. Kennedy's assassination; that orphans in Third World countries were being used as sources of body parts for children of wealthy Americans needing transplants; that the United States was behind the assassination of Indian prime minister Indira Gandhi; and that the AIDS virus was created in U.S. laboratories for use against Third World populations. The KGB's campaign of lies, deceits, and calumnies ultimately failed in its strategic objectives, but these and other allegations, which served to make America the enemy and placed blame on America for the ills of the world, still resonate in the Third World and within those who cannot abide constitutional democracies. To the extent that Soviet disinformation has generated a mistrust in the American government by its own citizens and created circumstances in which these citizens hold no hesitation in believing the worst about their own country, however, the KGB can indeed claim some measure of success. One result of this willingness to view the government's actions in a negative light is that "Americans have a distorted view of covert action" as a legitimate tool of statecraft. A more serious issue is that this "distorted view" causes Americans to question their government's activities and purposes more than is merited.[5]

A second objective is to present a cogent (but, I hope, a not too pedagogical) explanation of what covert action is and, as important, what it isn't. Individuals who presume to sit in judgment of sensitive intelligence operations and those who conduct these programs should do so on an informed basis. This is especially the case when the self-proclaimed judges do so before a national audience. It's not important whether they agree with the utility of covert action or even whether they like it, but out of respect for simple fairness and accuracy the critics should at least understand what it is they are critiquing. This is not an unreasonable demand, for there is already a plethora of erroneous material on covert action policies, programs, and methodology in the public domain, and no justification to add to it. Yet, as this work will show, there are opponents of covert action, both in and out of government, who are nonetheless unable to define covert action, outline its limits, or identify occasions when it might be appropriately and favorably used. Even less do these carpers seem aware that the history of the United States was greatly affected by covert actions undertaken by American icons such as Washington, Jefferson, Madison, and Monroe. Likewise, it seems that few can name a successful covert action program (should they actually seek to find one), although the successes are more numerous than realized and the failures fewer than usually asserted.

Third, an accurate historical record of post–World War II foreign policy demands the inclusion of covert action operations, and so those writing the histories should be able to identify which presidents were successful in using covert action and which weren't. Several chief executives relied on covert action as a mainstay of their foreign policy programs—among them Eisenhower, Kennedy, and Reagan, with varying degrees of success—and full comprehension of American foreign policy must recognize the contributions of covert action. During these administrations, CIA covert action contributed to the fall of the Soviet Union and the end of the cold war nuclear nightmare, while enabling millions of oppressed ethnic and religious minorities to sustain their cultural identities under Soviet domination through means such as Radio Free Europe/Radio Liberty and the publication of written materials for infiltration behind the Iron Curtain. There was also assistance to Western European trade unions and political parties to counter Soviet-supported political parties, as well as the extensive publication of literary and political journals, and sponsorship of dozens of conferences to undermine the supposed attractions of the Soviet Union in the 1950s and 1960s. It's hard to imagine any American being upset over these actions of the CIA, which were undertaken in response to the policies and directives of the president of the United States.

In the 1990s, CIA covert action programs assisted in the capture of major international terrorists such as Che Guevara, Abimael Guzman (head of Peru's Sendaro Luminoso), and "Carlos the Jackal."[6] CIA officers engineered the capture and extradition to the United States of over fifty major terrorists between 1983 and 1995 and disrupted literally hundreds of acts of terrorism over the past thirty years, including some from Osama bin-Ladin's Al-Qaeda organization. CIA paramilitary elements supported the United States's military operations and evacuations of American citizens in danger zones in Somalia, Liberia, the Persian Gulf, and the Balkans.[7]

But even the most cursory review of the media and literature on intelligence reveals that the public is much more likely to hear about the CIA's failures (real or otherwise) than it is of the Agency's successes.[8] This unbalanced emphasis on failure is harmful as it stimulates a misleading impression that covert action always and inevitably leads to folly. It also contributes to an inaccurate public record of the programs themselves and of the overt foreign policies they supported. Perhaps not as noticeable but still of import, the concentration on failure to the exclusion of success (or even of factors legitimately mitigating failures) has undermined the institutional reputation of the CIA and of its cadre of professional intelligence officers who, at presidential behest, managed the programs and conducted the operations.

With respect to the reputations of the Agency and the dedicated civil servants who work there, it matters greatly that the historical record shows the meaningful and often courageous contributions they have made to American national security. Further, for the sake of their professional reputations, it is important that history reflects that many of the most controversial covert action programs and worst failures of the Agency occurred not because the Agency proposed flawed programs, urged their inception, and then ineptly managed them, but instead because presidents insisted on pursuing politically risky—or, in a few instances, utterly foolhardy—programs against the sound and repeated advice of the intelligence professionals.[9] That said, the reader may be assured that this volume is not exculpatory of every allegation against the Agency or of covert action. Like any large bureaucratic organization, the CIA has made and will continue to make regrettable, and in many cases avoidable, errors. However, it should not be required to shoulder the burden of blame for programs and events for which others rightfully bear the responsibility, or for programs that have been wrongly characterized.

Arguably, many of the Agency's alleged missteps have occurred (and more will occur in the future, to be sure) because the intelligence business is at heart the business of taking risks. No matter how closely calculated or thoroughly analyzed these risks are, unforeseen—and often unforeseeable—complications that limit the odds of success inevitably insert themselves into even the best planned operations. Another inherent, often overlooked characteristic of the intelligence profession is the human factor. Murphy's Law, the inability to guard against the arbitrary, looms over every intelligence program and leaves case officers in the field to cope with random events they cannot control. Furthermore, the nature of the presidential directives that generated these programs in the first place should not be ignored. When political figures direct that ultra-sensitive, exceptionally high-risk programs be undertaken against the studied advice of the career intelligence professional, then ultimate failure should surprise no one.

There is one last reason for this book. I am able to add, however marginally, to the understanding of covert action as a tool of presidential statecraft through personal experience with covert action programs and policy. In the late 1980s, at the acme of the

CIA's cold war covert action experience, I spent two years on the Evaluation and Plans Staff (renamed the Operations and Management Staff during that period) of the CIA's Directorate of Operations (DO), where my principal responsibility was to oversee, on a continuing basis, every covert action operation run against the Soviet Union and Eastern Europe. This oversight included analyzing the programs' operational effectiveness by assessing compliance with the policy set forth by the White House and by joint CIA–State Department guidelines, evaluating observance of relevant federal laws and internal CIA regulations, and determining whether budgetary requirements were being satisfied.

I remained informed in detail by reading the daily operational activity in command-channel and, upon occasion, back-channel cable traffic. I talked daily, often several times each day, to the headquarters desk officers running the covert action operations; met frequently with the senior managers of the operational line component responsible for managing the operations; and sat in meetings with the most senior officers of the DO. I attended policy-oriented meetings and read memoranda for the record of many other such meetings, including those that occurred at the White House and on Capitol Hill. I perused memos on congressional interaction with Agency officers on such issues as program budgets and operational successes, problems, and future plans. I wrote annual reviews of the individual programs and of the component responsible for managing the programs for the associate deputy director of operations (ADDO).

My final assignment in the Agency, in 1995 and 1996, also dealt with covert action, this time from a policy and process perspective. I was privy to all of the current covert action programs then in progress, maintained a repository of all Presidential Findings present and past, and provided guidance to officers faced with responding to White House requests for new or proposed covert action programs. I arranged and participated in all internal reviews of current and proposed programs; attended numerous other discussions of these programs at the division, directorate, and director of central intelligence (DCI) level; and represented the Agency at the White House on the Interagency Working Group for Covert Action. I gave numerous briefings to various military elements and other U.S. government agencies on the intelligence discipline of covert action. In sum, then, in this volume I believe I have something relevant to contribute to the understanding of covert action and its relationship to foreign policy and statecraft.

GENERAL COMMENTS ON CONTENT AND RESEARCH

This work focuses generally on the nature of the intelligence discipline of covert action and the decision-making processes post–World War II presidents employed to approve and review covert action programs. By necessity, the book offers merely a cursory overview of selected covert action programs, which are intended to serve only as examples of how individual presidents employed covert action as a tool of foreign policy statecraft. An astute reader might notice that a number of (alleged) covert action programs that have appeared in public sources (e.g., newspaper articles and books) have been omitted from this work. As a retired CIA officer, I was obligated to submit the manuscript to the CIA's Publications Review Board to insure that it did not include any classified data. Beyond that, as covert action programs are truly presidential programs, further review by the National Security Council (NSC) staff was mandated, rendering the review process doubly exacting. As a consequence, only programs that have been officially acknowledged by the U.S. government were permitted to be included, regardless of the publicity, or notoriety, of (alleged) programs that have appeared in open sources. No effort was made either to include or exclude programs based on their success or failure, or whether they were a credit to a president or an embarrassment. I have referenced as many programs as I was permitted to do by the review process; it's just that simple.

The requirement to submit the manuscript for multiple reviews also precluded the use of interviews from current, former, or retired intelligence and policy-level officials about individual covert action programs. Those most knowledgeable of particular programs would, for the most part, have had to contribute anonymously if they were to go beyond what little has been officially disclosed; otherwise, the material would have been excised and their careers possibly jeopardized. While academics and journalists may use anonymous sources with impunity, none of this material would survive a review of a manuscript by a former Agency officer. Due to a shortage of officially cleared documentary sources from the Reagan, Bush, and Clinton administrations, in 2001 I placed requests for the declassification of more than five thousand documents through the Freedom of Information Act. The request to the CIA was flatly and quickly denied. Requests to the Bush and Reagan presidential libraries are still in the queue awaiting the time when the overworked staffs can cull the documents from the files—following which time the CIA and NSC will review the documents for declassification. I do not expect to see the requested material anytime soon.

The reader who is looking for details of covert operations from the Korean and Vietnam wars or other conflicts will find only disappointment. Likewise, those seeking information on covert technical programs, like the U-2 and SR-71 or the MKULTRA project, will have to look elsewhere, for the scope of this book is limited to traditional peacetime covert action operations managed by the Directorate of Operations. Readers interested in covert operations in Southeast Asia, the Studies and Observation Group, and OpPlan 34-A are directed to the many books and articles on these subjects that have appeared during the past decade. Likewise, readers should seek additional information on technical programs from other sources, for these programs were neither covert action nor were they products of the Directorate of Operations.

ACKNOWLEDGMENTS

I am indebted to a number of people who assisted in various ways with the preparation of this manuscript. First, I wish to extend my immense gratitude to the wonderful folks at the University Press of Kentucky, present and past, who had a hand in the publication of this work. Included are Directors Ken Cherry and Steve Wrinn; Acquisition Editors John Zeigler, Joyce Harrison, and (especially) Gena Henry; and Manuscript Editor Nichole Lainhart. I am grateful to Nichole for passing me along to Robin Roenker, who did an absolutely masterful job as copy editor for the manuscript; I cannot thank her enough for her contributions, which were many and significant, to this effort. The talents and vision of the graphics department are manifestly obvious in the terrific dust jacket design. Working with the UPK has been a uniformly wonderful experience, and I feel very lucky to have had the opportunity to do so.

There were some two dozen academicians, former intelligence officers, and some who are both who read either parts or all of the manuscript at various intervals depending on what portions had been cleared at what times. They know who they are and that I appreciate their contributions.

At Armstrong Atlantic State University's Lane Library, research librarian Caroline Hopkinson again worked her magic in locating articles and documents that were essential to this volume, doing so with her inevitable cheerful enthusiasm and exceptional professionalism. I am, as always, grateful to Caro, and I am already looking forward to working with her on my next book.

Overdue thanks go to Matt Easterwood, a gifted baseball player and genuinely excellent student who steered his independent study courses on the presidency and American foreign policy in the direction of valued research for this book. Matt is one of the finest students whom I've had the privilege of mentoring, and I hope he learned as much from me as I did from him. I wish him all the best as he faces the rigors of law school.

I am especially indebted to the following: Hayden Peake, who may know more about the CIA than any living person. Hayden not only plowed through the manuscript in record time, providing insights and details that no one else could have, but also graciously reread portions of it in follow-up and was kind enough to answer what must have seemed to be a series of never-ending questions from the important to the trivial. Dr. Jeffery T. Richelson, of the National Security Archives at George Washington University's Gelman Library, interrupted his own full schedule several times to send useful documents and identify errors, adding much to the finished product. Jeff also provided much appreciated encouragement and support at every step. Dr. Roy Godson of Georgetown University likewise took time out from his busy agenda and generously proffered advice and encouragement. And Dr. John Stempel from the University of Kentucky Patterson School of Diplomacy and International Commerce reviewed the manuscript several times, providing essential guidance and enthusiastic support. The inspiration, assistance, and goodwill I received from these four eminent intelligence scholars will be valued long after the life of this book.

Needless to say (but I will anyway), I am deeply appreciative of the love and support received from my lovely wife, Susan, who accepted her all-too-frequent status as a "book widow" with great good humor—usually. I would promise that my next book won't be so demanding, but it probably will be. I apologize in advance. Visits from Kelly and Amy, while too infrequent, were always welcomed and fun respites from the computer; they never fail to bring joy into my life, and I am so immensely proud of them.

This is normally the place where the author accepts full responsibility for any and all errors in the manuscript. I would have no hesitation in doing that, but Stafford Thomas, in an astonishing act of unparalleled generosity, has blithely offered to serve as "the fall guy." At least that's how I remember the e-mail, so please direct all criticisms to him. What a sport.

INTRODUCTION

We have come to two basic conclusions. Our first is that
covert action inherently conflicts with . . . our democratic aspirations, not merely because it is secretive and
deceptive but because it is intended to avoid public accountability. . . . At the same time, the world remains a
dangerous place in which threats to the United States, its
interests, and its citizens continue to exist. . . . Therefore,
we also conclude that covert action may be justified when
a prospective threat creates a compelling national interest that cannot be met prudently by overt means alone.[1]

Twentieth-Century Fund

The intelligence discipline known as covert action has been employed as an instrument of statecraft by our nation's leaders
since Revolutionary days. It added significantly to our nation's
growth and security in the early years; served both ably and poorly
as a tool to contain the expansion of communism and to counter
Soviet adventurism on four continents during the cold war; and
enabled some peoples of the world to remain free and, undoubtedly, kept others under the foot of dictators for the four decades
that were the cold war, albeit in the cause of a greater good. Covert
action has been used cleverly and effectively by some presidents,

accomplishing much. It has also been used poorly—even ineptly—for the wrong reasons and in the wrong places by presidents who did not understand its limitations and weaknesses, creating disaster for the United States and its image as a world leader. This has resulted in Americans' understandable confusion about the value of covert action: "For a nation whose birth was assisted by successful covert operations—the secret provision of arms by the French . . . and brilliant deceptions by George Washington—America has traditionally evinced a profound ambiguity towards the hidden dimension of statecraft."[2]

There are well-meaning supporters who urge the application of covert action to an expansive range of foreign policy problems, and there are detractors who call for it to be banned, statutorily or otherwise, claiming that it is ineffective, counterproductive, immoral, or some combination thereof.[3] Both sides are wrong, simply because neither group fully understands what covert action is, what its limitations are, and when it is appropriate to employ it and when it's not. Unfortunately, adherents of both sides have also included more than a few senior U.S. government officials, whose lack of precision regarding covert action has led, at the least, to embarrassment for the United States and, at the worst, to crisis.[4]

Since the overthrow of the government of Iran in 1953—the first major post–World War II covert action program to become openly known—this tool of presidential statecraft has been the subject of a vast number of books, articles, and editorials. While this mountain of literature has attempted to enlighten—or to proselytize to—the American public about the positive or negative sides of covert action, the main result has been to generate a public record replete with errors and misconceptions about this intelligence discipline. There are understandable reasons for this problem (e.g., materials that remain classified), as well as reasons more perfidious. Some critics have deliberately distorted the record or facts in order to support their personal, anti-CIA agenda, despite clear and convincing evidence contrary to their assertions. This introduction will, inter alia, put forth some of the myths, mistakes, and misconceptions found in the literature on covert action, laying the foundation for the detailed examination of selected events in later chapters, so that they may be accurately and honestly evaluated. It is intended that when the reader reaches the end of the book, a balanced and infinitely more correct picture of covert action as a tool of presidential statecraft will have emerged.

THE MYTH OF THE "ROGUE ELEPHANT"

While the most serious or persistent of the myths revolving around covert action are discussed in chapter two, it is appropriate here to highlight the most prevalent misconception about covert action: namely, that covert action is initiated in isolation by the CIA and executed without the knowledge of either the White House or Congress. Stated more vividly, the Agency is asserted to be an independent actor acting out of control, without oversight by either branch of government, a "rogue elephant," in the (too) oft-repeated words of Senator Frank Church. At the time of this statement, Church was heading a senatorial investigation of the Agency, of which he was already a voluble critic; this particular criticism was uttered by Church at a well-attended press conference and has since been cited by a multitude of critics as evidence of Agency perfidy. It is noteworthy that Church was also a candidate for the presidency, engendering an obvious political connotation to the hearings. Unfortunately, the senator's final conclusion, included in his committee's written report but pointedly not broadcast to members of the media, is rarely mentioned. The CIA, Church determined, was not out of control but rather acted at the express personal command of the president. He could have added in regard to covert action—indeed, he was obligated to add, if he was concerned about airing the full truth—that the CIA had acted at presidential order even when Agency officers thought the program to be impossible, undesirable, or unwise.

Two interrelated myths allege that the CIA is enamored of covert action programs and that covert action constitutes a major portion of the Agency's budget and mission. Nothing could be further from reality. For the most part Agency officers in the DO, who manage the covert action programs, have always shied away from this side of the business as quickly as a pony shies from a rattlesnake. While it was bad enough that covert action was never career enhancing in the DO, there was an even more problematic drawback to these programs: they were just not exciting enough to draw the average street case officer. Covert action operations involving propaganda and political action were considered too "intellectual" by many field case officers, with far too much writing and far too little street work.

As for budgetary figures, one of the harsher critics (writing a decade ago) estimated that a reported $3.5 billion CIA budget was "on the far side of conservative," implying that it was much greater. He would be chagrined to know that his figure—wherever he found it—is much more accurate than he imagined.[5]

THERE IS SUCCESS, AND THEN THERE IS SUCCESS . . .

As this work does not concern itself much with the theoretical, it delves even less into the philosophical. Yet there is one question, one notion, that begs serious consideration: What, exactly, constitutes "success" in a program? One obvious response is that a successful outcome is one in which foreign policy objectives sought by the president are obtained. Perhaps the most successful covert action program regardless of standard of measure was the support of the Polish labor organization Solidarity during the 1980s and related operations to deter Soviet intervention in Poland, which eventually led to political reforms there. The Reagan administration's conviction that a democratic Poland would lead to a free Eastern Europe must be viewed as one of the most successful foreign policies ever, a combination of skillful overt diplomacy and methodical, resourceful, and imaginative covert action. The almost complete omission of this story in the writings of critics of covert action and the CIA is telling. Other clear successes of CIA covert action were the creation and use of Radio Free Europe and Radio Liberty, assistance to Western European trade unions and political parties to counter Soviet-supported internal political parties, the publication and infiltration of books and magazines behind the Iron Curtin, the clandestine exfiltration of Chinese dissidents after the Tiananmen Square massacre, and the capture of major international terrorists like "Carlos" Che Guevara, and Abimael Guzman.[6] Additional successes such as the destruction of several of the world's largest and deadliest narcotics cartels and the disruption or prevention of literally hundred of acts of terrorism through the 1980s and 1990s underscore the value of sound covert action programs to policy success.

A second, more parochial definition of success is having a program that is well managed from an operational standpoint—with no compromises, no tradecraft errors—regardless of whether or not the policy objectives are obtained. Others might deem an outcome successful only after observing the long-term results after a period of years. For example, the Iran and Guatemala programs, while at first seemingly successful, to many did not appear to be so twenty years later. Former staff director of the House Permanent Select Committee on Intelligence (HPSCI) Mark Lowenthal wonders, in addition, whether the "human costs" of a program should be considered as a measure of success and refrains from placing time limits on the evaluation. (For example, was Guatemala an unmitigated success regardless of what occurred during the next thirty years, or did it become less so as the death toll mounted over the decades?)[7]

Intelligence expert Dr. Angelo Codevilla points to one other measure of success: Has covert action actually made a significant difference in shape, nature, or condition of the world? He acknowledges that "American covert action has been perhaps the most important influence in the world since 1945," but he also asserts that "there is no evidence that, absent American covert action, the important conflicts of the 1940s and early 1950s, never mind those in subsequent years, would have turned out differently." He argues that many of the indigenous peoples who became enmeshed with CIA programs thusly exposed themselves to their enemies and suffered for it once the Americans left. Additionally, he asserts that covert action programs "fostered the growth of political parties and elites" around the globe "who do not wish American well."[8]

There is much truth to what Codevilla states, at least when the covert action programs considered are paramilitary programs. But when reviewing political action programs, the conclusions are arguably different, if for no other reason than there is no way of knowing what would have transpired had there been no American intervention. Would Italian democracy have been undermined in the 1940s and 1950s by Communist subversion if there had been no CIA counter-program? No one knows for certain, of course, and it is quite possible—even probable—that the only difference the political action operation made was to give the non-Communists a larger margin of victory. But what would have been the consequences not only for Italy but also for other European democracies with large Communist parties, such as France, had the Italian Communists in fact won either a majority or sizeable plurality? Could the United States as well as pro-democratic forces in Italy and throughout Europe have risked a Communist victory? If the United States had not supported a conservative Japanese party in the 1950s and 1960s, would a leftist government have evicted American military forces from that country? If so, what would that have meant for our defense posture in the Far East? Maybe nothing, but then again, maybe a great deal. Is that a risk the United States would or should have taken?

And consider Iran without the American intervention: would internal unrest under Mossadegh have become sufficiently severe due to the economic consequences of Britain's oil boycott against Iran to have invited Soviet intervention in Iranian politics, if not the reoccupation of Iranian territory (which we know the Soviets desperately desired)? If the latter had occurred, what would the United States have done then? In 1952 Truman signed NSC-136 and NSC-136/1, which stated as a matter of policy that a Soviet invasion of Iran would be cause for war. Would the United States have gone to war in such an event, or would it have accepted Soviet political or military domination of Iran? In that case, would Iraq still have allied itself with the Soviet Union later in that decade, and if so, what would that have meant for the region? Most important, perhaps, what of the American intelligence sites located in Iran that enabled the United States first to monitor developments of the Soviet Strategic Missile Forces and then later to validate Soviet compliance with arms limitations treaties? What difference would it have made to President Kennedy during the Cuban missile crisis, and to President Nixon's negotiations with the Soviets on the Strategic Arms Limitations Treaty (SALT) if those intelligence sites and the information derived from them had not existed?

It is, one concludes, easier to argue that covert action probably has not made a difference to the world when the scope of the argument is limited to those "small wars of liberation" and similar conflicts. It is harder to make that same argument when political action programs are considered, depending on what the program was and its results. This is especially so since, as discussed, it is impossible to know how a country or region and U.S. policy toward it would have developed differently had the changes wrought by covert action not occurred. This is one reason why covert action has been and remains so controversial.

ONE

The Role of Covert Action in Intelligence and Foreign Policy

Overt economic or military aid is sometimes enough to achieve our goals. Only a direct military intervention can do so in others. But between the two lies a vast area where the United States must be able to undertake covert actions. Without this capability, we will be unable to protect important U.S. interests.[1]

President Richard M. Nixon

There are three disciplines, or missions, inherent within the intelligence profession, which are separated by purpose and methodology: intelligence collection and analysis, counterintelligence/counterespionage, and covert action. To better understand the unique role of covert action within the intelligence constellation, it is useful first to define the other two disciplines, each of which possesses certain characteristics both individual and shared. With this comparison clearly in mind, the reader will more easily see how and why the general discipline of covert action is so different from the other two. A later chapter will detail the various types of operations and missions within the covert action discipline itself.

The first discipline is that of intelligence collection and analysis. Collection consists of the clandestine utilization of human or technical sources to gather privileged information that the adversary wishes to keep secret, and which cannot be acquired any other way (referred to colloquially as FI, for foreign intelligence, or as PI, for positive intelligence). The immediate resulting product, whether from one clandestine agent meeting, one satellite photograph, or one conversation acquired over a tapped telephone line, is referred to as "raw" intelligence—an unevaluated report from a single source, lacking cogent analysis as to content and circumstances, cross-checking with other information, corroboration with material from other sources, etc.

When raw intelligence, regardless of source, is melded with intelligence from multiple sources—satellite imagery, signals, or electronic intelligence; human assets; or "open source" materials—and evaluated in its totality by skilled analysts, the product is referred to as "finished" intelligence. It's calculated that, on average, only about 8 percent of the material in finished intelligence is acquired clandestinely by human sources, while 12 percent is acquired through various clandestine technical methods. The remaining 80 percent of the finished product is from "open sources"—material available to anyone that may be found in the published reports of foreign governments, academic or scientific journals, research papers or findings, technical manuals and data, industry literature, geographic and topographic data, speeches or televised statements of foreign leaders, media reporting on foreign government or business affairs, and so forth. The finished intelligence report or assessment, often referred to as "strategic intelligence," is then delivered to policymakers, including the president.[2] Interestingly, in the last decade multisource analysis has also been employed increasingly to generate "tactical intelligence" useful to operations officers in devising surveillance detection routes, selecting meeting sites, discerning patterns of the opposition (such as foreign intelligence or security services, terrorist groups, etc.), and a host of other operational support activities.

Counterintelligence/counterespionage (CI/CE) is the second intelligence discipline. CI is the employment of clandestine operations, including those for the recruitment of hostile intelligence officers, to collect information that can then be used to neutralize the opposition's own collection operations. CE is intended to thwart the acquisition of secrets by hostile intelligence services. CI/CE took an interesting twist in the 1980s as the CIA, the Federal Bureau of Investigation (FBI), and the Drug Enforcement Administration (DEA) found that narcotics cartels and terrorist organizations were using many of the same defensive measures that intelligence and security services do. Specifically, these criminal organizations were employing such operational security skills as surveillance detection methodology, penetrating the "opposition" (e.g., bribing law enforcement or judicial officials) to learn what police forces knew and to acquire tip-offs of impending raids, communications security, safe houses, cut-outs, accommodation addresses, and the like. As a result, a new breed of CI officers emerged who specialized not in foreign intelligence or security services but in international criminal organizations.

An additional facet of this "new CI" was the movement of monies by narcotics traffickers and terrorist groups. Narco-traffickers are in business to generate profits, and terrorists need money to finance their activities. Thus the narcotics cartels must launder funds earned from drug sales, while the terrorist groups must generate income from legitimate front companies as well as illegal activities (narcotics, theft, etc.) and then move those funds to operational and support elements. As with the Watergate scandal—"Deep Throat" urging Woodward and Bernstein to "follow the money"—operations officers and intelligence analysts found that following the money of traffickers and terrorists served both FI and CI purposes in attacking the organizations and preventing terrorist attacks. Now, collecting intelligence from banking circles and becoming knowledgeable in such arcane areas as international financial procedures, offshore accounts, and the tricks of money laundering are as much a part of a CI officer's job as are wiretaps and surveillance.

Both intelligence collection and counterintelligence share many operational techniques and tools and are, of necessity, purely clandestine in nature. By this, one means that the actual operations, their participants, and their results are intended to be, and to remain, hidden from view.

THE THIRD DISCIPLINE

It is the third intelligence discipline, however, that interests us here—an intelligence mission separate and distinct from the others. While opinions differ on the "correct" definition of covert action, in simplest terms covert action is influence. It is a program of multiple, subordinate, coordinated, interlocking intelligence operations, usually managed over a long period of time, intended to influence a target audience to do something or to refrain from doing something, or to influence opinion (e.g., of the general public, business elites, or political or military leadership). At times, individuals, as opposed to sovereign national governments, are worthy targets of a covert action program simply because they *are* the government. One needed only to influence Hitler, Stalin, or Saddam Hussein to move the entire government. Covert action programs may likewise be initiated to influence organizations such as terrorist groups or narcotics cartels, or, again, individuals in the group (to induce defections, for example).[3]

Influence operations may take place in peacetime, in that twilight period between peace and hostility known to the military as "preparation of the battlefield," or in actual war. For the CIA, however, the vast majority of covert action operations are peacetime missions, conducted against either hostile audiences who stand to hinder or hurt American foreign policy interests or, more rarely, against neutral or friendly audiences who might be influenced to support our policy interests. The resultant acts are, perforce, overt and apparent in nature, for without a visible act no audience could be influenced or affected. The covert aspect is that the "sponsor" (i.e., the government behind the program) remains hidden, leaving observers to believe that the actors are indigenous citizens acting entirely of their own volition in events that are local in origin.

LEGAL CHARACTERIZATIONS
OF COVERT ACTION

President Ronald W. Reagan articulated in Executive Order 12333 (1981) the first official definition or explanation for covert action. Still in effect today (2003), it was eventually to serve as a guide for future congressional legislation. EO 12333 states in part that covert action is:

> special activities conducted in support of national foreign policy objectives abroad which are planned and executed so that the role of the United States Government is not apparent or acknowledged publicly, and functions in support of such activities, but which are not intended to influence United States political processes, public opinion, policies, or media and do not include diplomatic activities or the collection or production of intelligence and related support functions.[4]

First, the Order makes it clear that "[c]overt activity is not fundamentally an intelligence activity; rather, it is a foreign policy option" that the CIA executes only after the White House initiates it.[5] Traditional intelligence missions (i.e., FI and CI) and all diplomatic activities are excluded from the covert action rubric, meaning that these activities may be conducted under established routine legislative and executive authorities, and require no special authorization—the Presidential Finding—that has been a sine qua non for covert action programs since 1974. Second, the order directs the CIA to keep all elements of any covert action program focused overseas and beyond the ken of American citizens and media. (The inadvertent—and decidedly unwelcome—replay of foreign-targeted propaganda in American media is known in the parlance as "blowback.") EO 12333 also accomplishes a third, signal task: it explicitly and unambiguously assigns all peacetime covert action missions to the CIA, unless the president specifically assigns another agency to do so. To date, no chief executive has ever officially or legally given a peacetime covert action assignment to any U.S. government agency other than the CIA.

EO 12333 proved to be such an imminently workable definition and policy standard that in 1991 the U.S. Congress enshrined most of the language and intent into the Intelligence Authorization Act of 1991, one of the most important pieces of intelligence legislation ever. As now defined in federal statute:

> Covert Action is an activity or activities of the United States Government to influence political, economic, or military conditions abroad, where it is intended that the role of the United States Government will not be apparent or acknowledged publicly, but does not include: (1) activities the primary purpose of which is to acquire intelligence, traditional counterintelligence activities, traditional activities to improve or maintain the operational security of United States Government programs, or administrative activities; (2) traditional diplomatic or military activities or routine support to such activities; (3) traditional law enforcement activities conducted by United States Government law enforcement agencies or routine support to such activities; or (4) activities to provide routine support to the overt activities [other than activities described in paragraph (1), (2), or (3)] of other United States Government agencies abroad.[6]

Significantly, the law also requires that the president notify Congress whenever any "third party" (e.g., foreign country, private organization, corporation, or individual) is to finance any covert action program or operation, or even participate "in any significant way"—an acknowledgment of Iran-Contra misdeeds.

While the EO and the 1991 Intelligence Authorization Act are generally straightforward in intent, they are nonetheless written in legal language utilizing terminology that may be confusing to some outside of the intelligence or legal professions. As the 1991 Intelligence Authorization Act was intended to embed into federal law the primary provisions of EO 12333, these documents are complementary in content so that reading both together provides the fullest understanding of covert action's limits and missions. Yet despite a joint reading of the two texts, there is still ample room for misunderstanding.

First, the rules apply to something broader than pure covert action programs and operations. "Special activities," first defined in EO 12333 as "covert action," now—by dint of the 1991 statute—encompasses any intelligence activity, in addition to covert action, that does not fit the rubric of traditional FI or CI. This can be sufficiently confusing to cause even learned individuals to see covert action and special activities as synonymous.[7] But they are not. Included in special activities are programs such as, inter alia, the training of foreign military, security, and intelligence services; the provision of intelligence materials or special support to foreign governments; field support to operational counternarcotics and counterterrorism forces of a foreign nation; exfiltration by sea or air of a sensitive defector; or rendering inert a cache of terrorist explosives. The "security-assistance and intelligence-training" special activities programs have been especially important to presidents not because the programs seek change in a hostile regime, but because they work to preserve a friendly regime.[8]

Also under the special activities umbrella is the much more restrictive role of "special operations," which, to the CIA, means paramilitary operations—military-type actions utilizing non-military personnel—including commando-style raids, long-range reconnaissance, and sabotage operations. For the CIA, all of its "special operations" are also "special activities," but not all (indeed, only a few) special activities are special operations. Stated differently, special activities constitute one subset of covert action, and special operations are a subset of special activities. Another distinction between covert action and special activities is that the latter are not intended to produce any overt event to influence an audience, but instead are operations that are meant to remain clandestine in all aspects.

Covert action is distasteful to many Americans who see it as a violation of the "norms of democratic accountability," which run "counter to the country's moral conscience."[9] They view covert action as antithetical to our constitutional belief in government openness and accountability, to the rule of law, and to American ethical values. These earnest citizens argue that U.S. government activities should be open to public scrutiny, certainly a noble ideal. Yet in practice such openness for intelligence programs and covert action would be manifestly unwise. Covert action programs remain justifiably covert whenever knowledge of U.S. participation or sponsorship would make the program unfeasible or impossible. Examples of such situations include instances when knowledge of a program would invite retaliation or escalate hostilities or when other countries' governments participating in the program specifically request that the U.S. government keep the program covert, deeming the American connection deleterious to their own interests.[10]

One definitive example is found in President Harry S Truman's policies to influence European politics in the late 1940s to prevent or counter Soviet programs intended to undermine European democracies. A senior CIA officer who was deeply involved in the management and policies of these programs has noted that "European political and cultural leaders who solicited our aid in their unequal struggle with the Soviet-subsidized apparatus made it a condition that there be no publicity, since the Communist propaganda machine could exploit any overt evidence of official American support as proof that they were puppets of American imperialists."[11] Another informative example, albeit one not involving the American government, was the relationship between the Jewish state of Israel and the Muslim nation of Iran during the time of Shah Mohammad Reza Pahlavi. Not only did the two countries maintain normal diplomatic and trade relations, but the shah allowed Israel to use Iran for the clandestine infiltration of agents into neighboring Arab nations while assisting with the exfiltration of Jews from these states. The shah, for obvious reasons, demanded that this aspect of the relationship remain secret, and Israel naturally complied. The overall relationship was covert, rather than clandestine, because there was some awareness of them among segments of the government and, perhaps, in public circles, but "it sufficed that [any] affront to [Iranian] Muslims not be blatant."[12]

COVERT ACTION: A DISCIPLINE OVERVIEW

In meeting agents recruited for covert action programs (often referred to as "assets") and as support resources, the intelligence service's operations officer will use many of the same clandestine techniques that he/she would in meeting an FI-producing agent, so there is this tradecraft factor in common. But unlike the FI operation, where all elements are intended to remain secret, it is vital that the results of the covert action operation be visible to the intended target. One outstanding text on intelligence and espionage gives the reader a classic case:

> If, for example, it is decided to strengthen a political party in a neutralist country which is wavering in the face of Communist subversion, the reinforced efforts [i.e., results] of the party are not and cannot be hidden or disguised, nor is it even desirable to do so. What is covert is foreign government involvement in the process, whether it is in the form of subsidies or advice—and the two are rarely separated in practice. Since cover is limited to but one essential point—the relationship to government—it is obvious that the choice of cover, the choice of agent, the forms of communication, and the nature of the case officer-agent relationship are all affected . . . the cover

possibilities in political operations are more flexible than in secret intelligence, the choice of agent is more difficult, the forms of communication are equally restricted, and the case officer-agent relationship less prone to duplicity.[13]

As noted, the target audience is often—but not always—another government, usually hostile, but occasionally neutral or even friendly. One transparent example of the last are the little-known programs by the British government in 1916–1917 and again in 1940–1941 to influence the U.S. government and American people to support the British war effort in both World Wars, to undermine the isolationist sentiment in the country, and ultimately to entice the United States to enter each war on the side of the British. The British lesson serves to underscore that successful covert action is "intelligence-intensive work" in that it "requires precise knowledge of whom in the target government [or other audience] would be receptive to what threat or blandishment; it requires cover; and it requires protection against hostile CI."[14]

There are other important factors that separate covert action, in kind and in degree, from collection/analysis and counterintelligence/counterespionage. Arguably most important, the CIA's employment of covert action operations is predominantly a peacetime function for use against enemies. But in highly selective and carefully considered instances in which the gain clearly outweighs the risk and consequences of exposure, covert action is also an appropriate tool for employment against neutrals and even against allies. For this reason, a range of potential political dangers exists for the government engaging in covert action that does not inhere in the more traditional intelligence disciplines. For while target governments will accept being spied upon as a natural adjunct of a nation's foreign or national security policy (and likewise will accept the defensive requirements of counterintelligence as a routine responsibility of governing), covert action involves the deliberate, planned intervention in the sovereign rights of a nation by an outside government to influence or coerce a change of state policy. As such, covert action is not only in contravention of the laws of the government being targeted, but also contrary to international law and the United Nations Charter, both of which prohibit the "interference in the internal affairs" of other nations. Moreover, paramilitary operations used in covert action programs, especially those involving destruction and assassination, are apt to be considered by the adversary leadership as an act of war—which is rather ironic, in as much as covert action is as likely to permit the two sides to avoid war as to cause it.

Still, covert action has its place in American foreign policy and presidential statecraft, empirically proven by the fact that all post–World War II presidents have relied on it. Thus, it is of value not only for American citizens but also (it should go without saying) American government officials to understand its uses and limits without the hindrance of misleading concepts and erroneous information. By nature, covert action often involves America's secret intervention into the policies of sovereign nations, and so it is often labeled as "undemocratic" by critics. Yet a study group led by the exceptional presidential scholar Richard G. Neustadt found that while "covert action inherently conflicts with democratic aspirations," there are circumstances in which, with proper controls and oversight, it can be used to further national objectives when overt policies would be marginal or ineffectual.[15]

In point of fact, covert action can be, and often is, effective when it is employed within the limits of its capabilities and in support of established overt policies. In the words of one national security expert: "Covert action is only one of the tools of foreign policy, but it is not a negligible one: in certain conditions it may be decisive. It is not an option to be chosen lightly, but in the absence of such an option a global power may be doomed to impotence."[16]

The value of covert action to a president is that it offers a "third way" or "quiet option," a middle ground between overt measures on the one hand (diplomacy, trade incentives or sanctions, foreign aid, etc.) and the use of military force on the other. Covert action gives the president an alternative that may be more effective than diplomacy and a bit "less noisy and obtrusive than the overt use of force." Writes one intelligence scholar, "If a covert action capability exists, all kinds of possibilities are open." During the cold war, covert action was often the option of presidential choice, a "prudent alternative," for it allowed the United States to resist Soviet expansionism in Europe and the Third World without the threat of war that a direct confrontation would carry. From the onset of the cold war, covert action had almost equal seating with diplomacy and military force at the policy table, for Presidents Truman and Eisenhower "preferred covert action to a possibility of a general war in Europe." Looking backward from 1976, David D. Newsom, deputy secretary of state at that time, analyzed that critical period and noted, "In a world where the movements of U.S. troops in any sizeable numbers risked superpower confrontation . . . and where traditional diplomacy seemed cumbersome at best and counterproductive at worst, covert action seemed a godsend."[17]

The origins of the CIA's covert action operations in Europe following World War II began, as former deputy director of central intelligence (DDCI) Dr. Ray Cline has noted, as a way to curb Soviet expansion:

> In 1947 and 1948, many thoughtful and patriotic people urgently searched for ways to forestall Soviet use of either local Communist parties or nearby military forces to intimidate and dominate the governments of Germany, France, and Italy. . . . This was a conflict short of war, the zone in which the United States would use covert political and psychological efforts to counter Soviet influence. The United States was able to supplement its diplomatic efforts with assistance to moderate, non-Communist groups.[18]

One illustrative example of the use of covert action as a "third option" was President Kennedy's introduction of CIA paramilitary forces in Laos in 1962: JFK, "for national policy reasons, did not want to use the uniformed forces of the United States . . . but also did not want to be limited to a mere diplomatic protest against the continued presence of five thousand North Vietnamese troops in Laos in violation of the Geneva Accords, and their expansion of control over communities who wished to resist them." In this manner, the United States was able, with the full knowledge and approval of the Laotian government, to help those Laotian villagers without "confronting North Vietnam and its allies with a direct and overt challenge."[19]

Covert action can be subtle or confrontational; it can be long-term, short-term, or something in-between. It may rely on the power of the pen, the power of public demonstrations, or the power of the sword. It offers the president the ability to deal with a foreign policy problem unilaterally or with the secret assistance of foreign governments. In all but the largest programs, covert action permits the president to subtly push foreign governments or leaders in directions that benefit American national interests, while hiding the origins of that force. In this respect, one ancillary attraction of a limited covert action program being integrated into a larger overt policy effort is that the likelihood of the covert action program's coming to public attention is significantly reduced.

Further, covert action can be surprisingly inexpensive compared to the costs of overt military action or foreign aid programs. U.S. covert action programs in Chile began under John Kennedy in 1963 and continued almost until the end of the Nixon administration; the costs were less than $2 million a year for extensive propaganda and political action programs in election campaigns. Numerous programs involving the infiltration into the USSR of materials keeping alive minority cultures and history, or providing accurate accounts of world events—to counter the false stories put out by the Soviet government—ran for decades at costs of no more than a few hundred thousand dollars a year, per program, and often less.[20]

Thus, covert action is a foreign policy tool that is more flexible and responsive, and often much less costly to the U.S. treasury, than many other options at the chief executive's disposal. It's no wonder then that so many presidents—even those who come into office predisposed against it—find covert action to be such a useful lever to move foreign governments.

TWO

The "Romances" of Covert Action

Romances: Fictitiously embellished accounts or explanations; constantly reiterated misstatements, myths, and misconceptions.[1]

American Heritage Dictionary

It is perhaps ironic that the instrument of statecraft known as covert action has come to be seen by many in modern times as an odious practice unworthy of the world's leading democratic government. Somehow the knowledge that covert action was employed to further the interests of the American colonies before they became the United States—notably by George Washington as commander-in-chief of the Continental Army and by patriots Ben Franklin and James Monroe serving as diplomats to France and Spain—has evaporated from our national memory. Presidents Washington, Jefferson, Madison, and Monroe relied on covert action programs as an adjunct of American national security and foreign policy to win military victories, expand the boundaries of America, and help sustain the security of its borders while avoiding open warfare. The last point is critical, for the avoidance of full-scale wars allowed the energies of the new nation to be directed to strengthening and growing its economy—a sine qua non for the establishment of an enduring democracy. Yet in the latter half of the twentieth century, this significant aspect of American history is mostly ignored, especially by covert action's detractors.[2]

Before dissecting this secrecy-shrouded, controversial policy option, a review of the more frequently voiced criticisms of covert action will be helpful. These are the "romances" of covert action: the myths, misunderstandings, misrepresentations, and just plain wrong information about this intelligence discipline that exist in the public domain as "conventional wisdom," and which no doubt contribute much to the opprobrium that surrounds covert action. This is not to claim, of course, that all the negative or unflattering information the public sees about covert action programs is wrong— far from it. There have been programs that should not have been ordered by presidents, or that should not have been conducted as they were by government officials in or out of the CIA. Yet a good deal of information also exists that shows the alleged failures were not such in reality or that, in the least, places the failures in an enlightening context. Much of the material will be further discussed in later chapters, but to set the stage it is useful now to look at the more egregious "romances" that repeatedly draw closed-minded critics as the flame draws the moth.

As noted earlier, the most pervasive myth is that of the "rogue elephant"; and as such, it is appropriate to begin with that point: *The CIA initiates and executes covert action programs according to its own agenda, without the president's knowledge or approval, and often at cross-purposes to the president's own foreign policy.* This allegation is the most damaging and misleading of the romances, especially when discussing covert action programs after 1974. To be sure, there was an era extending from Presidents Truman to Ford in which the CIA was allowed by the president and National Security Council (NSC) to initiate and run low-level, low-cost, low-risk covert action programs as long as they were in line with established foreign policy. However, major programs—which were defined not only by cost or scope, but also by potential political consequences for the president if compromised—were closely supervised by the presidents and their most trusted aides. An exception was John F. Kennedy's lack of close oversight of Operation ZAPATA, the Bay of Pigs, a lesson that was not lost on him and his successors.

The truth of the matter, though unacknowledged by critics, is that federal law has mandated since 1974, three decades now, that the president personally approve every covert action program and report it to Congress within forty-eight hours through a document that is known as a Presidential Finding. Even if there were not an abundance of evidence to support this basic fact—which there is, as will become clear in this work—one should consider this telling point: given the enormous amount of damage a failed or ill-advised covert action program can bring to a president's doorstep, in terms of domestic politics and international relations, no serious observer of government can reasonably conclude or believe that a modern chief executive would allow for one minute any organization, or officers within that organization, to conduct its own foreign policy totally independent from White House control. Anyone who has worked at the mid- or senior levels in Washington's foreign policy/national security arena has seen and understands just how jealously protective policymakers are of their prerogatives, and how unwilling they are to let others put their policies and political futures in jeopardy. Moreover, there is absolutely no record of any modern president's willingness to accept such a situation—indeed, just the opposite has been the case.

The persistent belief that the CIA runs covert action programs without control or oversight as though it is a "rogue elephant" in foreign policy has its origins in a public statement by a senator who was by no means a fan of the Agency. During the congressional investigations of 1976 the Agency was freely accused, in the Capitol and in the media, of secretly pursuing its own policies outside the control of either of the political branches of government. The Agency was, charged Senator Frank Church (D-Idaho), a "rogue elephant." The claim was an attention-grabbing sound bite that has lived on as the sacred shibboleth of all who view the Agency with a jaundiced eye. While heading the Senate investigation of the Agency, Church tossed this statement out at a highly publicized and well-attended press conference held early in the life of the committee, long before it had completed its investigation. Clearly, Church came to the committee chair having already prejudged the Agency as a source of governmental misconduct.

Yet when the investigators wrote their report after all the evidence was in and all the witnesses were heard, the official conclusion was just the opposite: the Church Committee had definitively determined that the CIA was not, and never had been, out of control. Indeed, the committee provided indisputable evidence that the Agency had in all events acted at the express personal command of the president. Regrettably, the senator's acknowledgment of this fact was buried in the committee's written report and pointedly omitted from any public statement to the media. But the damage was done: the idea of the "rogue elephant" resonates to this day in the public's mind.[3]

As mentioned above, the simple fact is that while presidents have at times disingenuously denied responsibility for failed or otherwise controversial covert action programs, not one president has ever accused the CIA of acting independently or of having its own secret agenda. Bolstering this point is the fact that the two presidents who were the most critical of the CIA and the most philosophically and morally opposed to covert action—Carter and Clinton—not only continued covert action programs they inherited but also initiated new programs while in office. The programs Carter established in the last eighteen months of his presidency served as the basis for many of Ronald Reagan's thirty-plus covert action programs, including the controversial Central American programs, although Carter rarely receives credit (or blame). It only stands to reason that if presidents of such strong character as Eisenhower, Johnson, and Nixon—or those who were as morally opposed to covert action prior to assuming office as were Carter and Clinton—ever found the CIA acting independently, they would not have hesitated to pillory the Agency or even to call for its dismantlement.

As a corollary, Agency detractors also take issue with activities of the Agency officers, alleging or implying that these intelligence professionals act on their own volition. Critics condemn CIA officers for having "propped up cruel dictators" or for "collaborating with the most degenerate governments in the Third World."[4] They seek to leave the impression that the CIA opted, through the making of its own policies, to deal with these odious governments, and that Agency officers doing so were engaged in immoral activities to the detriment of the United States. But invariably these condemnations omit reference to the Agency's having been obliged to pursue these relationships by the direct order of the president of the United States (as recorded, since 1974, in Presidential Findings).

Also missing is any acknowledgment that the Departments of State and Defense, the Agency for International Development, and the Departments of Commerce and Agriculture were likewise directed by the president to maintain and support these governments in fulfillment of established U.S. foreign policy. Nor should it be forgotten that almost all of these policies were carried out by both Republican and Democratic presidents. Moreover, these criticisms fail to point out that the vast majority of American officials, especially including CIA officers, were as disgusted with the behavior of these regimes as the critics themselves.[5] Nor is there, within the critical arguments, ever any mention of compelling national security issues at the heart of the United States's relationships with these unsavory regimes. One example was Iran, where vital intelligence listening sites eavesdropped on the Soviet missile test ranges to collect critical intelligence on the performance characteristics of various Soviet intercontinental ballistic missiles, and, later, to verify Soviet compliance (or lack thereof) with arms reduction treaties. Finally, the critics ignore—indeed, deny—the intensive and extensive congressional oversight *and approval* of these relationships that have existed since the early 1970s.[6]

One telling anecdote demonstrates that even highly educated, senior officials within a presidential administration do not understand or realize that covert action programs are truly the president's. In the Clinton years, there was a fairly senior official who was both a lawyer and Rhodes Scholar and at the time serving, as he would extol, as "counselor" to one of the administration's highest officials. This individual attended most interagency meetings on covert action programs as a representative of his cabinet-level superior. During one White House meeting in which a particular covert action program of very limited scope and cost was soundly disparaged by CIA and State Department officers, this individual questioned why the CIA was running the program when it was obvious that its CIA managers believed it to be ineffectual and worthless. His surprise was genuine after it was pointed out to him that the program existed because, and *only* because, the president of the United States directed that it be done. He had participated at interagency meetings on covert action for months and still had not realized that it was not the CIA but the president who decided what programs to run.[7] (This individual later went on to an assistant secretary position at the Department of State.)

But it is not only the presidents who know of and embrace covert action: Congress also is a willing partner in this element of foreign policy. This fact leads to the second most pervasive romance: *Covert action programs are not subject to congressional oversight.* This was strictly the case between 1804 and 1974, from Thomas Jefferson's administration through Gerald Ford's. In the early post–World War II era, members of Congress expressly wished not to be informed of these programs (see chapter 6). But for three decades now the president has been required to report every covert action program, without exception, to Congress and to provide frequent, detailed briefings to the intelligence oversight committees—the Senate Select Committee on Intelligence (SSCI) and the House Permanent Select Committee on Intelligence (HPSCI). This requirement has been in place for so long that there is no excuse for critics not to know of it. One director of central intelligence (DCI) has stated with authority that "the CIA receives more oversight from the Congress than any other agency in the federal government."[8] But it's much more than mere routine monitoring by Congress: "In no other country—including the parliamentary democracies of Western Europe—has intelligence been subject to so much investigation and review by the legislative branch as it has been in the United States."[9] The ink on the 1974 legislation that mandated congressional knowledge and oversight of all covert action programs, the Hughes-Ryan Amendment to the Foreign Assistance Act of 1961 (chapter 6), was hardly dry before the DCI at the time, William E. Colby, confirmed that in just the first three months of 1975 CIA officials had already testified about covert action before eighteen congressional committees on twenty-eight different occasions. The intensity of congressional oversight is derived from "a procedural framework for monitoring Executive actions and occasionally through the adoption of specific policies." And this level of oversight certainly includes all covert action programs.[10]

Yet much of the literature on covert action published since the Hughes-Ryan Amendment continues to assert that presidents are attracted to these programs because they are cleverly able to slip around the legislative branch, evading Congress's constitutional and statutory oversight responsibilities. As such, presidents are allegedly able to avoid the "need to make messy, unsatisfying compromises" with Congress or to evade answering "hard questions" from legislators.[11] On this latter point, the author's personal observations of congressional briefings in the late 1980s and mid-1990s revealed that neither staff nor members had any hesitation or reluctance whatsoever in asking tough questions. Despite writing a full seventeen years after the requirement to report covert action programs to Congress was enacted, Christopher Hitchens, a particularly harsh critic of the Agency and covert action, claimed that the CIA is "unlawful" because it has "managed to exempt itself from all manner of scrutiny, be it from Congress, the press, or the public." This statement is so far removed from reality that one can only speculate about ulterior motives. Writing four years earlier than Hitchens (but still more than a decade after Hughes-Ryan), Morton Halperin, a White House official under Nixon and a Defense Department official under Clinton, urged statutory action to prohibit any president from utilizing covert action in statecraft. Presidents, asserted Halperin, rely on covert action because they "become wary of all of the requirements imposed by various laws and they become reluctant to consult with Congress." If Halperin had confined his observations to the period prior to Hughes-Ryan, he would have had a valid point; however, because the only attempt to avoid congressional consultations and other legal requirements since the passage of Hughes-Ryan was the Iran-Contra scandal—which was neither a legitimate covert action program nor a CIA program (see below)—Halperin's claim is manifestly, egregiously, and, perhaps deliberately, inaccurate.[12]

In fact, covert action programs receive far more congressional scrutiny than any other CIA activity. Faultfinders inevitably overlook (deliberately or otherwise) the fact that federal law enforcement agencies refuse to tell Congress about their undercover operations. Likewise, Department of Defense (DoD) officials routinely deny their congressional oversight committees details of their "black" operations or sensitive weapons developmental programs. And Congress accepts this. But Congress does not allow the Agency such privilege when it comes to covert action.

Critics' allegations that the CIA's covert action programs receive no congressional scrutiny indicate either their complete lack of understanding of the import of Hughes-Ryan or that they possess a permanent (and intentional) blind eye to the post-1974 reality. Hitchens asserts that Congress "has been routinely deceived by the Agency," but only cites the Iran-Contra scandal as evidence, adding that Iran-Contra proves that the CIA holds "unrelieved contempt for the American public." Hitchens has conveniently ignored a particularly telling comment made by the national security advisor to the president, Vice-Admiral John Poindexter, under oath before the Congressional Select Committee investigating this disgraceful event. Poindexter, who of course was not a CIA officer but a navy vice-admiral working directly for the president as a national security advisor, stated candidly that he deliberately "excluded" Congress because he "didn't want any interference" from that body. Arguably, it is not the CIA, but individuals like Poindexter and his Iran-Contra coconspirator Oliver North who show contempt for the American Constitution and American people.[13]

Critics who believe that the CIA runs covert action programs without the knowledge of the president or Congress subscribe perforce to the third pervasive myth: *Covert action is illegal under American constitutional and statutory law.* This allegation is as convenient to critics as it is utterly wrong.[14] First, absolutely nothing in the Constitution prohibits the president from utilizing covert action as a tool of statecraft. Indeed, the history of our first presidents limns an appreciation for maneuvers that would today be termed covert action in gaining our freedom from Great Britain, sustaining our national security, and enlarging our borders. As Washington, Madison, and Monroe were all instrumental in drafting the Constitution, it reasonably follows that they would not have engaged in covert action had they believed it to be unconstitutional. Critics who argue that covert action is also "undemocratic" should remember that Jefferson—the ultimate democrat and advocate of a presidency of limited powers—was also a believer in and practitioner of covert action during his administration. If any of the early presidents were apt to question the legitimacy of covert action, it would have been he.[15]

Detractors point out that the Agency's first general counsel, Lawrence R. Houston, advised DCI Roscoe Hillenkoetter in 1948 that there was "no specific statutory authority language authorizing the conduct of covert action" as proof of the illegality of the CIA's covert action mission. The issue arose when Hillenkoetter requested a legal opinion as to whether the authority given to the CIA in the National Security Act of 1947 to "perform such other functions and duties related to intelligence affecting the national security that the National Security Council may direct" included covert action operations. What the critics omit is that Houston also told the DCI that "if the president, with his constitutional responsibilities for the conduct of foreign affairs, gave the Agency appropriate instructions and if Congress gave it the funds to carry them out, [then] the Agency had the legal capability of carrying out the covert actions involved." Since then, presidents, attorneys general, DCIs, and Congress have all accepted the CIA's legitimacy to conduct covert action.

This has especially been the case with Congress, which, had it any doubts about the legality of covert action, either would not appropriate the funds for such missions or would enact legislation explicitly denying the Agency any covert action duties.[16] Too, Congress has had ample opportunity during the past fifty years "to forswear the use of covert action," yet has never done so.[17] Any lingering doubts about the legality of the Agency's mission to conduct covert action have since been erased by congressional action via passing of the Intelligence Oversight Act of 1980 and the Intelligence Authorization Act of 1991, each of which did indeed formally recognize covert action as a proper tool for the president. Further, in the past two decades Congress has established public entities to do overtly some tasks previously done covertly by the CIA (e.g., the National Endowment for Democracy), and in doing so "has elected not to subject covert programs to the statutory constraints that govern their overt counterparts." Thus, allegations that covert action programs are somehow "illegal" or "unlawful" under U.S. law are proof of nothing more than the ignorance of those making the allegations.[18]

One common romance among both critics and the general public is that *the CIA exists mainly to run covert action programs and is a strong advocate for these operations.* The primary missions of the CIA are the provision of strategic intelligence to policymakers through the clandestine collection of secret information and the subsequent independent, all-source analysis of that material, and counterintelligence/counterespionage. Covert action—and, now, the broader range of capabilities known as "special activities"—runs a far distant third to the two principal missions.

Hence, assertions that the CIA prefers covert action to other intelligence activities, and that it urges a covert action agenda on the White House, diverge significantly from reality.[19]

While some of the politically appointed heads and deputy heads of the Agency exhibited a predilection for covert action programs during their tenures, career officers have rarely shared their fondness.[20] While it was problematic enough that covert action was never career enhancing in the DO—traditionally, advancement in the DO is through the recruitment of foreign nationals to provide intelligence and the management of those intelligence collection operations—there was an even more severe drawback to these programs: they were just not challenging, or even exciting, enough to attract most field operations officers. For substantiation, one need only look at the makeup of the DO office responsible for most propaganda and political action programs during the heyday of covert action during the Reagan-Casey years.

In the late 1980s the DO's Propaganda and Political Action Staff (PPS) headquarters element had just slightly fewer than forty officers ranked GS-9 and above either running or managing these operations; of this group only a very few were career DO case officers with full operations training and overseas field experience. The great majority were either converted analysts from the Directorate of Intelligence (DI) or Eastern European language translators who had moved into operations. None received more than a much-abbreviated introductory operations training period and some not even that. While not a desirable situation, it was nonetheless a necessity; no qualified field-experienced case officer cared to do that kind of work. Without the aid of retired covert action specialists from the 1950s and 1960s who came back to work as independent contractors, PPS would have found itself trying to operate without any experienced specialists and ignorant of that vital element known as institutional memory.[21]

An additional—and significant—reason why DO officers dislike covert action programs is that "they feel that the chances for the CIA to be misused are never greater than when it is told to carry out a covert action." This belief was prevalent throughout the Nixon era (when Nixon clearly did misuse covert action in Chile and Kurdistan) and while William J. Casey was DCI in the Reagan administration. By the mid-1990s and the end of the cold war, personnel engaged in purely covert action had diminished to a mere handful.[22] (As this book was being written, however, the terrorist attacks of September 11, 2001, were causing a rejuvenation of covert action programs against the terrorist target and Iraq.)

Because the Agency's finances are secret, a prevalent myth is that *covert action programs consume the lion's share of the CIA budget.* As with personnel, the extent of the Agency's mission and budget devoted to covert action is consistently overrated. While it is generally accurate that perhaps as much as half of the Agency's budget was dedicated to covert action during the 1950 and 1960s, that percentage steadily decreased in later years. During the Casey period—a benchmark because it constitutes the Agency's most active period with respect to covert action programs since the Kennedy years—only about 5 percent of the Agency's budget was being spent on covert action. In some years during the 1970s and the 1990s, the covert action budget didn't even break the 3 percent level; one informed observer has asserted that, in 1990, the Agency funds spent on covert action came to only about 1 percent of the total Agency budget.[23] Expenditures of this amount are practically insignificant in the Agency's budget (much less in the overall budget of the intelligence community) and by no measurement constitute a significant slice of the Agency's overall mission.

Because CIA officers were involved in the Iran-Contra scandal, the inevitable conclusion, and continuing myth, is that *Iran-Contra was a CIA rogue covert action operation.* But Iran-Contra was neither a true covert action program nor a CIA program of any sort. In short, it "was a desire to evade all statutory and constitutional supervision and even *to exclude the normal intelligence agencies* in order to keep illegal activities secret" [emphasis mine].[24] Whether or not it was truly a "rogue operation," meaning that it was executed without the knowledge or direction of the president, is still uncertain, and may never be known for sure. But without question it happened because those on the White House staff—either with the president's approval or without it—deliberately ignored both a standing presidential directive and federal law that required that all covert action programs navigate an established interagency approval and review process, and be reported to Congress after receiving the president's signature. It's the simple story of disaster striking because those who wrote the requirements broke them.[25]

At heart, Iran-Contra was a criminal activity that utilized secrecy and deception, albeit one also intended to influence people or events. But merely because covert action programs share the same characteristics as the Iran-Contra fiasco does not magically make Iran-Contra a true covert action program. Nor was it a CIA program, for the Agency *as an institution* was never assigned any official responsibility whatsoever to manage and direct either of Iran-Contra's two components—selling or otherwise providing weaponry to the Iranians in return for the release of Americans captive in Beirut, and then utilizing proceeds from those sales to fund the Contras despite a congressional ban on such aid.[26]

There is no doubt that had the Agency, as an institution, been officially asked by the White House or by DCI Casey to do these activities, Agency lawyers and many operations officers would have immediately recognized the illegality of each of these two projects. And there can be no doubt but that lawyers would at some point have been involved, because all covert action programs receive legal scrutiny at four different levels, and because case officers by the 1980s had grown accustomed to seeking legal guidance any time they had questions about the legitimacy of an operation. Without doubt, show-stopping objections would have quickly been registered, and, probably, leaked to Congress for good measure. Indeed, Casey chose deliberately to exclude the Agency from this affair because he "feared that the professionals within the CIA would refuse to lie to Congress or break the laws," a conclusion borne out by the angry reactions of large numbers of career officers once they learned of the scandal.[27] The very few CIA officers, active and retired, who did work with Casey did so outside of Agency channels, utilizing office space in the Executive Office Building next to the White House for their work on "the Enterprise," as it came to be called by those involved. And while the provision of a CIA propriety aircraft to move Hawk antiaircraft missiles to Iran was a combination of poor judgment and misinformation, it is difficult to argue that this one act serves to make Iran-Contra a "CIA" operation.

The American public does not realize the depth of anger and the feelings of betrayal experienced by the majority of operations officers in the Agency when details about Iran-Contra surfaced. While some very senior officers rallied around and made excuses for their fellow senior DO colleagues who participated with Casey, at the lower levels, and particularly in middle management, there was a great deal of hostility toward those who had participated in the affair. When Iran-Contra was first exposed in the early fall of 1986, senior leadership in the DO first—but not surprisingly—denied any CIA involvement whatsoever in a cable sent to DO offices worldwide. When a bit more information about a possible Agency connection appeared in the press, the leadership sent another cable that in effect said, "Yes, this little item is true, but that's the only CIA involvement." When the next tidbits were exposed, the cycle repeated again, with still more high-level messages to rank-and-file DO officers admitting nothing more than a small amount of marginally inappropriate involvement. Then, when the story broke wide open and it was clear that Casey and his hand-selected Agency officers were far more involved than had been acknowledged, there were no more palliative comments from on high, only silence.

Many DO officers felt betrayed by their leadership, and they strongly resented being deceived. Morale in the DO plummeted. More than a few DO officers were greatly disappointed when President Bush eventually pardoned the Agency employees indicted in the scandal, preferring instead to see them pay not only for breaking the law but also for bringing shame and discredit to the Agency and their directorate. To this day, those officers who participated in Iran-Contra (with but one or two exceptions) deny that they were engaged in any inappropriate behavior. This did not stop them from accepting President Bush's pardon, however.[28]

Finally, the fact that these Iran-Contra "operations" were deliberately kept from Congress by the White House further undermines any argument that they were a CIA operation. Agency policy and regulations—in addition to the strict requirements imposed on the CIA by the president through various NSC directives—demand that Agency officers comply fully with all federal statutes, including the Oversight Act of 1980 (and, now, the Authorization Act of 1991), which levied the additional legal duty to report covert action programs to legislative oversight committees. While NSC staff in the White House may have felt comfortable deviating from federal law or presidentially imposed rules, few Agency career officers would have felt the same, although apparently Casey found those whose personal motivations permitted their turning a blind eye to legalities. When all is stripped away, it is clear that Iran-Contra was a criminal enterprise, directed and managed by White House staff, which was contrary to written presidential directive and federal law, and executed in a manner intended to keep it secret from the CIA as well as from everyone else.

One romance that does have something of a logical foundation is that *covert action programs are, ultimately, harmful to United States interests.* Some covert action programs have been harmful to U.S. interests, to be sure, but many more have been unalloyed successes, both at the time they were undertaken and when reviewed retrospectively years later. History and the actions of historical figures can only be correctly understood if they are viewed in the light of their times. Critics of the decisions and policies of past presidents too often conveniently forget that they are privy to knowledge through hindsight that presidents didn't have access to when making their decisions. More important, the critics know how the decisions played out—whether the policies succeeded or flopped, whether the long-term interests of the United States were well served or harmed.

Anyone wishing to analyze the covert action programs of earlier times must first bear in mind that neither the CIA nor the presidents themselves saw covert action as "dirty tricks." Covert action as a tool of presidential statecraft supported the three general cold war policies that grew out of NSC-68: prevent the spread of Communism to non-Communist governments; undermine regimes that were Communist with the hope of creating a more pro-West government; and help non-Communist regimes fend off efforts at Soviet subversion. As such, covert action programs, as well as the overarching foreign policy they supported, were intended neither to create democratic regimes nor to propagate democracy as the government of preference.[29] As with any category of foreign policy program (e.g., political, economic, financial, or military), determining whether covert action programs were either harmful or helpful to U.S. interests is not subject to a blanket assessment but instead must be assessed on a case-by-case basis.

Presidents are not clairvoyant; they cannot see the effects of their policies decades into the future. They act on what they perceive to be the best interests for the country and world at that time and can only hope that history will prove them wise. The threat of a Communist takeover in Iran was considered to be far more damaging to world peace and security in 1953 than the return of the shah to the Peacock throne, and the same can be applied to Guatemala a year later. Criticism of these two operations that placed dictators in power only arose years afterward.

The arming of the Afghan resistance in the 1980s with the highly effective Stinger shoulder-fired antiaircraft missiles became a focus of criticism a decade later only with the rise of stridently anti-American Islamic fundamentalist groups that were formerly members of that resistance. By the early 1990s pundits began deploring the Reagan administration's decision to give Stingers to the Afghans, seeing the retention of the weapons by these fundamentalist groups as a potential threat to American airliners. Now, it may be that some members of the Reagan administration were sufficiently prescient to recognize this possible future threat in the mid-

1980s, but if so they remained silent, for there is no record of any presidential policy advisor registering this concern. One must recall that driving the Soviets from Afghanistan was only the administration's intermediate goal; of much greater import was the Reagan White House's strong belief that a military defeat would deal the Soviets a crushing blow in terms of world influence—and Stingers were seen as the key to that defeat. So even if someone in the White House had raised the potential, long-term possibility of a Stinger being used against U.S. interests a decade later, the very real, short-term opportunity to accelerate the decline of the Soviet Union and all that this would hold for world peace would doubtless have outweighed that concern. And so it was with other covert action programs, including Iran and Guatemala.

In any foreign policy initiative, whether involving diplomacy, economic sanctions, military assistance, trade agreements, or covert action, there is always risk involved—including unforeseen consequences long after the conclusion of the program. The question becomes, then, should covert action be categorically ruled out as an option for immediate and real issues posing dangers to American security interests out of fear that these operations might, twenty or thirty years later, engender unforeseen and unforeseeable consequences?

History leaves no doubt that all post–1945 presidents, without exception, have used covert action in the belief that it would not only resolve the immediate problem but would, in the longer term, be beneficial to the United States and to the nation in which the covert action program was conducted. And is this not the same belief, the same hope, that presidents hold when they authorize any type of foreign policy program? Until presidents become convinced beyond any doubt that *all* covert action programs will *always* end up inimical to U.S. interests, no president will eschew this capability. No president was ever more opposed to covert action than Jimmy Carter, and yet his record of reliance on covert action programs is as robust as any president's.

Another understandable myth is that *covert action programs are either expensive, paramilitary programs or involve the over-throw of governments that inevitably ends up reported in the media.* The truth is not so, on all accounts. Only a very few covert action programs have even a modest paramilitary aspect to them. Historically, the great majority of covert action programs involve only propaganda and/or political or economic operations and cost very little, often but a few hundred thousand dollars a year to run. As for being compromised in the media, all but a few of the programs targeted against the Soviet Union and the former Eastern European bloc ran literally for decades without once appearing in the press. For some reason, too many critics assume, without further reflection, that the large paramilitary programs that easily become public knowledge are the *only* covert action programs ever executed.[30]

Of the hundreds of covert action programs run since the end of World War II, only a few have resulted in the overthrow of an established government. Moreover, there have been more failures in covert action efforts to reverse hostile regimes (Indonesia, Cuba, Guyana, Iraq) than there have been successes (Iran, Guatemala). In the 1970s, if not before, many professional intelligence officers came to realize that reversing governments not only is harder than they imagined, but that doing so often created more problems than it solved. The professionals concluded that you should overthrow a government *only* if you can control what comes afterward—and too often such is virtually impossible.[31]

One of the lesser romances is that *covert action was renamed "special activities" to obscure its meaning, thereby hiding the true nature of these programs.* The term "special activities" was coined early in the Reagan administration, in Executive Order 12333, in which it was essentially synonymous with covert action. But during that administration, operations evolved that were seen as "non-traditional" intelligence activities (see chapters 1 and 5), or, as Professor Roy Godson has labeled them, "intelligence assistance activities." These operations were clearly not covert action programs and yet equally clearly were not of a collection or counterintelligence nature. What distinguished them was that they relied on the assets and resources of the CIA's covert action infrastructure to accomplish the mission, and that they were almost always in support of friendly governments rather than against hostile regimes. Acting conservatively, agency lawyers have since required that many of these special activities be included in Presidential Findings, especially in light of the language in the 1991 Intelligence Authorization Act, which clarifies reporting requirements (see chapter 6).[32]

There is, for some unfathomable reason, a segment of our society that always sees America as the source of the world's problems, and which believes that America acts in ways far worse than its foes. This has led to the myth that *only the United States engages in this undemocratic meddling in the internal affairs of other countries.* There is indisputable proof that covert action operations were a staple of the Soviet Union in the cold war against the West. Indeed, any advanced country, democratic or otherwise, that possesses a political, economic, or military stake in events in foreign countries or regions relies on covert action operations at one time or another.[33] As one intelligence officer has noted, in their relations with the United States, "virtually every nation in the world supplements its open diplomacy with various forms of covert action . . . attempting, with varying degrees of success, to influence our opinions and actions in ways congenial to the nation in perceptions of its interests."[34]

It is important to remember that the United States never sought to create conflict with the Soviet Union and has, at least in terms of desire, tried to play a positive role in the world. For American presidents and in most instances, "U.S. covert action was a defensive reaction to Soviet expansionism and the massive Soviet active measures program [consisting of] a well-organized, systematic effort to influence outside developments overtly, as well as covertly." In other words, most covert action operations up through 1990 were ordered by presidents "only in response to perceived foreign (typically Soviet or Cuban) intervention, and often not until perceived Leninist 'clients' had taken repressive measures against democratic opposition groups . . . [t]he objective, in many instances, was to 'level the playing field' by offsetting the perceived Leninist influence." For just two examples, among many, there was no intervention in Italy in 1940, nor in Nicaragua in 1980, until it became clear that the Soviets or Soviet clients were actively seeking to undermine the local government or to overthrow neighboring governments.[35]

A rather silly, but nonetheless enduring, myth is that *the CIA was involved in Watergate.* As noted in the introduction, DCI Richard M. Helms refused to go along with the White House cover-up, an act of integrity that cost him his position. Howard Hunt, a former CIA officer who was then working in the White House as a political operative and manifestly *not* as a CIA officer on detail, did obtain disguises for the "Plumbers" from the CIA, but he did so deceitfully by claiming that the materials were required for a highly classified matter of "national security." Nevertheless, some authors persist in citing this one act of deception as proof positive of Agency perfidy in Watergate. As a result, readers are misled, the amount of erroneous information in the public domain unnecessarily increases, and the reputation of the CIA is unjustifiably sullied.

After the 9/11 terrorist attacks, one myth that gained additional currency was that *the CIA trained Osama bin-Ladin.* This accusation is absolutely wrong. Bin-Ladin was a financier of several of the anti-Soviet Mujahedin elements, but he was never a fighter, and he never personally received any training or assistance from the U.S. government, although undoubtedly some individuals or groups that he supported financially did receive such training.

A favorite and completely erroneous romance is that *the CIA has conducted political assassinations of foreign government leaders and is responsible for abetting others.* In the unvarnished words of former DCI Richard M. Helms, "the CIA has never assassinated anyone." Added Helms, "There were many of us who never liked any idea of assassination. Plotting such an act is one thing and committing it is another. . . . But the fact remains, none of this [assassinations] happened."[36] This assertion, as well as proof that the CIA never attempted to assassinate a foreign leader absent White

House direction, was confirmed by the Church Committee investigations and is backed up by, among others, historian John Ranelagh in his excellent history of the CIA.[37] But despite presidential authorization to assist in or carry out assassinations in the cases of, for examples, Patrice Lumumba (who was killed by his political opponents before the CIA could act) and Fidel Castro, the Agency never succeeded. This obviously raises the question of whether it's better to be incompetent or effective when the goal is the murder of another.

As a result of the congressional investigations into Agency activities during the 1970s, President Ford issued Executive Order 12333 banning assassinations. It was never clearly stated whether the order was limited to foreign government leaders or whether it applied across the board (e.g., terrorists or narco-traffickers), and so without that clarification the working premise, until 1989, was that no one was to be assassinated. In that year, President George H.W. Bush, in response to increasingly deadly Colombian drug cartels, modified E.O. 12333, holding that deaths of terrorists, guerrilla forces, or others who constituted a "national security threat" during CIA or military operations would not constitute assassination. After September 11, 2001, President George W. Bush authorized the CIA and the military to target specific terrorist leaders. In each case, the general ban on assassinating political leaders remained. It is noteworthy that Congress has never acted through legislation to prohibit government-sponsored assassinations, whether by the CIA, the Defense Department, or any other government agency.[38]

The deaths of President Ngo Dinh Diem of South Vietnam and President Salvador Allende of Chile are the two that are most often attributed to the CIA, and both are asserted to have been the product of CIA coups in those countries. The lifespan of these two allegations seems to be endless, although both were thoroughly explored by the Church Committee—composed of a fair number of both senators and staff members who would dearly have loved to pin murders on a "rogue" CIA—which exonerated the CIA both of sponsoring the coups and of the deaths that ensued.[39]

Documents from the Kennedy administration declassified since

1990 show beyond doubt that while the CIA—and the State Department—knew that a coup was being planned in South Vietnam, the U.S. government was neither instigator nor perpetrator. Indeed, the administration wasn't even primarily interested in getting rid of Diem; it actually sought the ouster of his powerful brother, Ngo Dinh Nhu, and if that meant allowing the South Vietnamese generals to stage a coup against Diem, then so be it. Adding to the record are recently released White House tapes and documents from the Kennedy years that prove conclusively that while Kennedy and his advisors welcomed the coup, they never actually considered the possibility that the Diem brothers would be murdered. The most significant lesson the Kennedy group learned from the coup was that they "vastly overestimated their ability to control the generals who ran the coup. . . ." Nevertheless, as recently as November 2002 a major news network would bill a story as the "anniversary of the CIA–backed coup in South Vietnam," a headline that was in fact contrary to the content of the story. The CIA station in Saigon reported the planned coup and was directed not to interfere by the Kennedy White House. The coup then took its own course.[40]

Likewise, two exhaustive investigations—the Church Committee in 1975 and the Hinchey Committee in 2000—found that the United States had "tried unsuccessfully to foment a coup against the democratically elected Allende government but had not been directly involved in the 1973 coup" that ultimately led to Allende's death.[41] Although Nixon and Kissinger had ordered the CIA to work with the Chilean military in 1970 to prevent Allende's assumption of office, it was soon realized that there was little or no ability to control the high-level military officers plotting the coup. The CIA was ordered to back down and ultimately retained only limited contact with senior military officers. Because of these contacts, the Agency probably learned of additional plotting by the military, which was distressed by Allende's mismanagement of the economy in the spring and summer of 1973. A successful coup that did result in Allende's death was eventually conducted by Chilean officers who were, in all probability, known to the CIA, but—as conclusively demonstrated in both the Church investigation (no friend of the Agency) and the Hinchey Committee—there was no Agency involvement in either the coup or the assassination. One can be assured that if either investigation—especially the Church Committee—had been less than absolutely certain in its exoneration of the Agency or Agency officers in this matter, the issue and the surrounding doubts would have in the least been left open to question.

For some mystifying reason, authors of works on the CIA keep saying that *Desert One was a covert action operation.* The mission officially designated Operation Eagle Claw, but more familiarly tagged Desert One, was a military operation devised and managed by the Department of Defense and executed by American military forces in uniform to rescue American hostages in Iran. Eagle Claw employed only modest, although important, paramilitary support from the CIA. The fact that it was a secret operation no more makes Desert One a covert action than secrecy made the D-day landings a covert action operation. (That said, there were certainly some in Congress who thought that Desert One should have been treated as covert action with respect to reporting requirements.)[42] Likewise, there is no comparison between Eagle Claw and the "secret" or "paramilitary" wars in Indochina in the 1960s or Central America in the 1980s. Those earlier programs were genuinely covert action, in part because the CIA was specifically assigned the mission (with DoD in a supporting role) and because the combatants were either CIA officers or third country nationals instead of uniformed U.S. military forces. Other differences will emerge in a later chapter, but these two just mentioned are distinctive.

In sum, erroneous and misleading information has created in the minds of many Americans a flawed image of what the Agency does and how it does it, as well as what covert action really is. The above "romances" are a combination of this material and the "conventional wisdom" that has been bred in the public's mind. It is now time to set the record straight.

THREE

Covert Action Policy and Pitfalls

The CIA conducts such activities only when specifically authorized by the National Security Council. Thus, CIA covert actions reflect national policy.[1]

DCI William E. Colby

Whether a covert action program ultimately succeeds, fails, or lands somewhere in between is often rooted in the degree to which a president and his advisor understand the limits and capabilities of covert action operations. Covert action can be a highly effective tool of presidential statecraft when knowledgeably employed. But no matter how appropriate or effective a covert action program may be in any foreign policy scheme, the absolute first imperative must be that it is conceived and managed in full compliance with the Constitution, federal statutes, executive orders, and CIA internal regulations—including the requirement that Congress be fully informed. Beyond this desideratum, any decision to use covert action should generally include considerations of whether the "intentions and objectives are clear, reasonable, and just"; whether the means employed are appropriate in costs and methodology to the objectives sought; whether the Congress generally supports the president; and whether there is a favorable public consensus about the overall foreign policy objective the covert program supports.

An unambiguous comprehension of the capabilities and limits of covert action is essential for presidents and their key advisors. Covert action works best at the margins; it is not a magic bullet that will, by itself, solve a particularly thorny foreign policy problem. Without this understanding, intelligence officers will be forced either to attempt to convince the White House not to employ an inappropriate covert action program or to pull together an inherently unsuitable operation to please an insistent president or advisors. Should the president nonetheless order a covert action operation that lies outside the discipline's capabilities or limits, program failure is virtually guaranteed—and often so is public embarrassment for the president and the Agency.

Some presidents—Eisenhower, Reagan, the first Bush—enjoyed an excellent understanding of covert action and initiated a number of successful programs. Nixon and his national security advisor, Henry Kissinger, understood covert action but, arguably possessing a flawed sense of morality, seriously abused it in Chile in 1970 and with the Kurds in 1972. While Jimmy Carter believed covert action to be immoral, just as he did much of the CIA's overall mission, he nonetheless placed the highly knowledgeable Zbigniew Brzezinski as his national security advisor to superintend the initiation of viable covert action programs when the time came. Bill Clinton cared nothing for covert action, disdaining it as he disdained the CIA in general, and the same charge can generally be levied against his advisors, as well.[2]

Under Clinton and his national security advisor, Anthony Lake, who likewise was unacquainted with covert action specifics and prejudiced against the general concept, the administration's first term saw a series of false starts and unwise initiatives that ate up valuable time but went nowhere. Intelligence professionals were repeatedly directed to find covert action solutions to issues—not infrequently the same issues time and again—that were manifestly unsuited for such. Even Tobi Gati, Clinton's choice to head the State Department's Bureau of Intelligence and Research (INR), the component that served as the coordination point for covert action programs, had virtually no comprehension of this statecraft tool. In a briefing to the Senate Select Committee on Intelligence (SSCI) in the spring of 1995, Gati stated that she was very much against covert action programs because (in her opinion) they always failed or resulted in disaster. Asked to name some of these "disasters," Gati, who was several years into her tenure at INR and thus could be reasonably expected to be knowledgeable about covert action programs and capabilities, then proceeded to list several counterintelligence failures and at least one flap resulting from an exposed intelligence collection program! The CIA's deputy director for operations (DDO), attending the same briefing, noted for the record and to the amusement of the senators present that none of Gati's alleged "covert action failures and disasters" were in fact covert action programs.[3]

Likewise, President John Kennedy and his brother Robert, the attorney general, were enamored with covert action, but whether or not they fully understood it is questionable, even after the Bay of Pigs disaster. CIA official Sam Halpern related how the Kennedys "chewed him out" when a sabotage operation inside Cuba that "blew up a small power plant or generator" made the front pages of newspapers in Cuba and Florida. The Kennedys were angry over the publicity and apparently couldn't understand why things a secret agency did in secret became public. Halpern then had to explain that when you blow something up, "it's going to make noise, people are going to see it, it's going to be on television, and it's going to be in the newspapers." Added Halpern, "That's the kind of stupidity we were getting from the White House, from the president and his brother."[4]

Foreign policy initiatives consist of multiple subordinated, overt programs managed by the different agencies within the foreign policy or national security community. These overt elements may include diplomacy, military assistance missions, trade incentives or sanctions, low-interest loans or potential debt forgiveness, agricultural assistance, infrastructure aid, etc. There may or may not be a covert action component to the policy initiative, depending on the objectives, the target(s) of the policy, and the attitude of the president toward covert action. But whenever an administration is at a loss for a substantive policy, policymakers must not turn to covert action as some sort of magic "problem-solving" bullet. If there is one cardinal rule of covert action it is this: covert action cannot and must not serve as a substitute for an established overt policy that has been unambiguously enunciated and for which objectives are clearly and firmly established.[5] As Roy Godson writes with succinct clarity:

> Covert action, when integrated into coherent policy, can be remarkably effective—as exemplified by the covert "annexes" to the Marshall Plan and NATO, and to the Afghan resistance. But covert operations are not a substitute for coherent policy; they provide but one of the arrows in the national security quiver. Effectively utilized in conjunction with other tools, covert operations can play a valuable, even decisive role. . . .[6]

This fundamental principle has a number of equally vital corollaries:

A. Covert action is not and should not be a mechanism for resolving a crisis.

B. Covert action programs must be fully coordinated with the other relevant government agencies (e.g., State, Defense, etc.) and seamlessly integrated into the overall policy.

C. The goals to be attained by the covert action program must be clearly stated and reflect both "an accurate understanding of the prevailing conditions and sound logic."

D. Covert action is not an appropriate "last resort"

option, to be employed in the complete absence of any viable overt measures.

E. "Covert action . . . should never be used to rescue a failed policy," as though it can magically correct an overt policy that probably should never have been attempted in the first place.

F. The operational components of any covert action program should not be randomly chosen by policymakers, as though they are "mix-and-match" fashion accessories, to be individually employed without an overarching integrated intelligence architecture.

G. Covert action programs should never be expected to achieve results immediately; a viable program requires long lead times for planning, for establishing necessary infrastructure, for recruiting necessary agents, and for budget development. Once begun, programs require additional time for the influence to be felt and acted upon by the target audience.[7]

H. The program goals should be compatible with American values and interests; if the program were to be compromised the American public should be able to say, "That was a worthy objective."[8]

The first term of the Clinton White House shines as the best—or worst—example of misuse of covert action among modern presidents, as Clinton's foreign policy team consistently violated each of the above "rules" (save perhaps for A and H) with respect to directives to initiating new programs. Consider the administration's inability to gain a consensus on policies for Bosnia, Serbia, Haiti, and the tribal massacres in central Africa. The crux of the problem for the CIA managers was that Clinton's advisors, unable to reach consensus on how to handle these crises—and the president unwilling to step in and make a firm decision on which option to employ—attempted numerous times to fall back on covert action as a substitute for an overt policy or to defuse a crisis.

The "process" in the White House became frustratingly routine: Clinton's advisors would first seek an easy solution to what was perforce a complex problem with the objective of presenting the president with a team consensus. This was especially acute in the Clinton White House as consensus would eliminate the need for the tough decisions that the president always so desperately sought to avoid throughout his tenure, no matter what the issue. From the outside, this factor inevitably appeared futile, for (even as college sophomores understand) there are never any easy solutions to foreign policy problems.

Then, unable to develop the desired policy consensus—and the president unwilling to make a decision when his advisors were divided—Clinton's national security advisor, Anthony Lake, would ask the CIA to develop a broad menu of covert action options with the intention of selecting whichever options appeared to be the most promising. CIA managers were then left to spend excessive manhours pulling together all possible operations when a clearly stated overt policy would have guided the CIA officers in winnowing out options unsuited to the overt policy. Agency officers would then make the presentation to a White House–based interagency review committee, which inevitably recognized the same inherent problems that the Agency did. These problems entailed high political risks as well as potential for risk of life, excessive financial costs, an undesirable necessity for coordinating with other governments (particularly acute in the central African crisis), and ultimately very little chance of any measurable success, much less an ability to significantly reduce the crisis. And yet, with some of these lingering crises, several months after presenting their findings to the interagency committee, the Agency would again be tasked by the White House to do the same thing, mostly because the crisis continued, the Clinton policy team still could not attain consensus, and the president still would not step in to make a decision. This, even though virtually nothing had changed with respect to the crisis to permit the creation of a viable covert action program.

Fortunately, during my fifteen months immersed in covert action policy, every single case in which the above deficiencies were present resulted in a final decision by the White House to forego a covert action program, although that did not prevent the same proposals from being raised repeatedly by NSC staff.

These repetitive results should have signaled to the White House that other foreign policy mechanisms (e.g., diplomacy or trade sanctions) in lieu of intelligence programs were much more appropriate, and occasionally the point was made. But not always. In one instance, a mid-level NSC staff member succeeded in having three separate reviews over a period of months for the same issue, despite the fact that no one at the Department of State (either in the Bureau of Intelligence and Research [INR] or in the geographic area bureaus), the CIA, or Pentagon (whether from the Office of the Secretary of Defense or the Joint Chiefs), nor the U.S. ambassador in the country involved, was able to identify one single objective any possible covert action operation could accomplish. This NSC staff member was yet another Rhodes Scholar and, like her previously mentioned colleague (the "counselor" to the senior official), also later became an assistant secretary of state. The fact that this NCS staffer's "expertise" in the region in question was obtained mostly through her academic experience did not, however, deter her from denigrating the knowledge and advice of career officials who had actually lived and worked for two or more decades in the countries, knew the cultures and languages involved, and understood that there was little if anything the United States could do. This arrogance was highly reminiscent of that displayed in the mid-1960s by Lyndon Johnson's "Euro-centric" advisors when confronted with experts on Southeast Asia.

A senior CIA analyst has placed this shortcoming in perspective: "The abuse of the intelligence service by political leaders who weakly grasp at spy-novel tactics for pulling political chestnuts out of the fire shows a misunderstanding not only of covert action but also of the essence of international politics. Cases such as these serve to illustrate deceitful or incompetent politics rather than another intelligence failure."[9]

In fairness, however, it must be noted that the Clinton admin-istration continued to manage covert action programs begun in earlier administrations, which were producing positive results, with relatively little problem.

In contrast to the Clinton administration, Ronald Reagan's national security team was usually on top of covert action initia-tives. However, there was one program that escaped the detached, objective, professional management that characterized so many of their others: the Nicaraguan program. Regarding the controversial initiative, one longtime White House insider has observed: "[T]here was a covert action in Central America because the political sup-port was lacking for an open U.S. confrontation with the Sandinistas in Nicaragua. The truest believers tended to be the handful of people that [DCI William J.] Casey brought in from the outside, and those directly involved in running the program." This program disturbed many Americans —among whom there was no consensus about the initiative's necessity or productivity—and polarized Congress to the point that it would eventually lead to the Iran-Contra scandal.[10]

When covert action is expected to play an effective support-ing role in a foreign policy, it should be included early in the inter-agency policy development process and implemented in concert with the components of the policy. If a covert action element is shoe-horned into the overall policy program near or at the end of the planning phase, the result will be much like trying to insert a single domino into the middle of a long chain: one clumsy move can dis-rupt the entire scheme. None was better at integrating covert ac-tion into policy schema than Ronald Reagan and George H.W. Bush and their foreign policy teams. Again, Clinton stands out as the least effective. In one case during the Clinton administration, the confusion caused when a CIA covert action program was added at literally the last moment to a large-scale military operation brought about structural and personnel changes in the CIA and gave impe-tus to a greater Department of Defense (DoD) influence in the Agency.

Covert action programs are at times a source of conflict between the president and Congress, and a compromised or poorly managed program will inevitably exacerbate that relationship. As an example, one need only review the animosity that was publicly generated by Congress over the mining of several Nicaraguan ports in the 1980s. Although Congress was informed of this operation in advance, there was a measure of miscommunication that apparently left key senators in the dark.[11] A firestorm resulted on the Hill, which came very close to ending prematurely the tenure of DCI William J. Casey. It should also be noted, however, that some of the public discord was political showmanship: in a closed, secret briefing of the House Permanent Select Committee on Intelligence (HPSCI), liberal Democrats applauded the Agency and the operation, only to castigate the CIA later in the media.[12]

But the Reagan administration's covert programs for Nicaragua in particular, and Central America more generally, were sufficiently problematic, even without the spectacle of Soviet ships being blown up in Nicaraguan ports, to generate consternation within Congress. First, the covert action programs, one for Nicaragua and a second covering the rest of Central America, were exceptionally expensive, with the Nicaraguan program funded at about $100 million a year by the late 1980s and the Central American program at a bit less. Second, the administration insisted that the goals of the Nicaraguan program were to interdict the movement of arms through Nicaragua and to support the Contras as a way to force the Sandinistas to moderate and/or reform their dictatorial policies. The overthrow of the Sandinistas was ostensibly *not* a program objective, although the White House of course hoped for that exact outcome. Congress reinforced the administration's stated goals through legislation in late 1982 that specifically prohibited covert action operations from ousting the Sandinistas. But soon after, and to the great unhappiness of a number of officials, the Contras themselves, in a case of exquisitely poor timing, openly declared that their goal was to bring down the Nicaraguan regime, thus further eroding program support in Congress.[13]

A third element, complicating issues even more, was that Congress altered legislation regulating or limiting U.S. goals and operations in Central America five times in less than four years, with each piece of legislation more confusing than, and at times contradictory to, the last. This served only to create uncertainly among those who were executing the programs as to what their missions were and what they were permitted, or not permitted, to do. For example, in 1985 Congress voted to sustain the prohibition on any aid to the Contras, but then fourteen months later reversed course by voting to permit military assistance to the rebels. And what can one make of a situation where the president of the United States, in an Oval Office meeting, congratulated a Central American chief of station for doing a great job, only to see him indicted for violating federal law months later?[14] The end result was that the Nicaraguan/Central American programs created and sustained one of the most acrimonious periods in the history of the congressional-executive intelligence relationship. Moreover, not only were some Agency officers unfairly tarnished by the madness that accompanied efforts to interpret the ever-changing legislation, but the quality of the Nicaraguan/Central American programs themselves no doubt suffered because excellent officers who had much to contribute in the way of expertise literally ran the other way when offered the chance to work on them.

ANCILLARY DIFFICULTIES INHERENT IN COVERT ACTION PROGRAMS

The Nicaraguan program delineates a collateral difficulty with the development and management of covert action programs. While covert action programs are, by executive order, required to be "conducted in support of national foreign policy objectives," it is often unclear what precisely those objectives consist of or are intended to accomplish. And even when these objectives are clearly enunciated by the president, there may be those in Congress and within the body politic who disagree with the direction or substance of the policy. Inevitably, "when policy is debated, those who question the legitimacy, efficacy, or wisdom of covert undertakings will almost certainly be present."[15] Often, then, the only way essential compromise or consensus can be attained is through a deliberate obscuration of the issues by all parties concerned, leaving the field operatives and headquarters officers alike confused.

Another inherent difficulty or problem with covert action is that if compromised, it can be publicly embarrassing to the president, especially if it is a failure or even perceived to be such. An exposed program can affect not only the president's relations with Congress, but also U.S. policies toward allied, neutral, and hostile nations, and their leaders. King Hussein of Jordan, the United States's closest Arab ally and longtime friend, was livid in 1985 upon learning that the Reagan administration had transferred arms to Iran, a country against which the United States had successfully led the fight in the United Nations for a total arms embargo due to its terrorist activities. The ultimate source of the king's ire was that the United States had previously denied his own military the I-Hawk antiaircraft missile, only to send that same weapon to a country that was decidedly hostile to the United States. Similarly, European allies who sought and were denied permission to view satellite photography were incensed in 1984 to find that the United States was routinely providing this overhead imagery to assist Iraq's Saddam Hussein in the prosecution of a war that he had initiated without provocation against Iran.

Compromised covert action programs may also affect the president's standing with the American people, and they may become a significant issue in an election year. While it is generally accepted that public discord will be minimal if there is widespread approval with the program's cause or objective (e.g., Poland and Afghanistan), on issues where the public and Congress are divided, covert action and presidential policy are much more likely to be criticized.[16] And not least of the consequences of a failed or exposed program is that it will always involve, and thus affect, the CIA's relations with other U.S. government agencies, such as the Departments of State, Defense, and Justice.

FOUR

The Military and Peacetime Covert Action

The three worst Directors of Central Intelligence ever were John Deutch, John Deutch, and John Deutch.[1]

John Millis, Staff Director, House Permanent Select Committee on Intelligence

Following the creation of the CIA and the Department of Defense, there were suggestions within the Truman administration that Defense assume responsibility for covert action operations. After all, during World War II the armed forces undertook operations that are now recognized as classic covert action, such as propaganda and deception (called "psyops" in military argot, for psychological warfare), political action, and behind-the-lines paramilitary action, including with indigenous native groups, sabotage, raids, and assassinations. Assigning covert action to Defense seemed logical. But that department wanted no part of this nontraditional military role. Hence, through default, covert action landed in the lap of the CIA, and there it has remained.[2]

By dint of federal statute, presidential executive order, and operational methodology, the U.S. military has since been limited to playing only supporting roles in peacetime covert action programs. DoD components have provided training, airlift, and divers materials required by the CIA for various programs, but they have neither assumed nor exercised full operational responsibility for any program. This does not mean that the military establishment is excluded from the covert action arena, however. Whether or not military support is required for a covert action program, DoD representatives from both the Office of the Secretary of Defense (the civilian side, known as the "suits") and the Joint Chiefs of Staff (the military side, the "uniforms") sit in on the coordination and approval process at the various interagency levels in addition to participating as needed at CIA headquarters in the operational planning aspects of the program.

The CIA's covert action missions are in marked contrast to the military's use of identical or similar methodology principally because the CIA utilizes these techniques in peacetime against nations that may or may not be hostile to the United States. Further, these operations are conducted as ordered in writing by the president and with full knowledge of Congress. Military operations, in contrast, are undertaken in anticipation of hostilities and targeted against an enemy's military forces and infrastructure; they are not reported to Congress. The most important distinction, however, is that the CIA's peacetime role incurs a heavy political burden not faced by the military in wartime or in preparation for hostilities. Mark Lowenthal, who has three decades of experience as an intelligence professional, raises the collateral consideration that often covert action "is an alternative to military operations" and questions whether Defense "might find it difficult to keep the two options separate."[3]

As the Agency was assigned more and more covert action programs during the cold war, and as it developed and refined its covert action capabilities and infrastructure, the need to consider the military as an alternative covert action manager diminished. As a result, the passing years have seen the imposition of legal and policy restrictions that, today, essentially prevent a president from assigning exclusive control of a peacetime covert action mission to the military, although at times DoD officials have advocated that.

But there are sound reasons why the president has not given the Defense Department full responsibility for covert action. First, DoD does not possess nor has it ever possessed any statutory authority to conduct classic covert action, with these critical exceptions: during a war formally declared by Congress; during any period covered by a report to Congress by the president under the 1973 War Powers Act; and during times that the president specifically tasks DoD with the mission on the basis that the military would be more likely to achieve a particular objective (as permitted by EO 12333).[4] Additionally, although the special operations military units gathered under the United States Special Operations Command (USSOCOM) may well have the capability of performing many of the same peacetime covert action operations undertaken by the CIA, the statute establishing USSOCOM specifically states that its component military forces do not possess the "authority to conduct any activity which, if carried out as an intelligence activity by the Department of Defense," would require an explicit presidential directive (i.e., a Finding) and the subsequent notification to Congress.[5]

Second, the CIA is used in covert action because it allows the sponsorship of the United States to be much more easily concealed—the most crucial element in all covert action operations. The CIA has at its disposal civilian-registered aircraft and maritime vessels that can easily and without drawing notice transit the sovereign airspace or waters of foreign nations as legitimate civilian craft. Under international laws, before entering sovereign space, military aircraft and vessels must first obtain permission from the governments of the nations being transited. Obtaining such permission, it should go without saying, would make it obvious that the United States was involved.

Third, the CIA uses third-country nationals to carry out the required operational activity in overseas lands. These recruited agents are trained and supported by CIA staff officers and are then sent out to do the actual in-the-trenches work. Thus, the hand of the U.S. government remains hidden. Were U.S. military troops to conduct the operations, they would be required under international law to be in uniform and carry appropriate identification. If these troops were captured while, say, blowing up a bridge or sabotaging an electrical station, the target government would have legitimate grounds to consider the deed an act of war.[6]

Fourth, the CIA has a presence in many of the 190 sovereign nations in the world, while the U.S. military does not. As such, the CIA is likely to have case officers on the ground who speak the local languages, understand the national and regional political scene, and are learned in the local customs. These officers will often have access to an existing network of human intelligence and support assets that may be used to establish and serve a separate operational network for a covert action program. Moreover, the CIA's overseas facilities have nearly instantaneous communications with the impressive analytical and operational support capabilities found at CIA headquarters outside of Washington. This is an essential, singular capability, which would be difficult for the military to replicate.

Because of its relatively small size, flexibility, and can-do attitude, the CIA's directorate of operations is able to manage programs at less cost, with far fewer personnel, and with much less visibility than the military. For one thing, CIA officers in the field do not need all of the supporting personnel that accompany the military. Two examples will suffice. Decades ago in Laos three CIA officers living with, and in the lifestyle of, a local mountain tribe were conducting sabotage operations against the Communist Pathet Lao; the CIA costs for the operation were minimal, measured in hundreds of dollars a month. The Defense Department thought that the operations would be better conducted by a U.S. military detachment. But an Army evaluation of the living and battlefield conditions produced a requirement for air-conditioned huts, cooks, clerks, guards, individual experts in various subspecialties, and on and on. Ultimately the costs of a military-run program were placed at more than a quarter of a million dollars per month with a contingent of several dozen personnel.[7]

And in 1994, after DoD had spent billions of dollars and more than a few years attempting, with negligible success, to develop a long-range, high-endurance, multi-mission capable intelligence collecting "drone"—an Unmanned Aerial Vehicle, or UAV—the CIA succeeded with a platform costing less than $5 million. The first-ever overseas use of this forerunner to the Predator (which, beginning in October 2001, gained public notice in Afghanistan) involved fewer than fifteen CIA personnel, led by a relatively junior officer, in two back-to-back deployments to a region of critical importance to senior U.S. government policymakers. During these deployments, the platform collected tactical intelligence of great value to military commanders and policymakers without losing a single UAV. Subsequently, a military unit deployed to the same area of operations with eight Predators; that deployment was composed of two hundred men and women, led by a colonel, and lost two UAVs in the first weeks.[8]

Finally, the CIA has an almost instantaneous reaction or response time in a crisis situation. CIA officers can deploy in alias, under civilian cover, and travel with non-U.S. documents from Washington to anywhere overseas in just a few hours from the initial call, via commercial airliner or civilian-registered corporate aircraft. Upon arrival at the foreign destination, they will immediately receive the clandestine assistance of CIA case officers, operational support assistants, possibly technical officers and other special units, and a stable of intelligence reporting and support agents. Around-the-clock encrypted communications to Washington will be on call, including to the White House if necessary. The U.S. military can't match, much less improve upon, this clandestine capability.

The obvious conclusion is that those who advocate a transfer of covert action responsibilities to DoD simply do not comprehend all that managing and supporting covert operations entails. It should be noted, too, that the CIA has a core element of career covert action specialists in each of the four broad categories of covert action operations (propaganda, political action, paramilitary, and information warfare) who are uniquely qualified to manage peacetime covert action programs, yet another capability lacking at DoD.[9]

Traditionally, the U.S. military has not coveted authority in peacetime covert action—programs having a foreign government as the target and where the ends are strictly political. But during the Deutch tenure as DCI, senior officials in DoD did seek to achieve equality, or even assume primacy, in the conducting of peacetime covert action. While the ostensible reasons given were that the military could manage the operations more effectively and more cheaply, those well versed in covert action at the CIA and elsewhere knew better; rather, it looked far more like the Defense Department was seeking to expand its authority in foreign policy, acquire CIA technology cheaply, and increase its budget than anything else.

It began in 1995 when President Clinton named the deputy secretary of defense, John Deutch, to be his DCI, a nomination with near-disastrous consequences all around. It didn't take long before almost all observers agreed that Deutch was a DCI who didn't care about the Agency. Deutch had not wanted the position, and was said to have turned it down numerous times. Word in the Langley halls was that it was only the promise of the secretary of defense cabinet post in Clinton's second term that swayed Deutch to move to the CIA. As such, far too many of his decisions as DCI were assumed by Agency officers, rightly or wrongly, to be based not on operational requirements or on the best interests of the Agency, but rather on keeping himself in good graces with the White House and Congress so as not to jeopardize his desired future assignment. One serious collateral consequence was that more than a few operations officers were concerned about what would happen if they found themselves in serious danger overseas: would Deutch make decisions on rescue or other issues based on requirements for success, or would he bow to Clintonian pressure for inclusion (or exclusion) of options or personnel founded not on mission requirements but instead on irrelevant factors such as racial or gender diversity, the president's political standing, and a general aversion to risk-taking?

Deutch brought with him key protégés from DoD—Nora Slatkin to serve as the Agency's executive director, and Vice-Admiral Dennis Blair to fill the newly created position of Assistant DCI for Military Support—neither of whom knew anything about the intelligence business, much less covert action. Slatkin, previously an assistant secretary of the navy, owed almost her entire career progression to Deutch, and was therefore far more concerned about pleasing and protecting him than she was about the interests of the Agency. Worse, Blair came with an undisguised contempt for the CIA, but this did not deter him from either believing he knew better than career intelligence officers or from initiating action without fully understanding consequences. At one point Blair gave a press conference on Agency clandestine activities in the Balkans in which he related to the media intelligence sources and methods, including information that compromised the identity of several human sources. It cost the Agency nearly $10 million to exfiltrate the sources and their families and to relocate Agency case officers in-country, whose lives were placed in immediate danger, to safer areas (which concomitantly reduced their ability to collect intelligence). Blair was unapologetic and arrogantly asserted that he'd do the same thing again.[10] Apparently that resonated well at the Pentagon, for it wasn't long afterward that he was wearing the four stars of a full admiral and commanding all American forces in the Pacific theater.

But of course it was Deutch, as DCI, who had the most deleterious effect on the Agency. Deutch was determined to change the culture of the Agency, especially the operations area, by making it more like the military. Yet doing so would have unquestionably resulted in the degradation of the CIA's renowned, exceptional flexibility and responsiveness—characteristics one never associates with military bureaucracy, yet which are essential in covert action operations.[11] At one point he ordered a junior field operations officer to leave a briefing on an exceptionally sensitive matter, even after it was explained to him that the officer was in the room because she was handling the recruited agent and collecting the intelligence. Deutch countered that such a sensitive asset should have been handled by a more senior officer. It was then pointed out that this junior officer was the one who had actually recruited the asset and, therefore, was absolutely the best officer to handle him. Deutch was unmoved, unable to get past a military mind-set regarding the roles of senior and junior officers that simply does not apply to the CIA mission.[12]

One very obvious, and exceptionally detrimental, result of Deutch's intention to change the Agency culture was the proliferation of staffs and the concomitant need for experienced officers to fill staff positions. Unlike the vastly larger military services, the CIA does not have sufficient employees to conduct operations while also sustaining a separate category of headquarters staff officers whose sole raison d'être is to serve the individual needs of senior officers. Far too often, field operations officers—those folks doing the Agency's core mission of recruiting and running spies and collecting intelligence—were reassigned to headquarters staff duties, leaving fewer operations personnel either to run operations overseas or to manage the operations from Washington.[13] As the Agency was also downsizing in the wake of the collapse of the Soviet Union, the ranks of field operations officers thinned out dangerously while dozens of unnecessary staff positions were created.

Manifestly, responsibility for peacetime covert action was not immune from Deutch's intrusions. While at the Pentagon, Deutch had come to believe that the military could create and manage peacetime covert action programs better and cheaper than the CIA, although why this was so is unclear, save possibly for a visceral and general dislike of any competitor agency. But many CIA officers believed there were additional motives: a particular dislike of the CIA, a desire to garner the congressionally designated funds used to pay for covert action programs, and—perhaps most important— a hope of acquiring highly sophisticated new covert action technologies that the CIA had developed, but had not shared with DoD.[14]

The Military and Peacetime Covert Action

In short, Deutch, along with Blair (who knew absolutely nothing about the CIA's conduct of peacetime covert action), sought to involve the military in covert action, even though they had no knowledge of the reasons why, for nearly fifty years, president after president had assigned only the CIA to covert action missions. Indeed, they did not even realize that it was a key element of EO 12333. Early on in his tenure, Deutch attempted to initiate a covert action program, limiting knowledge of the program to but ten individuals—none of whom were from the Directorate of Operations! Eventually the deputy director of operations learned of the program, but by that time basic errors in operational tradecraft had been made, dooming the program to failure and wasting a large amount of taxpayers' money.[15] Over time, CIA officers experienced in covert action spent many long hours explaining and detailing covert action missions, Agency capabilities, and the laws and executive orders governing covert action to Blair and Slatkin. Finally, they began to see the light. But it was not an easy road.

Possibly the lowest period was Memorial Day weekend 1995, when the Clinton administration was seeking a policy to deal with the genocide and seemingly perpetual crisis in Bosnia. During the whole of that long holiday weekend, senior CIA, military, civilian DoD, and State Department officers met almost without break to work out a covert action program, despite the absence of any coherent policy. In this marathon conference the military sought to create—and thus control—a "covert" program for Bosnia. But the final military-generated "covert program" concept was not covert in the slightest. It involved CIA personnel openly working with large numbers of uniformed U.S. military in supplying huge amounts of materials and training local forces. The projected cost was, in a word, staggering, much greater than the gross domestic products of more than half of the world's nations. The "covert action program" went nowhere, resulting only in the total waste of an enormous amount of very senior government officials' time.

Nearing the end of their tenures in office, the Deutch clique finally came to understand the multiple reasons why the CIA was the presidential choice to conduct classic peacetime covert action, and from that point on, life for those Agency officers in the covert action business was a bit more comfortable. But those lessons may have to be learned all over again, as the United States fights the war against terrorism. As this was being written (a year into that war), Secretary of Defense Donald Rumsfeld was mulling over the use of the Defense Intelligence Agency and Special Forces troops to conduct covert action operations, normally the province of the CIA's paramilitary operatives, thus blurring significantly the line between peacetime covert action requiring a Presidential Finding and wartime special operations. The chairman of the Senate Select Committee on Intelligence at the time, Senator Bob Graham, was highly skeptical, indicating that he and the committee would be alert to any "end runs" by the military to attempt to subvert the Finding requirement, noting that "the fundamental reason the intelligence committees were created in the first place was because of covert actions that had run amok." This notwithstanding, Rumsfeld established the position of undersecretary of defense for intelligence, creating a separate intelligence evaluation process that is alleged to provide the secretary with conclusions that support his particular policy slant by evading the rigorous corroborative measures that professional intelligence analysts conduct as a matter of course. (As of spring 2004, serious questions have been raised about the DoD evaluation process in light of the failure to locate weapons of mass destruction in the wake of the Iraq war—weapons the Pentagon were absolutely certain existed.)[16]

Similarly, in early 2002 the Pentagon under Rumsfeld established a new Office of Strategic Influence dedicated to the dissemination of news items, both authentic and (selectively) false—in other words, disinformation—to foreign journalists; the office was quickly disbanded, however, when confronted with public criticism. Yet just eight months later, in October 2002, the Pentagon began reviewing the possibility of conducting covert influence operations as a component of the war against terrorism. Conceivably this would have entailed both propaganda and political action, targeted at the policy elites and the general public in neutral—and friendly—nations. The objectives would be to gain support for U.S. policies in fighting terrorism and to reverse public opinion hostile to the United States in the target countries. The Pentagon stated that its authority to conduct these operations stems from an existing DoD directive that permits similar operations but limits them to "adversary decision makers" (DoD Directive 3600.1: Information Operations); the creation of a covert peacetime capability, it argued, would only require amending the directive. DoD's reasoning, à la John Deutch of years past, was that the military possesses superior technological equipment, that the U.S. military has "important interests" in a number of countries, and that no other U.S. government agency is capable of conducting these missions.[17]

Of course, this proposal raises several issues. First, targeting neutral and friendly countries for influence operations in peacetime still requires a Presidential Finding under the Intelligence Authorization Act of 1991 and Executive Order 12333. The military should have no confidence that an internal DoD directive removes this statutory obligation. Second, much of what is accomplished in influence operations is not a matter of technology but of recruiting the human sources with the right access to serve as agents. And it is the CIA that has officers overseas and in contact with necessary third-country nationals, not DoD. Third, if DoD is allowed to pursue its own influence operations, where is the guarantee that they will be congruent with established U.S. foreign policy? All of the CIA's covert influence operations are intensively coordinated with the Department of State and reported to Congress to insure compliance and compatibility with established overt presidential policies. What are the odds that DoD would require that its own internal covert action programs be coordinated with overt diplomatic efforts by the Department of State and covert programs run by the CIA? Without this nexus, programs that should be complementary and synergistic are apt to be competitive and counterproductive.

Finally, the mission of favorably influencing allies belongs primarily to diplomats and elected officials. But if the U.S. government decided to do so covertly, then, again, current law stipulates that a Finding is required. One can only conclude that the war on terrorism combined with an aggressive secretary of defense has re-invigorated a dormant DoD desire to move into the peacetime covert action business through a mechanism (the DoD directive) that, in their eyes, precludes the need for a Finding. And that is, in plain talk, a terrible idea.

FIVE

The Discipline of Covert Action

When the President asks the CIA to undertake a covert program because he cannot obtain public support for an overt policy, the CIA will be left holding the Presidential bag.[1]

DCI Robert M. Gates

The intelligence discipline of covert action consists of three well-established methodological, or operational, subsets and one newly emerging category. Traditional covert action operations involve propaganda, political action, and paramilitary operations. Propaganda is the least visible, least expensive, least threatening, and most subtle of the covert action methodologies. It also usually requires the greatest amount of time to be effective. Political action ranges from low key, simple, and inexpensive events to the highly visible and provocative. Paramilitary operations run the gamut from low-cost, discreet training for foreign military and security forces to the clandestine exfiltration of defectors, and on to hugely expensive programs such as supporting the Afghanistan resistance in the 1980s. Any discussion of covert action must at least allude to deception operations, though they are not one of the primary operational methodologies. While rarely employed by the CIA, deception operations are an essential part of military operational planning.[2]

In addition to the three traditional methodologies, the emerging dependence of government bureaucracies, international businesses, financial institutions, worldwide criminal and terrorist groups, and individuals on computer systems in the 1980s created a new discipline of intelligence methodology, both in the collection of information and in covert action programs. The ability to clandestinely access data in computers to destroy or modify it, or even to destroy the hardware itself, is generically referred to as "information warfare," providing new operational vistas for the imaginative intelligence or counterintelligence professional.

PROPAGANDA

Propaganda is the systematic dissemination of specific doctrines, viewpoints, or messages to a chosen audience. Usually it is employed to foster the acceptance, by the chosen target audience, of a particular policy position or opinion, although at times propaganda may be used simply to denigrate or undermine a belief or position held by a foreign audience without advocating an alternative. University of Georgia professor and intelligence scholar Loch K. Johnson has described propaganda as the most "extensive" form of covert action: "whatever policy the White House may be extolling at the time . . . the CIA will likely be advancing the same slogans through its hidden channels."[3] Propaganda is often superior to other types of covert influence provided that there is sufficient time available for it to work, for intelligent minds are not quick to abandon strongly held beliefs. Initiating a propaganda operation may require months, for media assets—agents working in the news media, with academic journals or the Internet, or in other professions that give them an influential voice in the public arena—first have to be identified, recruited, and tested by field case officers before the program can commence.

Once the recruited and vetted agents begin placing the desired messages, success demands time for subtle thoughts and ideas to float through the various channels, attract the attention of the target audience, and, ultimately, influence or change their minds. The overall time required for a propaganda operation to work its magic depends upon a range of variables, including the number of channels available to disseminate the messages, the quality of the assets involved, the nature (e.g., openness) of the society, the character of the government, and so forth.

Depending on the type of propaganda, the originator or sponsor of the product may be openly identified, disguised, or falsely represented as some other source. Although a frequent presumption is that propaganda is composed of partial or total falsehood, in point of fact the best propaganda is the truth well presented and well argued. Nor does the source have to be disguised or hidden. Many governments have within their foreign ministries an official "news agency" that disseminates information about the government's policies and responds to critics of these policies.[4] This includes the United States, which has as its official voice the Office of International Information Programs in the State Department. Despite the official status of these agencies and the fact that the information they provide is accurate, albeit perhaps rather one-sided and often lacking complete objectivity, their products are propaganda nonetheless. After all, the intention of these government-sponsored, official "news" organizations is to promote their countries' national positions within the world community, to create and sustain a favorable image of their sponsoring government, and to provide news that may not otherwise be available to their audiences. Likewise, some governments also fund an overseas public radio network that provides news and other programming to various world regions, sometimes in the language of that region. The Voice of America, British Broadcasting System, Australian Broadcasting Company, National China News Agency, and Radio Moscow are all well-known examples of governmental radio networks that serve their sponsors' national purposes.

Perhaps the best-known official American propaganda organs

were Radio Free Europe (RFE) and Radio Liberty (RL), established early in the cold war to broadcast across the Iron Curtain to Soviet and Eastern European citizens. Through RFE and RL, oppressed populations, whose own governments provided only highly slanted and frequently false information to the public, could learn the truth about world events. Although funded and run covertly by the CIA for a number of years before being overtly managed by the United States Information Service, there was never much doubt among listeners as to the sponsoring government. Millions listened secretly to these broadcasts for decades, until the end of the cold war ushered in their own free media.

Simply repeating the truth, or the truth as one sees or understands it, is a highly underestimated form of propaganda. During forty years of cold war, there was never any need for the United States to lie to the Soviet people about the nature of their regime; they, far better than anyone else, knew that the Soviet government was corrupt, oppressive, and dangerous. The American government needed only to accurately relate world events to counter the deceitful lies the Soviet regime told its own citizens. Indeed, it would have been counterproductive for the United States to exaggerate or fabricate stories, for doing so would only have undermined the credibility of the United States and weakened its democratic ideals.

Included in U.S. propaganda operations against the USSR were the "Nationalities" programs intended to keep alive the heritage, culture, and languages of the ethnic minorities in the Soviet Union. These programs were doubly useful in that they also constituted an "attack on the internal legitimacy of the Soviet government." According to former director of central intelligence Robert M. Gates, among materials infiltrated into the USSR as well as other totalitarian governments were "Western literature (books, magazines, newspapers and the like) . . . [and] among other approaches the CIA has dropped leaflets from airplanes, tied transistor radios and Bibles onto balloons lofted towards hostile nations, and broadcast from makeshift radio stations in remote rain forests."[5] Also infiltrated in miniature version were banned works by prominent Russian authors like Aleksandr Isaevich Solzhenitsyn and Boris Pasternak. Unable to see any immediate positive results and disbelieving that such actions could assist in the dismantling of the Soviet system, CIA case officers specializing in Soviet intelligence operations were highly critical of these programs. But these programs were not intended to influence in the short term, nor were they ever touted as the key to the destruction of the Soviet regime. The value of these programs was ultimately seen in the pro-American, pro-democratic attitudes of more than a few former Soviet officials, many of the citizens, and some (but not all) of the governments in the new nations created from the former Soviet republics after the breakup of the Soviet Union.

Propaganda that presents facts in a generally accurate or truthful fashion (albeit perhaps one-sidedly) from official government outlets or from a clearly identified source is referred to as "white" propaganda in the argot of covert action specialists. White propaganda is used to present to foreign audiences the originating government's positions on issues, to explain policy decisions, to provide news unavailable from the local media, and generally to put a human face on the country and its people to the world. If the message emanates from a government agency, it may be considered the official position of that government. Regardless of whether the message is put out by a government or another source, however, if it is found to be untruthful, this fact soon becomes known and the source discredited.[6]

But not all propaganda presents the absolute truth, of course. The operational technique known as "gray" propaganda includes the subtle, or not so subtle, distortion of fact emanating from a source that is opaque or averred to be someone other than the actual author or presenter. "Gray" propaganda is the work of intelligence agencies and, like the overt product, is intended to further the policy interests of the originating government, albeit with disguised sponsorship. A government engages in gray propaganda when, for example, its intelligence agency recruits or induces a foreign newspaper editor or columnist to publish under his own name opinion pieces that coincide with the policies of the government that recruited him. These articles will purportedly reflect the writer's own independent thinking presented as the best policy for his country, but in reality much of the text may have been written at the intelligence agency's headquarters.[7] As these journalists are almost always in favor of the policies they are asked to support in the first place (or, at least, favorably disposed to the country for whose intelligence service they are now working), the fact that they may receive a secretly provided stipend usually serves only as an added incentive.

The attention of the intended audience—which is often, but not always, the general population—may be captured in any number of ways, through any medium that can carry a message: editorials placed in the press or on television, advertisements, television documentaries, tabloid-type exposés, political campaign speeches, books, articles placed in academic journals, weekly news magazines, music videos, radio programs, Internet "chat rooms" or other electronically accessed information sources, and pamphlets can all be utilized to carry a "payload" message. And just as a five-second shot of a particular brand of beer or automobile placed in a movie scene by an advertiser can influence the audience to buy that brand, likewise just a few seconds or minutes of "payload" message adroitly inserted by the propagandist in a documentary, video, newspaper editorial, or magazine article may generate a desired reaction on the part of the unwitting audience.

One excellent way to use gray propaganda to influence a country's elites is for a foreign intelligence service to recruit respected scholars, political figures, and other public figures who will publish articles in scholarly journals or commentary magazines that subtly support the foreign government's policies. In the United States, journals such as *Foreign Affairs* and magazines like *Atlantic Monthly* and *National Review* are read by policymakers and senior officials who work closely with policymakers. As such, an article written covertly at the behest of a foreign government and published in any of these periodicals could conceivably sway the thinking of a congressman, senior cabinet official, or White House staff member.

Articles that are well written, cogently argued, and in which the "payload" message is subtly stated or limited in presence—perhaps just one point in a much longer article that might be on an issue only tangentially related to the payload message—hold the possibility of affecting the perception or position of the reader. Likewise, publishers of scholarly journals are often policy-oriented research institutions (e.g., "think tanks") that may also sponsor issue forums, debates, discussions, and research projects, the results of which might reach policymakers. The ability to influence covertly the products of these institutions is perforce also the ability to influence the policy elites of the nation.[8]

It is "black" propaganda, the complete fabrication of message and source, known in the parlance of Soviet active measures specialists as "disinformation," that can be the most injurious. Black propaganda can reinforce rumor or unfounded beliefs in a population that is, in all probability, not largely literate or sophisticated in the first place and, therefore, at once the most likely to believe the lie and least apt to discern its provenance. This scenario explains the widespread acceptance in the early 1980s throughout the Third World (and especially sub-Saharan Africa) of the allegation—first propagated in India through a story in a pro-Soviet newspaper—that the U.S. government created the AIDS virus. The Soviets were also very successful in exploiting the willingness of South American poor to believe that their babies were at risk of being kidnapped at the behest of rich Americans who would then transplant body parts from those infants into their own sick children. Both stories were products of a KGB disinformation operation designed to discredit the United States in the Third World, and they both resonated for years, propagated by people who were already inclined to think ill of America.

The AIDS story is instructive for two reasons. First, it's a case study of the way a single story in one newspaper can spread throughout the world and influence large segments of the international population. Second, it demonstrates how a story can be so long-lived that it eventually creates unwanted difficulties for the regime that originated it. The AIDS story was generated in 1983 when U.S.-Soviet relations were at a nadir and endured for more than four years into the regime of Mikhail Gorbachev. After taking office, Gorbachev desperately sought to improve relations between the two superpowers, and he soon realized that this story and the negative image of the United States that it had created were beginning to cause problems at home and abroad for his new plans. The KGB then tried to deny the story, but not with unalloyed success. Both the AIDS and the "baby parts" story still lived on through the end of the twentieth century in some areas of the Third World.[9]

Two operations by the KGB to undermine Indian-American relations serve also as prime examples of black propaganda. In 1967, the KGB department responsible for active measures programs forged a series of communications supposedly originating from the U.S. Consulate in Bombay hinting that a major Indian politician, who was also anti-Communist, was both in the pay of the United States and involved in under-the-table dealings with the government of Pakistan. And in 1984 the KGB's effort to "prove" that the CIA was behind the assassination of Indian prime minister Indira Gandhi was a particularly potent operation given the Soviet Union's intense desire to drive a permanent wedge between the world's largest democracy and the West. The fact that the "official" U.S. government documents used to "prove" these stories were clearly fabrications—with very apparent discrepancies from authentic documents—had no impact on the target audience, many of whom were instinctively anti-American and, more importantly, illiterate. These stories resonated throughout sub-Saharan Africa, the subcontinent, and Latin America for years afterward.[10]

One notable exception to the general practice of first spreading black propaganda in the Third World was a highly successful Soviet intelligence operation in Europe using the Italian newspaper *Paese Sera*. An article planted in that daily in 1967 asserted that the CIA was behind the assassination of President John F. Kennedy, an allegation that even many Americans still believe today.[11] This one plant clearly shows the power of the written media with a literate audience and the willingness of a naive public to believe anything that both sounds credible and is aired in a medium that is likewise perceived as credible. This is particularly so when the story plays to a readership already prejudiced or predisposed to believe it.

It must be emphasized that the CIA does not create the propaganda in isolation and for its own purposes. A presidential requirement mandates that all propaganda must coincide with U.S. policy objectives. To insure that this is so, CIA, Department of State, and NSC staff jointly craft a guidance document clearly delineating U.S. government policies; thereafter, all propaganda messages are coordinated among the three entities prior to approval for dissemination by CIA field officers. The document gives policy thematic guidance on whatever issues are approved for propaganda operations, thus insuring that the propaganda supports overt foreign policy measures and objectives. As Georgetown University's Roy Godson asserts, propaganda must run in the same yoke as overall policy, for "[i]t serves little purpose to dabble in the trade unless there are important strategic goals to be achieved and tactical plans for carrying them out."[12]

DECEPTION OPERATIONS

A stepsister of propaganda is the deception operation, intended to confront a specific decision maker with a false reality or to "mislead an enemy by manipulating, distorting, or falsifying evidence to induce a mistaken perception."[13] Students of World War II are familiar with this type of program through Operation Fortitude, used by the Allies to convince Hitler that the D-day landings in June 1944 would take place at the Pas de Calais. More recently, in 1991 the presence of a large U.S. Marine Corps landing force off the Kuwait coast influenced Saddam Hussein to believe that the threat was from that direction rather than from the west—from whence came the Allied attack with devastating results. In these instances, deception, in the words of Boston University professor Angelo Codevilla, works to "ensure that the enemy's strength is wasted while one's own strength is matched against the enemy's weakness"; and because this is done, "deception can make the weak strong, and make the strong unchallengeable. In a close contest, it's the easiest way of tipping the balance."[14]

But deception operations are rarely used outside of the military, however, because they are such complex undertakings. Before a deception operation can be commenced, there must be in place a detailed, coherent policy so that the deception element can be specifically and precisely tailored to enhance and support the larger plan. Then the actual deception operation requires great attention to detail over a long period of time, a circumstance that is perforce a huge investment in manpower and multiple resources or assets in the target country (or countries) to acquire feedback on the effects of operations. In these endeavors, it is critical that the deception operation not only be fully integrated into the overall plan, but that it also be supported by other components having the responsibility of preventing the opponent from collecting accurate information that is contradictory to the deception plot.[15] The fabled Trojan Horse at Troy was a deception operation, while a modern day classic was the "Double Cross" operation by the Twenty Committee (or "XX," hence the double cross sobriquet), in which German spies in Great Britain were turned and used with astonishingly great success to deceive the Germans about Allied plans for the invasion of Europe in 1944. The Double Cross operation, as a case study, makes for exciting but also thoughtful reading for the intelligence professional.

The assets or resources necessary—overlapping human, technical, and open source information—for collecting details on the effects of the deception from within opposition territory must also be in place prior to the commencement of deception operations. This permits the deception program managers to observe the responses by the target audience as soon as they occur and to immediately refine the operations to solidify and sustain the deceptive acts. Moreover, accurate and timely feedback is necessary if unforeseen opportunities are to be exploited and for unforeseen difficulties to be managed before they become fatal.

While intelligence scholars Godson and Wirtz state that "deception is enhanced" when the deceiving power understands the history, culture, government, and sociology of the target country or individuals, it is more accurate to say that this knowledge is essential. Godson and Wirtz are absolutely correct when they recognize that "[f]alse information should conform to the [cultural] idiosyncrasies" of the target audience. Otherwise, readily apparent errors will undermine even the most elaborately designed deception program. In short, "deception planners 'need to know a great deal about the world view of those they are trying to manipulate, and recognize the human proclivity for self-deception.'"[16]

Finally, it is critical that deception material reach the target audience by multiple "creative" methods, including the unorthodox, to permit the target policymakers and intelligence services to corroborate the deception material, allowing the enemy to "confirm" the accuracy of what they're being fed.[17] Perhaps the prototypical non-wartime model of a successful deception program was "The Trust" (officially known as the Moscow Municipal Credit Association), run by Soviet intelligence between 1921 and 1927. The Trust had as its objectives the identification and elimination of anti-Bolshevik threats to the new Leninist regime, particularly among the exile organizations outside of the Soviet Union. Moreover, "the Trust was able to use its contacts with Western intelligence services to pass along misleading and false information on the internal state of the Soviet regime." By these deceptive operations, the Lenin government was able to construct a vastly more positive image of the Soviet regime than had previously existed, allowed time for the Bolsheviks to consolidate their control over the Soviet Union, and "distracted the West with unproductive operations."[18]

POLITICAL ACTION

Political action is a more visible and, often, more aggressive form of covert action than propaganda, although political action operations should be supported and intertwined, "working hand-inglove," with propaganda operations. These programs, in general, are the exploitation of secret contacts and/or the provision of funds in order to affect the political situation in a target country. To this end, the intelligence service of a foreign government will recruit nationals of the target country, or at times third-country nationals, to commit the overt actions while clandestinely providing the funding and requisite materials to these recruited agents. "Front" companies or organizations may also be established to provide cover for the agents and to facilitate the funding process.

Political action operations come in many forms and may include secretly funding political campaigns, with or without the knowledge of the candidate; extending subsidies to agents of influence (individuals who are trusted confidantes of key policymakers, whether or not they themselves hold a government position); funding labor demonstrations or strikes; instigating and funding street demonstrations, marches, or rallies; supporting friendship societies, social groups, or other similar civic organizations that may exert influence on a government; manipulating political events or personages; manipulating economic circumstances (e.g., inserting counterfeit currency to undermine the monetary system, sabotaging key industrial facilities or essential materials or foodstuffs, and "invading" computers and databanks to manipulate or destroy information); and instigating coups to overthrow a sitting government.

At times it seems as though intelligence officers managing political action programs have, as Dr. Loch Johnson says, "resembled nothing less than a group of political campaign consultants, producing slick materials for favored foreign candidates: speeches, brochures, handbills, placards, campaign buttons, and even bumper stickers for remote regions of the globe where donkeys and camels are more common than cars." And certainly political action operations (and propaganda, as well) have expanded in concept and capabilities as the characteristics of modern society—computers, communications, international finance, commercial air travel, and other aspects of a global community—have both facilitated operations and created new opportunities.[19]

For decades the secret funding of political organizations and party members was a staple of American foreign policy and covert action programs. In discussing a program supporting Japan's rightist Liberal Democratic Party, the assistant secretary of state for East Asian Affairs in the Kennedy administration, Roger Hilsman, has stated that the subsidy payments were "so established and so routine" that they played a "fundamental role" in U.S. policy toward Japan. This belief was also shared by America's ambassador to Tokyo in the early 1960s, U. Alexis Johnson, who acknowledged that "the principle was certainly acceptable" to him, for the United States was "financing a party on our side."[20] A few other notable CIA political action programs include intervening covertly in Italian political processes to prevent the Italian Communist Party (PCI) from winning elections between 1948 and the late 1960s, when the party was phased out; overthrowing potentially pro-Communist governments in Iran (1953) and Guatemala (1954); attempting to forestall a Communist government in Indonesia (1957); and providing funds, desktop publishing materials, and other means of support to the banned trade union Solidarity following the imposition of martial law in Poland after 1981.[21]

As mentioned, economic disruption and manipulations of markets are also staples of political action. For edification one need only look at an operation the Soviets executed against the United States in the Nixon years. According to a former director of international economics for the National Security Council, "in 1972 the Soviets surreptitiously bought 25 percent of the U.S. grain harvest, using phone intercepts of the grain dealers' network to listen to both sides of the market. The purchase led to higher grain prices for consumers, and taxpayers provided for a 25-percent-a-bushel export subsidy."[22]

Thus, a well-thought-out political action program, when employed properly and securely, and in consonance with an established overt policy, holds the potential to quietly further the national interests of the government that uses it. It is a means of exerting influence that is more visible and more direct than propaganda, but without necessarily escalating into situations that breed violence or possess the potential to do so. It is a means of placing discrete pressure on an enemy's government at his precise points of weakness without resorting to provocative measures or letting the target government realize that its opponents are other than its own citizens working for a better life. And an agent of influence, highly placed in an adversary's decision-making structure, can steer policies toward the direction that the government he's working for desires in a manner that either prevents hostilities or reduces the chances of hostilities occurring between the two countries. In sum, presidents are attracted to the political action option precisely because it allows them a variety and range of options that will advance their goals while permitting them to escalate their operations in a controlled and graduated manner as circumstances dictate.

PARAMILITARY

The words "covert action" often conjure up mental images of guerillas fighting in Afghanistan or insurgent Contras in Nicaragua—both cases employing force on a scale sufficient to make secrecy impossible but about which the government nonetheless pretended it knew nothing. It is thus understandable if the average American is inclined to believe that paramilitary operations are the raison d'être of the CIA. In point of fact, however, paramilitary programs are the least utilized of the three traditional categories, and they are usually so limited in scope that they seldom rise to public notice. Perhaps surprisingly, they are also quite often the least costly of all the covert action programs.

The CIA's paramilitary cadre is most often employed in training foreign military and security forces in such skills as small unit tactics and VIP protection, although of course beginning in 2002 actual wars in Afghanistan and Iraq have placed heavy operational demands on the paramilitary elements. In the last quarter of the twentieth century, however, training that falls under the rubric of special activities but which requires the support of the Agency's covert action infrastructure—rather than actual combat operations—was by far the most common mission for the paramilitary element. Even in the large, expensive, and well-known paramilitary programs just mentioned (and including the Bay of Pigs), the CIA's role was that of organizer, trainer, and logistician rather than actual combatant. But there have been times when Agency officers were indeed conducting combat operations. One obvious example was the "secret war" in Laos in the 1960s, where Agency staff and contract officers not only trained but led indigenous tribesmen, predominantly the Hmong, in combat operations against the Communist Pathet Lao.[23]

During the 1980s there were occasional criticisms of the training programs that CIA paramilitary officers routinely provided to security and military forces in the Persian Gulf states, even though the cost to the U.S. government of each round of training was often only in the low six figures. The value of these and similar low-cost programs to the U.S. government was proven in the days following the 1990 invasion of Kuwait by Iraq: when American military forces needed air, land, and sea bases and other support mechanisms for Desert Shield/Desert Storm, none of the Gulf States denied use of their territory. While these paramilitary training programs cannot claim all the credit for this, the personal and professional relationships that these programs established and nurtured over the years with senior officers and government leaders in the Gulf states helped to lay the foundation for generating a pro-U.S. attitude. In many ways, then, CIA paramilitary programs are not only specialized operations, but they serve also as force multipliers for U.S. government policies.

INFORMATION WARFARE

The use of the personal computer, communications networks, and electronic databases by government agencies and businesses of every ilk—not all legitimate by any means—has permitted creative individuals to engage in a new pastime. Private citizens, sitting at their home computers, soon learned how to intrude clandestinely into large institutional computer systems and databases, no matter how distant the site, to steal, alter, and destroy data, or to damage or destroy hardware and software in the target computer. When done by individuals acting on their own initiative and for their own reasons, the intrusive act is called "hacking." While definitions are malleable, the Japanese government has enacted a law defining hacking (or cyberterrorism) as "the unauthorized entry into computer systems through communications networks . . . and the damage caused to those systems as a result of the unauthorized access."[24]

When hacking is carried out by a nation's military, or by a government intelligence or security agency for national security purposes, the terminology is "information warfare."[25] Information warfare is a weapon applicable across the board against a country's governmental infrastructure, power and energy producers, banks and financial institutions, and media, as well as the supporting infrastructures of outlaw organizations such as terrorist groups and narcotics traffickers (which are, ironically, structured very much as legitimate businesses in order to track income, expenses, inventory, production, and so forth).

Information warfare is also used to describe attacks against governments and civilian institutions by terrorists, organized crime, and other outlaw enterprises (as opposed to the individual who hacks for fun or sport). In short, what differentiates hacking from information warfare is the affiliation (or lack thereof) of the person or organization committing the act and their motive for doing so.

One example of the potential threat cyberterrorists pose to governments took place in Japan at the hands of the terrorist group known as Aum Shinrikyo, best known for releasing canisters of poisonous sarin gas in the Tokyo subway system in 1995. In 2000, Japanese investigators were shocked to learn that the Japanese Defense Ministry, nearly a dozen other government agencies, and almost one hundred key Japanese businesses, including Nippon Telegraph and Telephone, were using more than one hundred software programs developed by Aum Shinrikyo and sold through front companies. Damage that could have been caused by these programs was potentially devastating: the terrorist group could have "compromised security by breaching firewalls, gaining access to sensitive information or systems, allowing invasion by outsiders, planting viruses that could be set off later, or planting malicious code that could cripple computer systems and key data systems."[26]

With the near-universal reliance on computer systems and databases by governments, businesses, and illegal organizations (e.g., front companies established by narcotics cartels and terrorist groups, or bank accounts utilized for money laundering), it was only a matter of time before governments began to look at information warfare (IW) for national security purposes. Complicating defenses against information warfare—while concomitantly facilitating the offensive work of IW warriors—is the very nature of the World Wide Web, which was, according to cyberterrorism expert Richard A. Love, "developed for efficiency, not security . . . [it] allows easy access [and is] difficult to control or exclude wrongdoers from committing illegal acts." The same can be said for multitudes of other computer networks of all sizes and types utilized by institutions, which could be significant targets for cyberterrorists. In the United States, "85 percent of critical infrastructure is privately owned, rendering government solutions [for security and protection] without private cooperation hollow and likely to fail." In Great Britain, a former foreign minister has allowed that "hacking could cripple Britain faster than a military strike" because the nation's military infrastructure is managed and controlled predominantly by computers.[27]

As a covert action tool, information warfare is a capability that has existed for some years but which has rarely been employed by American presidents (for reasons discussed below) until the terrorist attacks of September 11, 2001.[28] While the CIA and U.S. military forces have many of the same capabilities and methodologies to conduct information warfare as covert action, their objectives are vastly different. Should a U.S. military service, in peacetime, clandestinely and remotely enter a potentially hostile military force's computer system—for example, an air defense network or a command and control net—to alter or damage data, hardware, or software, this would be a technical or electronic form of "preparation of the battlefield," intended to allow our military to disable the computer and its data just before an attack. While this act would be at least partially analogous to covert action, no Presidential Finding would be required, for battlefield preparation unambiguously falls within the military's standing legal authorities. In contrast, were the U.S. military to be tasked by the president to use its capabilities to remotely and clandestinely enter, say, a database of a bank in a foreign nation to alter data in an account used by a weapons trafficker, then a Finding would indeed be necessary.[29]

It is a different matter if the CIA engages in a peacetime information warfare operation as covert action. As with any covert action program, it would manifestly require a Presidential Finding, be subjected to the intra- and interagency approval processes, and be duly reported to Congress.[30] While IW might appear at first blush to be an ideal tool for a president to employ in a range of areas, there is at least one serious consideration that argues against it: the bad guys can use information warfare, too, with potentially serious consequences for millions. Specifically, the United States Treasury Department is deeply concerned about the ability of computer experts, working for terrorist groups or other criminal organizations, to breach the databases of finance ministries, central banks, stock and bond markets, and similar enterprises through which the international financial world operates, believing such electronic invasions would have a devastating effect. Paper money rarely changes hands anymore in the world of high finance: "funds" are withdrawn, transferred, and deposited electronically, with computers "holding" or accounting for the monies. Similarly, stocks are bought and sold internationally via computer transactions and, like money, the "shares" exist only in databases. The fear is that, for example, a narcotics cartel that has seen its electronically transferred funds mysteriously disappear, as they pass through multiple financial institutions during the laundering process, might retaliate by attempting to erase or otherwise corrupt databases residing in an international financial institution or a nation's primary stock exchange. A successful attempt could create chaos in world financial markets.[31]

Thus, while computer intrusions as a covert action capability hold a great deal of promise and allure, as long as so many government and world enterprises are dependent on computer databases that have yet to be protected in an absolute manner, presidents will no doubt be wary of recommendations to resort to information warfare against other than military or terrorist targets. That said, information warfare has already been used on a limited scale, as "computer hacker technology has been used to disrupt international money transfers and other financial activities of [individuals in terrorist support networks]."[32] Clearly, information warfare is the covert action tool of the future.

SIX

Approval and Review of Covert Action Programs in the Modern Era

By authorizing covert action and surrounding it with procedural safeguards, backed by specific criminal sanctions, we may be able to construct a web of vested interests and prudent fears that will better protect against abuse of [covert action], both in foreign and domestic affairs.[1]

Walter F. Murphy,
Professor Emeritus,
Princeton University

Until the mid-1970s, there was very little congressional oversight of the CIA, and particularly of covert action programs. Senior members of Congress who chose to be briefed would be informed of programs in the very broadest of terms sufficient to justify funding requests, although often they deliberately chose *not* to be briefed on programs while nonetheless approving the requisite funds. Clark Clifford, close advisor to President Truman and other chief executives, commented that "Congress chose not to be involved and preferred to be uninformed." Likewise, former

CIA general counsel and distinguished intelligence historian Walter Pforzheimer recounted that "We allowed Congress to set the pace. We briefed in whatever detail they wanted. But one of the problems was you couldn't get Congress to get interested." And these opinions were corroborated by members of Congress themselves. The venerable Democrat and member of the Senate's Armed Forces Committee John Stennis, when offered a CIA briefing on a covert action program, hastily cut in: "No, no, my boy, don't tell me. Just go ahead and do it—but I don't want to know." And the ranking Republican on the Senate Armed Services Committee, Leverett Saltonstall, stated in 1955, "It is not a question of reluctance on the part of CIA officials to speak to us. Instead, it is a question of our reluctance, if you will, to seek information and knowledge on subjects which I personally . . . would rather not have. . . ."[2] Whether covert programs succeeded or failed was of little concern: these veteran legislators had lived through World War II, and, with the onset of the cold war, they not only believed that vital American security interests were at stake but also that the president had sole authority to conduct secret programs aimed at preventing Communist (particularly Soviet) domination of the world. Moreover, they realized that such programs entailed risk of failure and expected only that the risks be calculated beforehand and that no high-risk/low-gain operations be undertaken unless absolutely necessary.[3]

THE PRESIDENTIAL FINDING

But the general mistrust of the executive branch that arose from the Vietnam War was then exacerbated by other events, including but not limited to U.S. activities surrounding a military coup in Chile that replaced a democratically elected (albeit Socialist) government with a military dictatorship. These events, along with the revelations of earlier covert actions and the Watergate scandal, conspired to place the executive branch in a weakened position vis-à-vis a Congress that was intent on aggressively reasserting its constitutional prerogatives in foreign policy—including a more active role in intelligence matters.[4]

A growing civil war in the former Portuguese colony of Angola led to the Ford administration's decision to intervene covertly on the side of the anti-Marxist forces, and also heightened congressional interest in other intelligence operations. In the words of one CIA general-counsel: "In particular, the involvement of the CIA in various covert activities received considerable attention. Congressional reaction was an attempt to assert control."[5] But from the perspective of legislators on the Hill, the purpose behind "asserting" authority was not to control but instead to "ensure clear lines of authority and accountability."[6] The legislative mechanism for asserting control over covert action was the Hughes-Ryan Amendment to the Foreign Assistance Act of 1961—interestingly, the only intelligence reform measure passed by a Congress that had considered over two hundred such proposals.[7] (Moreover, in the quarter-century from 1949 to 1975, only two out of 150 proposals for reforming intelligence oversight passed the Congress.)[8] In short, Hughes-Ryan prohibited the expenditure of any funds by any U.S. government agency for covert action operations unless the president "found" that the operations were in the national security interest of the United States and reported this to the Congress, in writing. Not surprisingly, the reporting document quickly became known as a "Presidential Finding." Amendments to extant Findings were called "Memoranda of Notification," or MON.[9]

Enacted in 1974, the Hughes-Ryan Amendment had two immediate effects. First, it eliminated the president's ability to disclaim any knowledge of covert action operations. From Truman's time on, presidents had sought to strictly limit the knowledge of covert action programs, in part so that they could maintain "plausible deniability" of U.S. government involvement in case of public exposure or compromise. With the advent of the Finding, the president not only had to put his name to a paper directing that the operation take place, but that paper had to be transmitted to Congress in advance of commencing the program, expanding significantly the number of people aware of the program ("witting," in Agency parlance). Hughes-Ryan initially required that the Finding be reported to a total of eight congressional committees, four in each house: the Appropriations, Armed Services, and Foreign Affairs Committees and the new intelligence oversight committees—the House Permanent Select Committee on Intelligence (HPSCI), and the Senate Select Committee on Intelligence (SSCI). Thus, the total number of witting persons on Capitol Hill was not small, for selected committee staff were also read into the programs. The Intelligence Oversight Act of 1980 amended Hughes-Ryan by reducing to two the number of congressional committees requiring notification—the intelligence oversight committees—but nonetheless Hughes-Ryan was the practical death of "plausible deniability."[10]

The administrative demise of plausible deniability by dint of the Finding coincided with the arrival of William E. Colby as director of central intelligence, who asserted that he "proscribed the use of that term [because] I do not believe that we can tell the American people an untruth . . . we can give the American people true statements, and keep secret other matters that have to be secret, [b]ut I do not believe we can tell them an untruth."[11] From another perspective, accountability to Congress and, ultimately, to the American people is completely antithetical to the concept of plausible deniability.[12] This is as it should be in a democracy; with the advent of the Finding, accountability trumped deniability.

Second, Hughes-Ryan gave Congress constitutional as well as informal means to halt covert action operations in progress and prevent new programs from commencing. In essence, the amendment established the equivalent of a congressional veto over covert action programs, even though Findings technically only inform Congress and are not a request for program approval. Nonetheless, Congress holds this veto through its constitutional authority to authorize and appropriate public funds. Whereas presidents had previously been able to pay for covert action programs by tapping the general (and secret) Agency budget outside of congressional scrutiny, now Congress would know explicitly how the funds were being spent. If presented with a Finding that didn't meet its favor, Congress, through HPSCI and SSCI, could refuse the monies, thus stopping the covert action program dead.[13]

Members of the oversight committees could also take their objections directly to the president, who might find well-reasoned concerns sufficiently compelling to cancel a Finding. According to scholars, Presidents Carter, Reagan, and George H.W. Bush heeded the concerns of legislators and annulled Findings—but whether the presidents were convinced by the force of the legislators' argument or whether they were reluctant to buck powerful members of Congress and risk retaliation against other presidentially desired programs is unclear. A covert action program in Africa proposed soon after Reagan's inauguration resulted in the receipt of a letter from HPSCI of sufficient impact that it persuaded the White House to drop the plan. And both Reagan and George H.W. Bush floated to the oversight committees covert action proposals to overthrow Panamanian dictator Manuel Noriega. The legislators thought Reagan's plan, which reportedly had already been enshrined in a signed Finding that then had to be rescinded, might result in the death of Noriega. In Bush's case the proposal, which apparently was constituted in a briefing to Congress, was thought by the solons to be too "vague" and lacking in substance.[14]

And too, the intelligence oversight committees have the right to take to the full House or Senate any issues or concerns they have, which, in the case of covert action programs, would destroy the "covertness"—either forcing the president to drop the program or find a way to pursue it through overt mechanisms. And finally, a less-than-respectable but just as effective "last resort veto" could be achieved simply by leaking the existence of the Finding to the press.[15]

But the congressional oversight ensured by a Finding or MON isn't all negative for the executive branch by any means. When Congress favors a program it can be strongly supportive in a number of ways. It can, of course, insure that sufficient funds (or more) are always available. If the members and staffers understand fully the difficulties and risks involved in a particular program or operation, they can come to the defense of the Agency if there should be a compromise or failure. If unforeseen problems or circumstances arise, the overseers may be the first to step forward and ask, "What do you need? What can we do to help?" Members of Congress, and especially committee staff, often possess more knowledge about the programs than the Agency officers managing them, as those on the Hill tend to stay in their positions for years while Agency personnel usually change assignments every two to three years, if not more often. Thus, the overseers frequently have more long-term memory and understanding of a program than do their Agency contacts. This enables the committee members and staff to alert the intelligence managers to problems or developments that they might otherwise have missed. And if the Agency personnel involved have been straightforward and honest in reporting the accomplishments and other events in a program, the personal trust generated between the Agency officers and the committees will often pay dividends in the future.

Like the benefits of congressional oversight, there was another, delayed result of Hughes-Ryan that became apparent only in later years: Should Findings apply only to purely "classical" covert action programs, or should they be utilized also for intelligence activities that are either clearly *not* intelligence collection or CI and/or that constitute a "special activity" employing the CIA's covert action infrastructure (i.e., personnel and resources—aircraft, boats, technology, stocks—that are maintained under the CIA umbrella for use in covert action programs)? If the latter, then missions such as the foreign training programs in support of friendly governments carried out by the Agency's paramilitary/special operations cadre would require Findings.[16] By 1988 the broader interpretation prevailed, and Findings were written for any program that manifestly was *not* FI or CI, whether a classic covert action operation or simply a foreign government support program that utilized the covert action infrastructure (i.e., a "special activity").

More revisions of Hughes-Ryan followed with the Intelligence

Oversight Act of 1988, passed in the wake of the Iran-Contra abuses. One transgression that had caught in the legislative craw was the ten-month delay (perhaps at the urging of DCI William J. Casey) between President Reagan's decision to sell arms to the Iranians in exchange for American hostages held in Beirut and his subsequent notification of Congress of this program—which he gave only after it had been revealed to the world in a Lebanese newspaper. The Intelligence Oversight Act of 1980 had amended the original Hughes-Ryan notification requirements to permit the president to notify Congress of any new Finding in a "timely fashion," an opaque phrase that was not further defined (recall that the original language had required only advance notice). The Reagan administration had argued that "timely fashion" gave the president "virtually unfettered discretion to choose the right moment" to reveal a program to the legislative branch. Believing that this would allow any president to hide from Congress sensitive programs, thus undermining Congress's constitutional responsibility to conduct oversight of the executive, the 1988 Act discarded "timely fashion" in favor of a near-absolute forty-eight-hour period, although this stipulation did not preclude the president from acting absent congressional consultation in an emergency situation to protect the national interest.

The Intelligence Authorization Act of 1991 officially repealed Hughes-Ryan and replaced it with even stronger statutory oversight demands. It's obvious from even the most general reading of the Act's requirements that the abuses of power discovered in the Iran-Contra scandal lay at the foundation of the new legislation. The Act specifically mandates that the president be the final approving authority for covert action programs, that he sign the document specifically noting this fact, and that he affirm that the programs are in support of "identifiable policy objectives." No Finding may be signed retroactively and all must be in writing. No part of the program can violate the Constitution of the United States or any extant federal law. The president must list all U.S. government agencies that play a role in the program, as well as any foreign (i.e., "third party") countries involved. Finally, no program can be used to influence U.S. political processes, media, policies, or public opinion. The forty-eight–hour notification requirement remained.[17]

APPROVAL AND REVIEW IN
HISTORICAL PERSPECTIVE

From Truman to Nixon (that is, prior to Hughes-Ryan), only large-scale or politically risky programs received presidential scrutiny. The CIA had the standing authority to initiate and execute low-level, low-cost, low-risk "routine" covert action programs without prior presidential approval or even notification, so long as the programs were in consonance with presidentially established foreign policy objectives. These programs existed alongside those that manifestly did require presidential attention. For the major programs, presidents consulted only with the highest levels of the national security departments and agencies; rarely did any mid-level officers participate, as each president sought to strictly limit the number of people knowledgeable of the mere existence of covert action programs, much less their details. With only the president and his closest, most trusted associates aware of these programs, plausible deniability would be more effective in case of compromise.

But limiting knowledge of programs had one major drawback: it excluded experts on the geographic regions and on the key issues at hand who worked further down the chain—professionals who might have saved several presidents much embarrassment. For example, Cuban experts at the CIA and State Department could have explained why the masses would still support Castro rather than the invading rebels, and amphibious warfare experts at the Defense Department could have explained why the Bay of Pigs was an execrable site for landing an invasion force. But Kennedy's desire for secrecy and repeated assurances of senior officers who were not authorities on Cuba led to the exclusion of the true experts.

Although not covert action, the Iranian hostage rescue mission also serves as an example of what can result when a program is too compartmentalized. Eagle Claw, as it was named, was an operation that suffered gravely from secrecy and "need to know," but for a different reason than the Bay of Pigs. While plausible deniability was the predominant goal in the Bay of Pigs, with Eagle Claw the highest priority in the planning and rehearsal stages was operational security. Washington policy makers were certain that if Soviet intelligence were to learn of the mission, whether through human spies, satellite coverage, signals intelligence, or other methodology, they would alert their Iranian neighbors (the Soviets having nothing to lose and much to gain by doing so). Virtually all decisions made with respect to planning and rehearsing for Eagle Claw opted to err on the side of security, and this factor, combined with other misjudgments (e.g., the weather and the number of helicopters), reduced the chances of success significantly.[18]

With the advent of the Finding, the demise of presidential deniability, and the necessity of placing all covert action programs within the jurisdiction of Hughes-Ryan regardless of scope, cost, or risk, there was a recognized need at the White House for more scrutiny and control over the programs. For this to transpire, a systematic, institutionalized process both for approving new programs and periodically reviewing extant programs for effectiveness, risk, and policy adherence had to be created. As it has developed, the covert action approval and review process exists solely at the discretion of the president, who can make the reviewing group(s) as large or small, or as numerous, as he wishes (or dispense with any such group altogether); likewise, he can make the process formal, casual, or somewhere in between. The processes have been refined within the various administrations over the past three decades primarily because of deficiencies in the original Hughes-Ryan Amendment, the deliberate efforts to circumvent congressional oversight in the Iran-Contra scandal, and simply because, like any bureaucratic exercise, these processes were an evolutionary art form.

President Carter was the first to institute an official, specific, standardized process to approve and review covert action programs that required experts to participate at different stages.[19] It worked well for Carter, and it worked well for Reagan, so long as it was followed. After Iran-Contra, which was of course deliberately *not* subjected to the approval and review process (had it been, there would have been no scandal in the first place), Reagan's process was amended to exclude the National Security Council (NSC) and its staff from engaging in covert action programs (a statute later codified in the 1991 Intelligence Authorization Act). This revision was adopted part and parcel by George H.W. Bush, although the names of the various participating components were altered. Bill Clinton next modified the process slightly, bringing in officers at the GS-15/full colonel rank for a first cut at proposed programs. Since the Reagan years, the covert action approval and review processes have been such that (a) there is no possibility of a "rogue" operation by the CIA and (b) lawyers are present at every stage to ensure that constitutional requirements, federal statutes, executive orders, and internal Agency regulations are fully complied with. Critics who continue to accuse the Agency of running unauthorized operations or Agency officers of ignoring the Constitution and the law are either functioning on information that is more than a quarter-century out-of-date or deliberately ignoring the truth to pursue their own agenda.

APPROVAL AND REVIEW IN THE REAGAN/BUSH ERA

Once in office President Reagan promulgated a formal process governing the approval of new covert action programs and established an annual review for active programs. In response, senior CIA management as well as the Directorate of Operations established their own separate approval and review procedures. The intent was to ensure that all covert action programs reaching the president's desk for approval or renewal had been thoroughly reviewed by staff for policy congruence, operational effectiveness and security, interagency coordination, legality, and cost.

At the White House, a committee called the Planning and Co-ordination Group (PCG), which was composed of high-level representatives (often the deputies) from the Departments of State and Defense and other relevant agencies, was to review all covert action programs current and proposed. Once a proposed program had navigated the PCG, it was passed on to the National Security Planning Group (NSPG), which was essentially the statutory members of the National Security Council augmented by the heads (or their delegates) of other agencies having a stake in the program. A revision of this process was implemented on January 18, 1985, in National Security Decision Directive (NSDD)-159, *Covert Action Policy Approval and Coordination Procedures*.[20] The approval and review process was again amended after Iran-Contra on October 15, 1987, in NSDD-286, *Approval and Review of Special Activities*, the most important element of which was the prohibition against the NSC staff executing covert action operations. NSDD-286 proved so effective that Presidents Bush and Clinton retained it without substantive revision, save that the PCG became the "Deputies Committee" and the NSPG became the "Principals Committee," to reflect the status of the members in their respective agencies.

APPROVAL AND REVIEW IN THE CLINTON ADMINISTRATION

The procedure in place during the Clinton years for approval and review of covert action programs (and which was still essentially in effect in the George W. Bush administration at the end of 2002) was straightforward and composed of checks and balances at multiple levels.[21] First, the White House (i.e., the president or the national security advisor) transmitted to the CIA a directive to generate proposals for a possible covert action program. Only the president or the national security advisor could task the CIA to originate covert action planning, although any executive agency with foreign policy or national security responsibilities—*excluding the CIA*—was able to recommend this option to the NSC.[22]

That the tasking for modern covert action programs arises in the White House and *not* at CIA headquarters is a concept that to this day is still egregiously misunderstood by observers and denied by critics.

Indeed, even recent literature still places the onus for originating covert action programs on the Agency. For example, a report of a blue ribbon panel on covert action published by the Twentieth Century Fund in 1991 states that "CIA officers, not politically appointed officials or zealots in the White House, propose the bulk of covert action operations." The source for the panel's determination was the 1976 Church Committee report. Apparently no one on the panel considered that something might have changed in a decade and a half or felt compelled to question the Church Committee report's continuing validity. Other examples of this misconception abound in materials published as recently as 2000.[23]

Not only do covert action proposals originate in the White House; ideally, there should also be a comprehensive overt policy in existence in which to integrate a complementary covert element. Too, White House policymakers should have sufficient knowledge of covert action capabilities for their request to the CIA to contain at least fairly specific guidance. Les Aspin, a former congressman and Clinton's first secretary of defense, suggested specific questions for the president to consider before "buying into" a proposed covert action program. First, is the proposal based on sound intelligence, which presumably would be multiple-source and cross-checked? Second, is the proposal in "harmony" with established public policy? Perhaps the clearest example of covert action running contrary to publicly articulated policy was the Nixon administration's covert program in Chile. (Of course Iran-Contra was also completely at odds with established policies that prohibited negotiations for hostages and enacted the arms embargo against Iran.) Third, is the proposal merely "social engineering" rather than a viable foreign policy? Fourth, is the plan a hastily concocted response to some international crisis? And finally, are the intelligence folks "trying to run a war," something that perhaps should be left to military professionals? These are all valid issues for the president and his advisors to consider, and one assumes that Aspin worked to focus the White House on these concerns, although obviously without complete success.[24]

Often a Clinton request for a covert action program or, more frequently, a menu of covert action options to substitute for a policy—manifestly a poor utilization of covert action—would be communicated to CIA headquarters at Langley. Upon arrival at headquarters, the request would then be forwarded to the operations component—an area division (e.g., Near East or Latin America) or "issue" component (e.g., the Counternarcotics or Counterterrorism Centers)—that would have responsibility for managing the program. Appropriate officers from within the component, including a lawyer detailed specifically to that component on a full-time basis by the Agency's Office of General Counsel (OGC), would begin to work up possible options based on considerations and analysis of operational possibilities; resource availability, including personnel, funds, and assets from the covert action infrastructure; prospect of success; security and odds of public compromise; risks versus gains and costs versus benefits; whether and/or which foreign intelligence services could or should be involved; the need to acquire operational support from the Defense Department or other agency; and any legal issues that might pertain to the execution of the program. (In the risk-versus-gain category, danger to human life and damage to U.S. interests should the program become known are fully discussed. The latter does not encompass domestic political risks to the president, for that is the province of his White House policy advisors; it is, rather, a calculation of potential damage to U.S. interests in the target country or region should the operations become public knowledge.) Finally, once a set of covert action options had been compiled, all station chiefs in countries potentially affected by the program would be notified and their comments incorporated into the planning process.

Once the operational and supporting details were worked out, either a complete plan or a series of options were pulled together into one cogent proposal, which included a draft Presidential Finding. At that point a Covert Action Planning Group (CAPG) would be convened under the chairmanship of the deputy or associate deputy director for operations (DDO or ADDO).[25] Present were the component chief and the operations officer responsible for program management and representatives from the DCI Counterintelligence Center (CIC); the Operations and Resources Management Staff (ORMS), an operational oversight and budget planning component; the Special Activities Division (SA), which maintains the covert action infrastructure plus a cadre of covert action specialists; and any other potentially affected component. (For example, discussion of a counterterrorism or counternarcotics program that is to take place within a specific geographic region would find issue officers present as well as an officer from the appropriate area division to ensure that his/her component's equities are protected.) As within the individual operational components, the Office of General Counsel would assign an attorney to serve as the DO's legal advisor, who would play an active role in the meeting. The CAPG would then review in detail program goals, operational methodology, required assets (human and technical), costs, risks, compatibility with overt policy, chances for success, operational security, and consequences of blowback if compromised. It was not uncommon for the initial proposal to require amending once all the participants had contributed their knowledge and perspective.

Once a proposal received the blessing at the directorate level, the next step was a thorough scrub at the Agency level by the Covert Action Review Group (CARG).[26] Chaired by the Agency's third senior officer, the executive director, this group was established by Robert M. Gates during his tenure as deputy director of central intelligence (DDCI) in 1986 in the wake of Iran-Contra to provide coordinated advice to the DCI and DDCI on all aspects of proposed Findings and amendments to existing Findings (MON). In addition to the executive director, CARG membership consisted of the four deputy directors (Operations, Intelligence, Administration, and Science and Technology), the comptroller, the general counsel, the head of congressional affairs, and the chief of the Special Activities Division. The issues reviewed at the CARG were the same as those at the CAPG, with several significant additions: potential reaction from Congress was often on the agenda, both in terms of overall approval and with respect to funding issues; legal concerns, while discussed at the CAPG, were reviewed in more full detail; and needed support from the other directorates was hashed out. The result was a review that was at once wide-ranging and highly detailed, and as at CAPG, it was common for the CARG to meet multiple times before attaining consensus on the proposed program and Finding. With CARG concurrence, including a final approval by the general counsel with respect to legal issues, the presidential proposal was then passed up to the DDCI or DCI for transmittal to the White House.

It is essential to emphasize that there was substantive involvement by CIA lawyers at every stage of the covert action planning process—from the initial discussions of program development within the operational component, through the Directorate of Operations scrutiny, up to the approval at the most senior level of the Agency. Although one intelligence scholar asserts that while the DCI "has a sizable staff of lawyers, it is doubtful that he is truly kept informed about the more sensitive intelligence operations," this is an egregious inaccuracy, for the more sensitive the operation is, the more knowledgeable is the DCI.[27] Just as important, working-level operations officers and mid-level managers seek guidance, formally and informally, from these lawyers at all stages of covert action program development and execution.

With the arrival of the CIA's proposals at the Clinton White House, there began yet another multilayered review process for the proposed program incorporating all affected elements of the foreign policy community. The initial level was the Interagency Working Group for Covert Action (IWG), which had the responsibility of reviewing policy objectives, program risks, and legality, while ensuring interagency concurrence, coordination, and cooperation. As required in NSDD-286, as many as thirteen different executive branch agencies participated in this interagency process. Always present at the table were the NSC's director of intelligence programs (chair) and representatives from the Department of State, the Office of the Secretary of Defense, the Joint Chiefs of Staff, the Office of Management and Budget, the CIA, and the Justice Department. Others attended if the program fell within their domain—a representative from the Drug Enforcement Agency, for example, for a counternarcotics program. Although CIA officials consult with counterparts in the other agencies while developing the operational proposals, not every conflict or problem can be foreseen. Thus, it was at the IWG that conflicts were resolved. Multiple meetings were usually required before the NSC intelligence director was satisfied. And always present was the NSC's lawyer, who inevitably played a large and active role in the debates.

The State Department played a major role in the IWG, with representatives from the Bureau of Intelligence and Research (INR) as well as the geographical area bureau(s) having cognizance over the countries in which the program was to occur. Beforehand, as part of the State Department's own internal process, the views of the affected overseas ambassadors were also solicited for presentation to the IWG. If the program involved propaganda, the CIA-State Department joint thematic guidance, reflective of the president's policy positions, was reviewed to ensure the CIA's overseas agents knew the party line.

From the IWG (which might have met multiple times to discuss the program), the proposed covert action program and draft Finding moved up to the Deputies Committee, a grouping of the number-two officials in each of the relevant agencies (deputy secretary of state, deputy secretary of defense, vice-chairman of the Joint Chiefs, deputy attorney general, etc.), which was chaired by the deputy national security advisor. Again, program objectives and their relationship to policy goals were scrutinized, as were legalities, congressional reaction, consequences of program compromise, and—for the first time—domestic political considerations. Political considerations could involve the president's relationship with

Congress, his standing in popularity polls, results of other polls indicating preferences or positions of the voting public, the distance from or nearness to national elections, and pressures from various groups representing American citizens who have close ethnic connections to foreign countries (e.g., Greek-Americans or Polish-Americans). The final step was the Principals Committee, chaired by the national security advisor and composed of the heads of the relevant agencies (e.g., secretary of state, secretary of defense, chairman of the Joint Chiefs, attorney general, etc.), who added their own particular perspectives to the mix.

Once the proposed program and draft Finding navigated the rocks and shoals of these intensive and extensive reviews, the president would then sign the Finding for transmittal to Congress within the forty-eight–hour limit.[28] And the CIA would set forth on yet another mission. Of equal importance, the same process was utilized for an annual review of all existing covert action programs.

CONGRESSIONAL OVERSIGHT

Regardless of who is president, and separate from the procedures in the executive branch agencies, there was and still is an intense congressional scrutiny of covert action programs. Each spring both HPSCI and SSCI conduct an annual review of these programs, in which all facets are reviewed and critiqued. Then, throughout the year, congressional staff from the oversight committees and the appropriations committees hold quarterly reviews of the programs similar in scope to the annual review. Finally, members of Congress and/or their staff can call the Agency and "request" a briefing or update on any program at any time. These requests, which number literally in the hundreds every year, are met expeditiously by Agency personnel and result in the desired meetings, usually within forty-eight hours. Thus, key members of Congress and staff are kept au courant with each and every program, in detail and in a timely fashion.

Indeed, because (as mentioned above) intelligence officers

working the programs change assignments frequently while congressional staff members may remain in their positions for years, it is common for the staff to be much more familiar with the programs than the officers working them. This at times can be an embarrassment to the Agency. By way of example, one might see a newly assigned program manager asking for an additional X hundred thousand dollars for something, and a veteran staffer then asking what happened to Y hundred thousand dollars that was given to the program Z years ago to meet the same need. Yet the new program manager would have no knowledge of the previous request nor of the disposition of the funds that were provided to meet the need.

Agency officers new to dealing with Congress usually begin by assuming that oversight committee staff know little and are unnecessary hindrances, if not deliberate antagonists. Staff briefings, once the bane of clandestine operators, are now seen by the wiser officers as positive measures. The intelligence officers soon learn that staff members are exceptionally knowledgeable, both about the program and about operational difficulties involved in running it; far more often than not the staff are interested in seeing good, well-managed programs succeed. The support for these covert programs from staff and legislators alike allows program managers to feel able to speak more freely about the operations, raise problems more directly, and solicit assistance as needed. And when staff (especially) as well as congressional members are knowledgeable about the programs, they are able to see possibilities for helpful legislative initiatives that program managers might not. Indeed, it is not uncommon in popular covert action programs for Congress to try to push the Agency to do more than has been authorized in the Finding or to proffer more funding than the program can use.

There is one additional benefit to congressional awareness of these programs. In case of a compromise or operational catastrophe, the staff and members will have a realistic knowledge of the risks involved and potential problems. If disaster strikes, they are neither surprised by the downturn nor automatically inclined to assume the cause was incompetence or negligence. If nothing else, this may save the Agency from unearned negative press pronouncements by some in Congress, against which the program mangers are unable publicly to defend themselves.

THE FINDING FORMAT

Findings, usually drafted in the operational component of the CIA that will manage the covert action program, are actually two separate documents: the surprisingly brief Finding per se, and a detailed supporting document. Findings must be placed in writing, signed by the president, and reported to the intelligence committees of Congress within forty-eight hours unless exceptional circumstances prevail. Findings may *not* be signed retroactively. While the president and Congress may have different definitions of "exceptional circumstances," there is a classic example from the Carter years that yields something of a guide. During the capture of the American Embassy in Tehran, Iran, in 1979, six embassy staff members were able to evade the captors and find refuge in the residence of the Canadian ambassador. In collusion with the Canadians, an elaborate covert action plan for their escape from Iran was devised. But as a desideratum for their cooperation the Canadian government, afraid of leaks that would endanger their own personnel in Tehran, forbade the president to notify Congress of the planned operation. President Carter agreed, and it wasn't until the six Americans were out of Iran that Congress was informed; Congress quickly agreed that this was a worthy exception to the rule.

The Finding always begins with the statement that the president "finds" this covert action program to be in the national interest—and then proceeds to state precisely the foreign policy objective(s) to be achieved. It also specifically and plainly assigns the CIA to conduct the necessary operations. If the president *were* ever to give a covert action program to another agency (e.g., the Department of Defense), this is where the authorization would be granted. Subsequent paragraphs include the "Scope," naming the country, region, or issue for which the Finding is approved; and the "Description," a statement of policy objectives accompanied by a very general overview of operational goals and methodologies. This document is rarely more than two pages in length, and often less.[29]

It is in the supporting document that one finds the details. There are four major sections of this document. "Policy Objectives" states precisely the foreign policy objective(s) to be achieved and again specifically authorizes the CIA to conduct the requisite operations. The "Plan of Action" provides the details, reach, and limits of the CIA's methodology. The "Risk Assessment" section provides just that, the combined agencies' best estimation of what might go wrong and the impact of compromise. If there is a possibility that the operations entail a risk to human life, even accidentally, or that such is a reasonable by-product (e.g., from a paramilitary operation), then the document is defined as a "Lethal Finding," and this characteristic is made clear in its transmittal to Congress. The final section details the "Resources Required." Depending on the program, this supporting document may be only a few pages, or sometimes much longer. The supporting document must explicitly state whether DoD support, or the assistance of a third party country, is required for the program.

SUMMARY

There are a number of important points here that merit summarization. First, and possibly most important, covert action programs are very much the president's programs: only he approves them, and since 1974 he has been required to do so by affixing his signature to the Presidential Finding. Thus, for three decades it has been impossible to label these programs as "rogue" operations, activities conjured up and run by the CIA for its own purposes and in the conduct of its own foreign policy independent of the president's official policies. Covert action programs are specifically requested by the president and receive at least five different reviews ranging from the operational to the policy level, including all government agencies having a vested interest in the program.

Second, these are not extra-legal operations but rather are operational programs integrated into the overall foreign policy plan and scrutinized by lawyers at all review levels to ensure congruence with the Constitution, federal statutes, and Agency regulations.

Finally, not only is Congress aware of every covert program, it is a willing partner, for without the appropriation of funds there could be no program. It is important to know that covert action funds are always "fenced," meaning that only these funds can be expended on the program, no additional funds from other sources can be added, and the fenced funds cannot be used for any other purpose. Once a program has begun, it is followed closely by Congress, with scheduled quarterly briefings to staff members bolstered by ad hoc briefings with members and staff as requested or required. There is also an annual briefing for members of both of the oversight committees each spring. When all of these processes are added up, it's clear that the days of any "rogue" activity are long gone.

SEVEN

Harry S Truman

And we were alarmed particularly over the situation in France and Italy. We felt that the Communists were using the very extensive funds that they had in hand to gain control of key elements of life in France and Italy— particularly the publishing companies, the press, the labor unions, student organizations, women's organizations, and all sorts of organizations of that sort—to gain control of them and use them as front organizations.[1]

George F. Kennan

With the end of World War II, the European continent was at peace for the first time in nearly six years. President Harry S Truman, just weeks into his administration, decided that the U.S. intelligence apparatus created during and for the war was no longer desirable. Despite pleadings from advisors, Truman truncated the intelligence community, disbanding many elements and limiting the size and charter of those that remained. However, Soviet mischief soon produced in the president's mind serious concerns about the willingness of the Soviet Union, and Joseph Stalin in particular, to sustain and promote a peaceful world. In a speech to the Soviet

Communist Party elite at the Bolshoi in February 1946, Stalin passionately declared that democratic capitalism and Communism could not live together peacefully and that Communism would eventually overcome the West. Soon thereafter, the Soviets solidified control over Eastern European nations in contravention of the February 1945 Yalta Agreements (or, at least, what the United States had thought had been agreed to at Yalta), turning the six countries into mere appendages of the Soviet Union itself. In Italy, France, Turkey, and Greece, local Communist parties began working with clandestine Soviet intelligence support to gain control of those governments as well.[2]

The local Communists in these and other European nations had "infiltrated a number of important non-governmental organizations, including labor unions [so that] by the late 1940s, Moscow had established in Europe the largest and probably the most skilled collection of covert operatives that the world had ever seen."[3] Soon after Stalin's speech, and in partial response to it, presidential advisor Clark M. Clifford authored a policy paper for President Truman asserting that the Soviet Union, with its expansionist Communist ideology, was "the gravest problem facing the United States," as the Soviet leadership "appear to be on a course of aggrandizement designed to lead to eventual world domination."[4]

In 1947 Stalin initiated serious attempts to force the Allied Powers out of West Berlin, resulting ultimately in a road and rail blockade of that city, engendering a crisis that could have easily led to a major war between the United States and the USSR. By that time, the Soviet intelligence service had also placed significant numbers of clandestine operations officers both under official diplomatic cover and as non-official "illegals" in such key Western capitals as London, Rome, Paris, and Washington, and also in New York to recruit and handle spies; but there were no intelligence officers from any of the Western intelligence or security services in Moscow.[5] The aggregation of these and other events between 1945 and 1949 in which the Soviets had acted in a hostile fashion—including the detonation of an atomic bomb years earlier than

Western intelligence had predicted thanks to a formidable spy ring in the American research program—acutely informed Truman of Soviet intentions and the threat Stalin posed to the West.

In consequence of these actions, and in response to recommendations of key advisors, the president initiated the first of a number of covert action programs intended to limit or "contain" Soviet advances in Europe and elsewhere in the free world. Here, Truman was advised and encouraged by such distinguished patriots as Secretary of State George C. Marshall, Undersecretary of State (and future secretary) Dean Acheson, Secretary of War Robert Patterson, Secretary of the Navy (and future secretary of defense) James Forrestal, and the eminent diplomat and Sovietologist George F. Kennan. These statesmen each believed that it was essential for the United States to possess covert political action and propaganda capabilities to counter similar Soviet programs, but none wanted these capabilities associated either with other "legitimate" diplomatic and foreign policy activities or with themselves personally. Truman heeded their advice, becoming the first modern president to endorse programs intended to counter "subversive political activities by giving covert assistance to those nations and groups which opposed Communist aims." In short, a proposal for the U.S. government to "employ psychological warfare to counter worldwide Soviet subversion" became a cornerstone of American foreign policy, one that was adopted and utilized by every one of Truman's successors, without exception, until the end of the cold war.[6]

THE FIRST STEP: NSC-1

On June 26, 1947, President Truman signed into law The National Security Act of 1947, establishing inter alia the National Security Council (NSC). Statutory members of the NSC were the president, vice president, and the secretaries of state and defense. By November 14, 1947, the NSC produced for the president its first policy document, the top secret NSC-1/1, *The Position of the United States with Respect to Italy*, with the president directing that "these Conclusions be implemented by all departments and agencies concerned, under the coordination of the Secretary of State." NSC-1/1 found that the internal political situation in Italy was worsening, with the Italian Communist Party (PCI) gaining strength against the democratically oriented political parties. NSC-1/1 was in part based on an intelligence estimate sent to the White House three months prior, which concluded that "The Italian economic situation is desperate and the political situation unstable."[7] The intelligence analysts foresaw a possible Communist victory in Italy in the forthcoming spring 1948 elections; such an event, Kennan opined, would erode governments throughout Western Europe.[8]

NSC-1/1 stated that "The United States has security interests of primary importance in Italy and the measures to implement our current policies to safeguard those interests should be strengthened without delay." The document called for the United States to support the Italian government through shipments of food aid and dollar credits, assist the Italian military, provide favorable foreign trade policies, and "[a]ctively combat Communist propaganda by an effective U.S. information program and by all other practicable means, including the use of unvouched funds." The nonspecific directive to combat Communist propaganda would soon open the door for the Central Intelligence Agency, also established four and a half months earlier in the National Security Act of 1947.[9]

The first days of the new year saw the U.S. government send to Rome "several hundred million dollars of military and economic assistance."[10] Several months later the original policy document was revised as NSC-1/2, appearing on March 12, 1948, under the same title as NSC-1/1. The revision further defined overt U.S. policy toward Italy and, like 1/1, ended with approval to commence a covert propaganda program intended to offset similar Communist efforts (using "unvouched funds"), following the axiom that covert action should support overt policy measures. NSC-1/2 differed from NSC-1/1 by instructing the State Department to utilize the overt United States Information Agency (USIA) to "actively combat" Communist propaganda. NSC-1/1 made allusion to any covert element in the policy, but NSC-1/2 did include a vague reference to counter-ing propaganda by "other practicable means, including the use of unvouchered funds." The opaqueness of this phrase notwithstand-ing, it was clear to senior policymakers that it constituted presiden-tial approval for the CIA to enter the business of covert psychological warfare. The covertly provided "unvouchered funds" eventually exceeded $10 million, the majority of which went to "get out the vote" operations for the Christian Democrats and, secondarily, to finance general anticommunist literature. NSC-1/2 was particularly forceful, advocating that the United States should not only apply political and economic power, but also military force if the threat of Italy's "falling under the domination of the Soviet Union" seemed imminent. In its text, NSC-1/2 follows without deviation the axiom that covert action should support overt policy measures.[11]

NSC-1/3, *Position of the United States with Respect to Italy in the Light of the Possibility of Communist Participation in the Government by Legal Means*, dated March 8, 1948, and presented to the president for signature concurrently with NSC-1/2 on March 12, 1948, stated that the "problem" was to "assess and appraise the position of the United States with respect to Italy in the light of the possibility that the Communists will obtain participation in the Italian government by legal means," and held that "United States security interests in the Mediterranean are immediately and gravely threatened by the possibility" of a Communist victory. The paper expressed fear that the "Communists will thereafter, following a pattern made familiar in Eastern Europe, take over complete con-trol of the government and transform Italy into a totalitarian state subservient to Moscow."

To counter the prospect of the PCI winning the election, or at least winning a plurality of seats in the Parliament, NSC-1/3 di-rected "as a matter of priority [to] immediately undertake further measures designed to prevent the Communists from winning par-ticipation in the [Italian] government . . ." and enumerated the steps the U.S. government should take to preclude such an eventu-ality. The very first action to be taken was to "[i]mmediately provide campaign funds from unvouchered and private sources to the parties at present represented in the Italian government." Later Kennan was to acknowledge that Italy was precisely the reason why the CIA was given covert action responsibility and capabilities.[12]

These NSC papers in toto advocated U.S. intervention, through the mechanism of covert action programs managed by the Central Intelligence Agency, to forestall a PCI victory. It must be noted, however, that the covert action programs—the financial support of Italy's political parties of the Center, Right, and selected Left, as well as tailored propaganda programs—were by far the smallest element in the United States's overall policy to help Italy remain democratic.[13]

THE NEXT PHASE: NSC-4

President Harry S Truman was "deeply interested" in the employment of propaganda, believing it to be an underappreciated tool of statecraft for the cold war. The National Security Council's concern over Soviet covert activities in the fall of 1947 led to the consideration of two "streams" of U.S. countermeasures. One stream would be "overt foreign information activities," while the second would be covert propaganda and psychological warfare operations. After staff massaging, the overt proposal was authorized by Truman on December 14, 1947, in NSC-4, titled *Coordination of Foreign Intelligence Information Measures*. In it, authority was given to the secretary of state to counter through overt methods Communist propaganda and disinformation throughout Europe.[14]

At the instigation of the secretary of defense, James Forrestal, NSC-4 was accompanied by a top-secret annex, NSC-4/A, which was signed three days later on December 17 and provided the DCI with up to $20 million in unvouchered funds for the CIA to "initiate and conduct, within the limit of available funds, covert psychological operations designed to counteract Soviet and Soviet-inspired activities which constitute a threat to world peace and security, or are designed to discredit and defeat the United States in its endeavors to promote world peace and security." (About half of this went to Italy for "anti-Communist propaganda and bribes to aid the [Christian Democratic Party].")[15] Operations authorized under 4/A included propaganda, sabotage, demolitions, subversion of adversary states, and assistance to indigenous, anticommunist underground movements. In NSC-4/A, Truman directed that control of covert propaganda (that is, "black" and "gray," as opposed to the overt "white" information programs managed by the State Department) be given to a new entity first known as the Special Procedures Group and then as the Office of Special Projects. Not to slight the State Department, however, Truman also directed that it establish an office dedicated to psychological warfare. Concerned like others in the administration about a Communist victory in the coming Italian elections, Forrestal believed the CIA to be the ideal U.S. government mechanism to influence the elections through covert political action while keeping the U.S. hand hidden. Although neither the DCI nor the Agency's legal advisor was particularly keen for the assignment, Truman agreed with Forrestal, personally authorizing the CIA's first covert operations.[16]

NSC-4/A provided the foundation for peacetime covert action as well as a clear assignment of that role to the CIA. The U.S. Congress quickly appropriated the funds for the Italian program, indicating approval of and support for the program, as well as an implicit acknowledgment of the CIA as the U.S. government agency best suited to conduct these types of operations. And appropriately, the covert program supported overt diplomacy, one element of which was Truman's threat to reduce or terminate Marshall Plan aid to Italy if the Communists won (a message that was not lost on the citizens of this war-devastated nation).[17] Interestingly, in later years and after other covert action programs approved by his successors were recorded as public failures, Truman denied responsibility for the CIA's eventual dominant role in covert action programs.[18]

An intelligence collection unit, the Office of Special Operations (OSO), was already in place and at work in Italy under the auspices of the Central Intelligence Group (CIG), the CIA's predecessor organization. It was thus no great leap of administrative logic to place within the OSO's Rome unit a subcomponent to devise and conduct political action operations against the PCI and in support of pro-democratic, pro-West factions. Initially named the Special Procedures Branch but soon changed to the Special Procedures Group (SPG), it adopted Soviet intelligence tactics such as bribery; recruitment of newspaper editors; co-opting of labor unions; the purchasing of politicians; and the printing of election-oriented posters, leaflets, and other materials. Support was an ecumenical exercise, with all non-Communist parties in Italy from the Left-of-Center to the Right receiving funds or other assistance.[19] The labors paid off in the May 1948 elections with the preferred party, the Christian Democrats, winning 54 percent of the vote and blocking the PCI from playing any role in the Italian government.[20] With the electoral victory in Italy, U.S. policymakers became convinced that "covert operations were both practical and necessary to thwart Communism."[21] This belief was manifested many times over during the cold war, as some propaganda and political action programs ran for literally the entire length of this ideological conflict.

Interestingly, the United States again provided covert support to democratically oriented Italian political parties in the 1960s; again these efforts met with positive results, effectively countering Communist subversive efforts.[22] At the same time, of course, the Soviets were funding the PCI, and they continued to do so well into the 1980s. Even though the PCI publicly announced a severance with Moscow following the Soviet invasion of Afghanistan and the suppression of the Polish labor movement Solidarity in the late 1970s and early 1980s, the only real change in the relationship was the method of payment: in something of an ironic twist, the Soviets began laundering the PCI monies through privately owned businesses.[23]

THE THIRD PHASE: NSC-10/2

Truman retained policy control of covert action programs in the White House, but this did not necessarily mean close supervision of actual operations. More important to him was the creation of covert action operational capabilities and the initiation of covert action programs to support overt diplomatic actions and foreign policy programs intended to contain the worldwide Communist threat, as urged by George Kennan. There was no mechanism in the White House for periodically reviewing the programs; once begun any "quality control" had to be done at the CIA. Part of Kennan's impetus for expanding covert action methodologies was derived from his assessment that programs set up under 4/A were not working well, particularly with respect to the bureaucratic divisions of labor in the covert propaganda/psyops operations. Specifically, the Department of State had serious concerns regarding the "psychological and political warfare" programs run out of the Pentagon, which coincided with "sentiment for a more encompassing program of covert activity" within the White House.[24]

Thus Kennan, in league with the CIA's deputy director, Allen Dulles, and Undersecretary of State Robert Lovett, introduced NSC-10 in early 1948 with a proposal for reorganizing the relevant offices with a role to play in covert action programs.[25] His new superior, Secretary of State George C. Marshall, also agreed with the concept but was adamant that the State Department not be the home agency of any covert action executive or other espionage-related entity. The State Department was the public voice of U.S. policy to the world and home of the nation's diplomatic corps; placing a covert or clandestine component within the country's official overt foreign policy establishment would erode the trust and confidence other nations might place in American diplomacy. More specifically, Marshall was fearful that an exposure of a covert action program in Europe would undermine the European economic recovery plan bearing his name, which promised the renewal of Western Europe and was critical to forestalling Communist subversion on the continent. Marshall's concerns were real, for already covert action programs were being used effectively to support the Marshall Plan as well as other diplomatic efforts.[26] Truman agreed with Marshall and shortly thereafter, in response to a study of CIA operations (NSC-50), authorized the establishment of an action office to develop and manage a variety of covert programs, in addition to psychological operations.

NSC-10/2, signed by Truman on June 18, 1948, cited the "vicious covert activities of the USSR" and validated the assignment of covert operations to the CIA as the organization to counter Soviet perfidy.[27] NSC-10/2 stated that it was "desirable" to place the responsibility for covert operations in the CIA and "correlate them with espionage and counterespionage operations under the overall supervision of the Director of Central Intelligence." This designation was additionally intended to preclude any attempt by the Defense Department to create its own peacetime covert action office, a move feared by officials at the State Department.[28]

NSC-10/2 directed the chief of OSP to report to the DCI (although the organization itself was to operate independently of the other components of the Agency); required that covert programs be consistent with established U.S. policy; and mandated that disagreements be resolved by the National Security Council—the first time any White House element was specifically charged with involvement in covert action programs. Covert action activities specified in 10/2 included paramilitary operations such as assistance to resistance and/or guerrilla groups and sabotage. NSC-10/2 also specifically required that the Agency conduct all covert programs in a manner that would allow the U.S. government to "plausibly disclaim any responsibility." Important to the conduct of American foreign policy, NSC-10/2 made it explicitly clear that the CIA was to be the "instrument of policy, not the initiator."[29] In other words, the decision to undertake covert action operations was to remain with the president and the NSC. Ultimately, under this authorization, the CIA "channeled funds and information to non-Communist political parties, newspapers, labor unions, church groups, and writers throughout Western Europe." The CIA also undertook to ensure that accurate news and political analysis reached not only Western Europe but Eastern Europe, where the populations sought greater freedom from Soviet domination.[30]

With the implementation of NSC-10/2, Truman relied on a

committee, naturally enough referred to as the 10/2 Panel, to evaluate and approve covert action programs. The 10/2 Panel membership initially included the DCI as chair and designated representatives of the secretaries of state and defense (George Kennan and Ivan Yeaton, respectively). Only when the 10/2 Panel was unable to reach consensus regarding the merits of a particular program was the issue passed up to the full NSC. Through his individual responsibilities as well as his membership on the 10/2 Panel, the DCI could initiate covert action programs, though he did not oversee or manage them, given that OSP was an independent agency. It must be noted, however, that the DCI did not have carte blanche to run any covert action operations he desired; he was guided by presidential policies established and laid forth in various NSC directives. As such, these covert action operations were responsive to presidential policies and may thus be justly considered to be presidential programs.[31]

Soon after NSC-10/2 was signed, OSP was transferred to the DCI's control and formally became the Office of Policy Coordination (OPC) on September 1, 1948.[32] OPC eventually operated not only in Europe but also in the Middle East, South Asia, and the Far East, with Latin America and sub-Saharan Africa of lesser interest. NSC-10/5, *Scope and Pace of Covert Operations*, issued on October 23, 1951, provided for "the immediate expansion of the covert organization . . . and intensification of covert operations . . . to contribute to the retraction and reduction of Soviet power and influence." NSC-10/5 added further to the CIA's covert action authority by giving it the responsibility for paramilitary (i.e., guerilla) warfare. OPC (covert action) and OSO (positive intelligence collection) remained separate until merged into the Directorate of Plans in the CIA on August 2, 1952.[33]

In an effort to impart more coherency to the world of covert action, Truman rescinded the NSC-4 and NSC-10 series of directives in March 1950 and replaced them with NSC-59, which divided responsibility for psychological warfare and propaganda between the Departments of State and Defense. Truman followed this measure with a program for national-level psychological warfare, which he authorized in NSC-74. Nearing the end of his tenure in office, in 1951 Truman created in NSC-10/5 a National Psychological Strategy Board (PSB), which was later merged into the group that approved covert action programs (the 10/2 Panel). Membership on the PSB, now called the 10/5 Panel, included representatives of the secretaries of state and defense, the CIA, and the Joint Chiefs of Staff. The staff director was Gordon Gray.[34] By the time he left Washington, Truman had put in place more than eighty covert action mechanisms and programs intended to thwart the expansion of Communism into the Free World.

The final word on Soviet expansionism by the Truman administration was recorded in NSC-141, written by the CIA's Richard Bissell. NSC-141 "advised that Western nations must resist expansion" by the Soviet Union and its proxies.[35]

OTHER COVERT ACTION OPERATIONS UNDER TRUMAN

From Truman's time through the Nixon years, covert action programs served only two purposes: they were intended either to stop the spread of Communism to countries that were not under the Soviet thumb by strengthening or supporting whatever regimes were in power, or to weaken Communist or Communist-supported governments by "eroding their internal support." The overthrow of Communist regimes or governments that were sympathetic to the Soviet Union was not part of the original thinking. Nor was the idea of actively promoting or spreading democracy given much thought, although occasionally CIA programs in democratic countries were "designed to maintain the democratic process." In sum, the overall goal of covert action in these initial stages of the cold war was simply to "Stop Communism."[36]

One of the most interesting and, later, controversial of these covert action programs was the Congress for Cultural Freedom, which was established in 1949 in Paris by the OPC. The idea was simple: use American writers, poets, musicians, and artists to help "negate Communism's appeal to artists and intellectuals, undermining at the same time the Communist pose of moral superiority." To do so, Congress, using funds supplied through covert channels by the OPC and, later, the CIA, published political journals and literary magazines and sponsored cultural events, music festivals, art shows, and lectures on a variety of high-brow issues. The objective was to demonstrate that American freedom was far superior to anything the Soviets could create in these same arenas. The result was that "[s]omehow this organization of scholars and artists—egotistical, free-thinking, and even anti-American in their politics—managed to reach out from its Paris headquarters to demonstrate that Communism, despite its blandishments, was a deadly foe of art and thought."[37] Although it may seem as if this program is one that could have been openly supported by the U.S. government, perhaps through the Department of State's United States Information Agency (USIA), two critical factors prevented this. First, with McCarthyism rampant in the United States, USIA was pulling "hundreds of American classics" from USIA libraries worldwide due to fears of subversive content—an act that would not have endeared the agency to the writers and authors taking part in the Congress. Second, many of the artists and writers involved were either apolitical or had political leanings that were even anti-American; they found the sunny picture of Communism painted by the Soviet propaganda machine intellectually appealing, despite what was known about Stalin's brutally repressive regime with its purges and Gulags. Thus, any hint of U.S. government sponsorship or participation would have seen the mass exodus of many, if not most, of those who were affiliated with the Congress for Cultural Freedom or who partook of its events or publications.[38] After their CIA sponsorship was exposed in *Ramparts* magazine in 1967, the Congress folded along with the National Student Association, an organization that had been funded by the CIA since 1952, which intended to counter the Soviets' attempts to indoctrinate world youth with Communist ideas and policies.[39]

In August 1948, Truman's signature on NSC-20 initiated behind-the-lines paramilitary operations, including assistance to resistance groups and sabotage missions inside the Iron Curtain and
in the Baltics using émigrés recruited in the West. The overall objectives were to "reduce the power and influence of the USSR to
limits which no longer constitute a threat to peace . . . [and] to
bring about a basic change in the [Soviet] conduct of international relations."[40] To accomplish the overall goals of NSC-20,
the U.S. national security establishment was directed to "place
the maximum strain on the Soviet structure of power and control, particularly on the relationships between Moscow and the
satellite countries."

The scope of NSC-20 was amended and expanded over the
next several months, emerging with the president's signature as NSC-
20/4, *U.S. Objectives with Respect to the USSR to Counter Soviet
Threats to U.S. Security*, on November 24, 1948. This version, a
seven-page document, concluded that the "gravest threat to the
security of the United States within the foreseeable future stems
from the hostile designs and formidable power of the USSR and
from the nature of the Soviet system." As such, it held that the U.S.
government must take steps "short of war" to counter Soviet expansionism and domination over the Eastern European satellites.
Besides the offensive guerrilla operations, Truman included an authorization for "stay-behind" organizations in Western European
nations and directed that weapons, munitions, and other supplies
for potential guerrilla operations be cached in the event of a Soviet
invasion. The stay-behind program was perceived to be so vital
that it endured until after the end of the cold war.[41]

By dint of NSC-20 and 20/4 the United States, unilaterally
and allied with the British Secret Intelligence Service (BSIS, colloquially known as MI-6), conducted paramilitary operations around
the periphery of the Soviet Union, with the goal of supporting "large-
scale regional insurrections" or nationalist movements during the
years 1949–1953.[42] CIA and BSIS teams worked with local émigré
movements in the Ukraine, Poland, Albania, and the Baltics to make

life difficult for the occupying Soviet forces, although without success. Though the problems with these programs were multifold, their predominant shortcoming was their foundation on the unrealistic goal of "rolling back" Communist domination. Too, organizers mistakenly assumed that that émigré groups could be made secure from Soviet counterintelligence penetrations, which led to the discounting of obvious counterintelligence concerns. Further, Soviet military and intelligence units conducted formidable counterinsurgency operations in the target countries, relentlessly hunting down the émigré guerilla forces. Last, these operations were betrayed by KGB double agent Kim Philby, who, as head of the BSIS station in Washington, was privileged to these operations and, hence, able to alert his Soviet handlers prior to the commencement of any operation or support activity. These operations were all run too long in light of their clear deficiencies and mounting death tolls, and they all resulted in abject failure. The programs dwindled away by 1955 with no successes to their credit.[43]

In the last months of the Truman administration, a major concern to the president and his national security team was the question of potential Communist governments in Iran and Guatemala. Truman gave consideration to overthrowing the Guatemalan leader, Jacobo Arbenz, with the support of Nicaraguan leader Anastasio Somoza, and in fact allowed the CIA to ship weapons to Nicaragua for the operation. Undersecretary of State David K.G. Bruce convinced his boss, Dean Acheson, to persuade Truman to cancel the program before anything further transpired.[44] Further action would wait until the impending Eisenhower administration. As for Iran, Truman initiated a covert action program in that country, at first limited to operations designed to diminish Soviet influence there. Fed up with the economic policies and intransigence of Prime Minister Mossadegh, Truman began to mull over the possibility of reversing the regime as his administration flowed into its last months.[45] Time ran out, however, and so the removal of Mossadegh would also await the Eisenhower administration.

The origins of a later CIA covert operation conducted in the

Himalayan kingdom of Tibet may also be traced back to the Truman administration. Immediately following the North Korean invasion of South Korea on June 25, 1950, and the concomitant increase in the United States's national security emphasis on Asia, the Agency was "instructed to initiate psychological warfare and paramilitary operations against Communist China; this order would affect Tibet in due course."[46] In the fall of 1950, the Chinese Communists invaded Tibet, but they announced their action to the world only some weeks later. As the year ended, it was clear to Truman's advisors that nothing could reverse the occupation of that tiny country, but, in the spirit of containment and in line with administration policy of confronting Communist aggression, it also was recognized that Tibet could potentially serve as a pressure point against the spread of Communism. Programs to train Tibetans to conduct intelligence collection and guerrilla operations were put in place by the CIA by the end of Truman's tenure.[47]

Truman also authorized paramilitary operations aimed at defeating the Hukbalahap Rebellion in the Philippines, cited by one former CIA officer-turned-scholar as OPC's "first major success." The Communist guerilla force known as the Huks first emerged to fight the Japanese during World War II. Once the United States granted the Philippines independence in 1946, the Huks turned their violence against the new democratic government in Manila. The legendary counterinsurgency expert Edward Lansdale (later the model for the protagonist in the novel *The Ugly American*) was ordered to the islands to lead the CIA's liaison team to the Philippine military, relying particularly on Defense Minister Ramón Magsaysay. The Lansdale-Magsaysay team led to a revitalized Philippine military and, ultimately, defeat of the Huks. History would show that defeating Communist movements and armies elsewhere would not be as (relatively) easy as it was in the Philippines.[48]

So it was that Truman, who was later disgusted with what he saw as excesses in the Eisenhower years and was eventually led to repudiate covert action, established the mechanisms for covert action operations whose progeny exist to this day. And just as Jimmy

Carter's administration was to quietly lay the foundation for many of the programs that grew in size and import under Ronald Reagan, so did Truman set in motion many of the projects that would eventually become associated with Dwight Eisenhower.

EIGHT

Dwight D. Eisenhower

[The Iranian coup] did not prove that the CIA could topple governments and replace rulers in power. Rather, it was a unique case of supplying just the right bit of marginal assistance in the right way at the right time. Such is the nature of effective political action.[1]

Dr. Ray S. Cline, DDCI

As a core element of President Dwight D. Eisenhower's cold war strategy, covert action in the Eisenhower administration "attain[ed] an importance among the CIA's missions that would not be equaled until the Reagan administration in the eighties."[2] For many years, the myth persisted that Secretary of State John Foster Dulles had conceived and managed the administration's foreign policy while Eisenhower played golf. But as declassified documents from that era began to receive scholarly attention, it became irrefutably clear that Eisenhower was very much in control of his administration's foreign and national security policies. Moreover, it became evident that he never hesitated to turn to covert action as a tool for achieving U.S. policy goals in instances where diplomacy alone was insufficient, but the risks and costs of overt military intervention were too great. Eisenhower believed that the CIA could be "more effective" and better utilized in covert action operations than in intelligence collection, and so he fully intended to use the Agency more actively than had Truman.[3] As supreme commander in the European theater during World War II, Eisenhower oversaw the employment of highly imaginative and daring special operations in support of traditional military forces to achieve victory over the Nazis. Relatively fresh from this experience, Eisenhower was not only familiar and at ease with special operations, he was able to envision their peacetime variants playing key roles in containing the spread of Communism. As such, Eisenhower was probably the first president since George Washington to understand completely the value of intelligence and covert action.

The most "covert" part of covert action programs under the Eisenhower administration was Eisenhower's role in them, for he was adept at, and personally comfortable with, allowing his subordinates to step forward into the spotlight and accept the credit—or the heat—for his behind-the-scenes direction. It is worth remembering, too, that like Eisenhower himself, many of Eisenhower's top advisors were veterans of World War II and were, therefore, predisposed to using a variety of alternatives—including covert measures—to achieve dominance over the nation's enemies. From the beginning of his administration to the final days, Eisenhower personally approved each and every covert action program, whether instigating a coup, resorting to paramilitary operations, or, in at least two instances, giving the green light to assassinations.[4]

Upon assuming office in January 1953, Eisenhower restructured the White House organization to suit his personal style (as is the habit of every incoming chief executive). This included the termination of the NSC-10/5 Panel and related committees. In the summer of 1953 Eisenhower's National Security Council took the first step in establishing a formal mission statement for the role covert action would play in his administration by drafting the NSC-162 series, policy documents that built upon similar authorizations from the Truman administration. The final version, NSC-162/2,

Basic National Security Policy, was signed by the president on October 30, 1953, and was intended to serve as the primary national security reference document for Eisenhower's first term. While addressing a range of national security issues beyond just the Soviet threat, it was clear that the Soviet Union and world Communism were the document's major focus.

NSC-162/2 identified the role of covert programs (using both U.S. and Soviet operations for reference) in terms that would later be recognized colloquially as the "third option": deniable operations executed in the shadows between overt diplomacy and military force. The paper asserted that the most significant Soviet threat came not from general war but from Soviet subversive measures, such as political and economic warfare, propaganda and "front activities," Communist-controlled trade unions, sabotage, exploitation of revolutionary and insurgent movements, and psychological warfare.

Between the Departments of State and Defense arose a serious difference of opinion with respect to the scope of operations under 162/2, which Eisenhower eventually had to defuse. Specifically, the issue at dispute was whether to employ long-term, essentially nonconfrontational actions against the Soviets or to be more aggressive in selected instances. The State Department, unhappy that the language of 162/2 didn't specifically prohibit aggressive actions, accepted a compromise that none would be undertaken except with the consideration of the NSC.

NSC-162/2 also served to sanctify one additional positive aspect of covert action operations: their low expense. Because the cost of covert action programs in tax dollars was minuscule compared to those incurred in large military operations, the programs had come to be viewed as a cost-effective tool to counter Soviet expansion. In short, with NSC-162/2, covert action also served as an instrument of budget control.[5]

In his later years, Eisenhower listed TPAJAX, the overthrow of the Iranian government in 1953, and PBSUCCESS, the removal of Guatemalan leader Jacobo Arbenz in 1954, as defeats for

Communists and among his proudest achievements in his two terms of office. (Until the late 1990s the CIA used a two-letter digraph and a codeword to identify operations or agents. For example, "XYCanine" might denote a country assigned the digraph "XY" and the agent named "Canine," who would either be a national of XY or who was of a different nationality reporting on XY.) Although Eisenhower was the final approving authority for these two major covert action programs, they were apparently considered on something of an informal basis, with no objective approval or reviewing authority in place to screen them before the president gave the final go-ahead. Eisenhower's sense of military regimentation eventually led to his unease with the absence of a set procedure for reviewing and approving covert action programs, however. Particularly chagrined by a mishap during PBSUCCESS— in which a British merchant ship was accidentally sunk because the participants exceeded presidentially established limitations— Eisenhower sought "more rigorous" control over individual covert action operations, and not just the overall program. His mechanism for this was the creation of a committee similar to the 10/2 and 10/5 Panels, which, founded on a new directive, NSC-5412, instituted a formal control and coordination process. A collateral result of this decision was an effective "narrowing of the CIA's latitude" in developing and executing covert action programs.[6]

NATIONAL SECURITY COUNCIL-5412

On March 15, 1954, Eisenhower signed the *National Security Council Directive on Covert Operations*, NSC-5412, to replace NSC-10/5. This document was important for "reaffirming the Agency's responsibility for conducting covert actions abroad," as well as instituting the Eisenhower administration's intent to impose process and discipline on the approval and review of covert action programs. NSC-5412 pointedly expanded the policy on the use of covert action programs from the earlier Truman guidance; while National Security Council-10/2 discussed covert action in but one paragraph, the successor 5412 devoted more than a full page to these operations.[7]

NSC-5412 was explicitly anticommunist, charging the CIA to undertake covert operations to counter similar Soviet operations (later known as "active measures"); "discredit" Soviet ideology; support anticommunist guerilla or paramilitary operations; "develop underground resistance" organizations; counter threats to Communist attempts to "achieve dominant power in a free world country"; and undermine or "reduce International Communist control of any area of the world." And as was by then the norm, the Agency was to act in a manner that enabled the U.S. government to "plausibly deny" any responsibility for sponsorship. In "reaffirming" the CIA's role in covert action, NSC-5412 further required the DCI to coordinate with the Departments of State and Defense to ensure that programs were not in conflict with U.S. diplomatic or military policy, and created an interagency working group named the Operations Coordinating Board (OCB) to focus not on the approval of covert action programs, but rather on their implementation.[8]

On the one-year anniversary of NSC-5412, Eisenhower signed NSC-5412/1, which established a White House-based mid-level Planning Coordination Group (PCG) to bring additional coherency to covert action programs worldwide. The PCG was to be advised in advance of all major covert action programs and was to serve as the "normal channel" for policy approval as well as coordinator of requisite support for the execution of these programs. But despite the seemingly clear language of 5412/1, the CIA managed to avoid the intent of the directive by arguing that the need-to-know principle allowed the Agency to brief the PCG only on parts of covert action programs, with the Agency being the arbiter of who needed to know what. This was unacceptable to Eisenhower, who eliminated CIA recalcitrance by signing a revision, NSC-5412/2, on December 28, 1955.[9]

This presidential directive created a committee—soon referred to as the "5412 Committee" or the "Special Group"—that was ostensibly to approve covert action programs. This group was composed of senior officials, appointed by the president and by the secretaries of state and defense, with the DCI as an ex officio member. The 5412 Committee was to vet and oversee all proposed covert action programs through the application of established procedures and criteria to ensure that the programs were in the national interest and compatible with presidential policies. There was no fixed agenda for the meetings: the choice of operations brought before the committee and when to bring them were at the discretion of the Agency. Eisenhower deliberately excluded himself from membership on the committee, which was chaired by the national security assistant, Robert Cutler (and, later, Gordon Gray), so that he would be insulated from "direct involvement."

Eisenhower was very concerned that such operations conducted in peacetime should not be attributable to the United States; more specifically, he believed that the president should be able to claim a lack of knowledge should the existence and ultimate sponsorship of these potentially politically embarrassing programs be alleged or proved. While leaving the intelligence organs to assume the blame, and, consequently, to pay a heavy price in credibility, the president would (theoretically, at least) be immune from adverse political consequences. However, Cutler and DCI Allen Dulles ensured that Eisenhower was in "constant" or "close" contact with the committee and informed of its deliberations, because—despite the committee's charter to "approve" covert action programs—the president was manifestly the final deciding authority.[10] In fact, Eisenhower exercised such close scrutiny over these sensitive programs that he even followed secondary operations that supported the primary covert action programs. To facilitate this he appointed Marine Corps Lieutenant General Graves B. Erskine as assistant secretary of defense for special operations and gave Erskine direct access to him in the Oval Office whenever necessary.[11]

As for the targets of the covert action programs reviewed by the Special Group and approved by Eisenhower, NSC-5412/2 focused on two dangers: the operations were to counter threats from "the USSR and Communist China and the governments, parties and groups dominated by them." For the most part, operational proposals that originated within the CIA were usually approved by the president, demonstrating the confidence he had in the Agency. In late December 1958, Eisenhower added additional structure to the 5412 Committee by directing that it meet on a regular weekly schedule rather than on an "as-needed" basis. Further, when Eisenhower learned that the group was in essence ignoring some programs once they had received initial approval, he mandated semi-annual reviews of all extant covert action programs and expanded the group's purview by requiring it to develop a system to evaluate operations while in progress and in the post-operational phase. The 5412 Committee worked sufficiently well that it or its progeny continued to exist, under one name or another, through the Clinton administration. Nonetheless, as late as January 1959, covert action operations continued to be executed by the CIA only on Eisenhower's personal authority, in the belief that the operations would be more likely to remain in the shadows.[12]

COVERT ACTION OPERATIONS UNDER EISENHOWER

The story of the TPAJAX program, the overthrow of the government of Iranian prime minister Mohammad Mossadegh in August 1953, has been told so many times that it need not be repeated anew here.[13] The president paid close attention to the Iranian situation after his election in November 1952, giving personal and final approval to the coup just a few weeks beforehand. Historian Zachary Karabell has accurately described Eisenhower's preferred method of managing foreign policy: "Ike maintained an airy detachment in public, in private he was focused, and involved . . . it was Ike who called the shots."[14] The success of TPAJAX stemmed from just the right amount of pressure on the right people, at the right time and place. But the CIA and, indeed, the Eisenhower White House soon began to see the Agency's role as far more determinative and decisive than it was. Kermit Roosevelt, the operation's

Agency manager, realized this and told senior officials, including Secretary of State John Foster Dulles, that the Agency succeeded only because the Iranian army and people supported the shah. In concluding his briefing to these officials, Roosevelt warned that if "we, the CIA, are ever going to try something like this again, we must be absolutely sure that people and the army want what we want. If not, you'd better give the job to the Marines." Foster Dulles paid no heed to Roosevelt's cautionary remarks, however. Soon after, Roosevelt was offered command of the Guatemalan program. When he saw the scope of CIA and American involvement, which was contrary to everything he had learned from the Iranian program, he resigned from the CIA.[15]

Like Iran, Guatemala and the regime of Jacobo Arbenz were of interest to the Eisenhower administration even before Eisenhower was sworn in. Just a few days after NSC-162/2 was signed, the NSC first reviewed the deteriorating situation in that Central American country, concluding that "it was a sufficient threat to national security to warrant covert action against it." The council produced a draft that stated a "policy of non-action would be suicidal, since the Communist movement, under the tutelage of Moscow, would not falter nor abandon its goals."[16] As planning for the covert program, named PBSUCCESS, moved forward, the administration began implementing the overt diplomatic, economic, and military measures that would set the stage for the covert operations. By then Arbenz had legalized the Guatemalan Communist Party, giving it seats in his administration, and had expropriated a huge banana plantation owned and operated by United Fruit.[17] These acts were highly disturbing for Eisenhower, who kept a close eye on PBSUCCESS, a multifaceted operation with paramilitary and psychological elements. On June 22, 1954, Eisenhower discussed details of air support for PBSUCCESS with the secretary of state and the DCI. Emboldened by the outcome of the Iranian operation, the administration moved ahead to repeat it in Central America, although the exact date and circumstances of Eisenhower's approval remain obscured by a lack of documentation.[18]

The great irony is that while PBSUCCESS was a covert action success—overturning a potentially pro-Communist government in America's backyard mostly through the psyops program and with only a "modest" push from the paramilitary side—it was ultimately a foreign policy tragedy. The removal of Arbenz allowed an oppressive and exceptionally cruel military dictatorship to hold sway for forty years, with hundreds of thousands of Guatemalans killed by their own government in that time. Also destructive to American foreign policy was that the CIA, as it had in Iran, took away from the Guatemalan operation a fundamentally misguided notion—this time that "Soviet subversion could always be effectively countered by American subversion."[19]

Although it was long believed by many that the nationalization of the United Fruit plantation was a principal justification behind Arbenz's removal (in other words, that American force had been called upon primarily to protect private corporate interests), this assertion has since been disproved. As the dean of cold war historians, Yale University's John Lewis Gaddis found, "the [sanctity of the] corporation had greater influence over the Truman administration than over Eisenhower's." Gaddis makes it clear that Arbenz "did rely heavily on support from the Guatemalan Communist Party and was very much under its influence."[20] But while Arbenz desperately sought recognition and help from Moscow, his desires were unrequited—objectively leaving doubt about whether Arbenz's regime could ever pose a genuine threat to hemispheric interests. But Eisenhower and Dulles had seen Soviet aggression and mischief upset the established order since before the end of World War II, and they were not about to accept even a remote possibility of a Soviet foothold in the Americas. What in retrospect appeared to be "a massive overreaction to a minor irritant" seemed to the administration in the tenor of the times a reasonable course of action to forestall potential Soviet advances. When Eisenhower held a congratulatory party at the White House for the CIA officials who conducted PBSUCCESS, he thanked them for "averting a Soviet beachhead in our hemisphere."[21]

The displacement of Arbenz and the resulting rule of Guatemala by the ruthless military dictatorship for forty years were not the only negative consequences of PBSUCCESS. In combination with the successful overthrow of Mossadegh in Iran, the Guatemalan program permitted the Eisenhower administration to place too much confidence in the CIA as an institution and particularly in the employment of covert action as a policy tool. The Iranian program succeeded almost in spite of itself, with the CIA giving just a little nudge at the margins to capitalize on events already unfolding, while the Arbenz coup hardly classifies as a masterpiece of international intrigue. Nonetheless, covert action came to be seen within the Eisenhower administration and the national security community as a "silver bullet" that could slay Communist-dominated puppet governments easily and almost with impunity. These two successes left in their wake an attitude of hubris within the Agency and the administration that would lead to one of the Agency's greatest disasters: the Bay of Pigs. The Arbenz coup also exacerbated anti-American sentiments in Latin America, serving to influence a number of future Latin American leaders, in particular Fidel Castro and Che Guevara.[22]

While the Iran and Guatemala programs have become well known (or notorious) to the public over the years, Eisenhower also instituted one of the least-known, quite possibly because it was one of the most successful, covert action operations. Indeed, it was so successful, as well as genuinely crucial to U.S. and Asian security interests, that it continued through the Kennedy, Johnson, and Nixon administrations. That is to say, both Democratic and Republican presidents equally found this program to be essential to U.S. foreign policy. In this still shadowy program, the CIA supported covertly the Japanese Liberal Democratic Party and individual members with financial aid. The program had both covert action and intelligence collection aims, specifically, the gathering of information on the Japanese political scene and the bolstering of Japanese democracy against Communist expansionism while "undermining the Japanese left." The program was both a covert action and foreign policy success, in that the LDP "thwarted their Socialist opponents, forged close ties with Washington, and fought off public opposition to the United States' maintaining military bases throughout Japan." On the negative side, though, are charges that the program allowed the LDP to become a corrupt organization that controlled Japanese party politics—at the expense of a genuine democratic process—for forty-plus years.[23] The exposure of this covert action program made headlines but no real controversy when it was revealed by the *New York Times* in 1994, complete with commentary by former Under-secretary of State Alexis Johnson and former Assistant Secretary of State Roger Hilsman. Likewise, no one seemed to notice the publication two years later by Vladimir Bukovsky that the Soviets had channeled funds to the Japanese Socialists during the same period.[24]

Concerns within the Eisenhower administration over Communist expansion in Indochina after the fall of Dien Bien Phu and the ouster of the French in Vietnam almost inevitably led to the same concern with respect to Indonesia, whose various islands had been in different stages of unrest since the Truman days. American policy in the first Eisenhower administration was to "woo" the Indonesian leader, Achmed Sukarno, into a more pro-Western posture, a policy codified in May 1955 in NSC-5518, which recommended to the president a number of training and assistance programs for elements of the Indonesian security and military forces, as well as various categories of economic assistance. The paper also, however, expressed concern over the "vulnerability of Indonesia to Communist subversion and a manifest willingness [of the U.S. government] to support non-Communist elements both within and outside the Jakarta government." As a counter to this, NSC-5518 authorized a small covert action program to support the Muslim (and noncommunist) Masjumi Party, to the tune of about $1 million.

The policy of attempting to attract Sukarno to the West continued through 1956, when Sukarno returned from a visit to the Soviet satellite countries of Eastern Europe in late summer manifesting an appreciation for a Socialist system. In November of that year, having won reelection handily, "Sukarno called for a prohibition on the capitalist system and for the circumscription of political parties." Three months later, in February 1957, he "assumed quasi-dictatorial powers with support of the one-million-strong Communist Party."[25]

The concerns in Washington over the future of the island nation occasioned by Sukarno's apparent rejection of the West were exacerbated in 1957 by the Indonesian president's open support from the Communist Party and by the increasingly aggressive actions by military commanders on the outlying islands against the central government, threatening political instability. A meeting of the National Security Council in March 1957, at which Indonesia was a principal topic, led eventually to a change in U.S. policy toward the Sukarno government, inspired by circumstances in Indonesia and by Indonesian dissidents seeking financial assistance and other aid from American officials. The most exigent concerns for the administration were the growing rebellion against the Indonesian government and increased representation of members of the Indonesia Communist Party in the cabinet. A National Intelligence Estimate (NIE 65-57) published on August 27, 1957, further bolstered the administration's worries by concluding that "there is an immediate and pressing danger" of increased Communist influence over the Indonesian government and its leadership."[26]

By this time, the Indonesian leader had come to be viewed by the Eisenhower administration as "the classic American 'enemy' of the 1950s," although a more benign observer might have seen only a "high-riding nationalist who exploited Russian-American hostility for foreign aid, which he then 'squandered' on wasteful projects." Regardless, Sukarno's rule, increasingly anti-American, along with his fairly decadent personal life, upset the "puritanical" Foster Dulles, who was irate over what he perceived to be Sukarno's "immoral neutralism."[27]

In response to the NIE, Eisenhower requested an interagency position paper on consequences and options. A "Special NSC Ad-Hoc Committee" submitted its findings to the president on September 3, and included the option of covert action programs to counter Indonesian leader Sukarno's plans to allow leftists in his government. At that point, so acute were Eisenhower's fears of a Communist takeover in Indonesia with the consequences of that strategic region falling under Soviet influence that he told his ambassador in Jakarta that, "given a choice between a single Indonesia under Communist rule and a divided entity with noncommunist elements, he preferred the latter."[28]

There was also, according to historians Kenneth Conboy (also an Indonesian expert) and James Morrison, a domestic "political dimension" to Eisenhower's actions and decisions. Mao Tse-Dong's Communists had gained power in mainland China in 1949, driving the pro-West forces of Chiang Kai-Shek to exile on the island of Taiwan. Additionally, the Communist Chinese had invaded the mountain kingdom of Tibet, the North Koreans had invaded their southern brethren, and the Viet Minh under Ho Chi Minh had beaten the French in Vietnam. Eisenhower was afraid that the "potential loss of Indonesia to leftist forces [was] likely to have negative ripple effects not just in Southeast Asia but across the free world."[29]

In response to the NIE, in November 1957 Eisenhower approved a new covert action program with a large paramilitary component to it, in which the United States was to support the emerging (and ultimately unsuccessful) rebellion during the next two years. The program ended "ignominiously" when an American-made B-26 Invader bomber was shot down and the CIA contract pilot captured while in possession of documents identifying him as an American and allowing the Indonesian authorities to "trace him back to the CIA," thereby undermining Eisenhower's plausible deniability of knowledge of the program. Former deputy director of central intelligence Ray S. Cline succinctly summed up the hazards of covert action, especially a paramilitary program, saying that the "weak point in covert paramilitary action is that a single misfortune that reveals the CIA's connection makes it necessary for the United States either to abandon the cause completely or convert it to a policy of overt military intervention."[30]

The Indonesian program was a multidimensional failure by virtue of the fact that it left the target—Sukarno—in power, while strengthening his hold. The president was unable to deny American involvement, plausibly or any other way. Worse, it failed to dampen the Agency's hubris with respect to covert action, nor did it lead them to be more deliberate and cautious in undertaking future projects. The Indonesian program was clearly not a fail-proof silver bullet, and there were indeed lessons to be learned—but they were ignored.[31] In point of fact, had the lessons that appeared from the Agency's own study of the Indonesian program been applied to the Bay of Pigs operation, the program would have either been significantly improved or, much more likely, cancelled, thus avoiding the disaster that followed.[32] Once humbled by the Bay of Pigs, it wasn't until the 1980s that the Agency again displayed such operational hubris, only to sustain counterintelligence disasters inflicted by Cuba, East Germany, Ghana, Yemen, and Iran. (But unlike with the Bay of Pigs failure, the hubris factor was so ingrained by the 1980s that the senior Agency officers managing these programs seemed incapable of feeling any sense of humiliation or seeing any failure on their part, with the Iranian disaster subjected to a cover-up at the highest DO levels.)

The Eisenhower administration undertook another covert action program in Asia, occasioned by the invasion and occupation of the small kingdom of Tibet by the Chinese Communists near the end of 1950. While the Eisenhower administration was interested in assisting the Tibetans soon after it took office, the Tibetan internal resistance movement was at that time "isolated and not sufficiently organized to justify" a covert program; however, an increase in resistance activities on the border with China in 1956 "indicated that more active U.S. involvement was warranted." Ultimately, a revolt by the Tibetans against their Communist Chinese occupiers began in the spring of 1956 and was quickly seen by the cold warriors in the Eisenhower administration as a way to counter Communist expansionism. From the summer of 1956 until terminated in 1969 by Richard Nixon (who sought a rapprochement with the leadership in Beijing, in part to play the Chinese off against the Soviets and in part to help end the war in Vietnam), the CIA conducted a covert action program to assist the Tibetans. The CIA provided weapons and communications equipment to the Tibetans and trained them in guerrilla tactics, small arms use, and intelligence collection.

The "impetus for the Tibet operations" lay with Foster Dulles at the Department of State and his undersecretary, Herbert Hoover, Jr. Told that the State Department "had no objection" to the program, DCI Allen Dulles insisted that State tell CIA unequivocally that it wanted the Agency to do it. The NSC Special Group and, perforce, the president, were unanimously supportive of the program. The great majority of U.S. foreign policy programs during the cold war were intended only to confront, thwart, or harass the Soviet and Chinese Communist governments in their expansionary designs, and this was also the case with the Tibetan program.[33]

Africa was also a locus of Eisenhower's anti-Soviet covert action programs. Circumstantial, but not conclusive, evidence exists to suggest that Eisenhower personally approved the (attempted) assassination of Patrice Lumumba, prime minister of the Congo and a Marxist whose political leanings automatically made him suspect as a potential asset to the Soviets—especially worrisome in light of the enormous quantity and diversity of strategically important natural resources found in the Congo.[34] The 5412 Committee convened on August 25, 1959, to discuss the situation in the Congo and options to deal with the pro-Soviet Lumumba. Contrary to his usual custom, Eisenhower sat in on the meeting, during which he expressed his "strong feeling" that the committee's original plan was too weak. Then, according to the minutes of the meeting, phrases like "getting rid of" and "disposing of" were made in reference to the African leader. (Later, though, several attendees suggested that the speakers—none of whom were the president—were only joking.) The committee finally agreed that all options would be on the table, presumably including assassination. In the end, Lumumba was indeed murdered, but not by the hand of the CIA.

One researcher, Ludo De Witte, investigated the event and has concluded that either the Belgian security service or the Belgian military intelligence organization actually was the "mastermind" behind the death of Lumumba.[35]

A revolution on the Caribbean island of Cuba in 1958 brought Fidel Castro, a lawyer, to power by ousting Fulgencio Batista, a dictator of exceptional cruelty and greed. Once in control of the island, Castro proclaimed himself a longtime Communist. Determined to stop another potential Soviet penetration of the Western Hemisphere, in March 1959 Eisenhower directed that the CIA produce a covert action program to topple Castro, despite having just experienced the failure of a similar program in Indonesia. DCI Dulles took the anti-Castro program, Operation ZAPATA, to the 5412 Committee on January 13, 1960, and obtained the committee's conditional approval. Eisenhower again deviated from his usual practice and personally convened the 5412 Committee in the Oval Office on March 17, 1960, to review the "Program of Covert Action against the Castro Regime." The plan essentially called for the clandestine infiltration of Cuban exiles to organize local insurgents, and the logistic support of those groups. Eisenhower accepted the plan, but in doing so insisted, as usual, that U.S. sponsorship remain concealed. Within months, however, it became clear that this program was failing—Castro remained popular, he tolerated no internal dissent, and efforts to supply the insurgents were ineffective. Rather than halt these covert efforts to unseat Castro and wait until circumstances were more favorable to begin planning anew, organizers "metamorphosed [ZAPATA] into an invasion plan" with a brigade of exiles.[36]

Eisenhower discussed funding for the Cuban program with his director of the Office of Management and Budget, Maurice Stans, and noted that he would also give approval in the future for other Cuban operations if he was "convinced" that the operations were "essential and . . . [wouldn't] fail."[37] Eisenhower pressed for strong action—even stronger than his 5412 Committee advocated—against Castro during his final years in office. According to Eisenhower's last national security assistant, Gordon Gray, even "drastic" measures (e.g., assassination) were to be considered.[38]

There was also trouble on another Caribbean island in the period. By 1959 Eisenhower had become personally and politically fed up with the strongman of the Dominican Republic, Rafael Trujillo, whose regime was as murderous as it was corrupt. Trujillo's rule was not only threatening American interests in the region but, worse, undermining the United States's anti-Castro policies. Leaders of Latin democracies such as Venezuela and Costa Rica were equally disturbed, especially as Trujillo "harbored and funded Latin American counterrevolutionaries, leading these democrats to insist, as a price for their support of anti-Castro policies, that the United States oppose all undemocratic regïmes, including Trujillo's." Eisenhower agreed.[39]

After a series of political and economic measures to convince or force Trujillo to step down, none of which had any effect on the tyrant, the administration began considering assassination. In a meeting with senior officials on May 13, 1960, the president referred to Castro and Trujillo and commented that he "would like to see them both sawed off." A month later the State Department authorized the U.S. ambassador in Santo Domingo to serve as a conduit for communications between the CIA and internal opposition groups, which made no bones about their intentions to kill the dictator. In August 1960 the administration severed diplomatic relations with the Dominican Republic (which, of course, was a republic in name only) and instituted economic sanctions against the regime. Discussions on how to oust Trujillo continued into the last days of the Eisenhower administration. With but a week to go in office, Eisenhower approved the provision of arms to the dissidents. As Eisenhower left office, Trujillo's days appeared to be numbered, through one means or another. He was assassinated five months into the Kennedy administration by Dominican oppositionists.[40]

At the very end of the Eisenhower administration, the CIA established a super-secret unit with a cryptonym of ZRRIFLE to conduct political murders at the (perceived?) behest of the White

House. The head of ZRRIFLE was none other than the legendary case officer Bill Harvey. Professor John J. Nutter thinks it is still unclear who authorized the establishment of this unit, opining that Eisenhower would not have done so with but days remaining in his term, and that it was probably much too early for Kennedy to do so. As such, Nutter finds the mystery behind the creation of this unit to be "unanswered, intriguing, and worrisome."[41] However, the CIA's director of operations at the time, Richard Bissell, recalled in an interview years later that he and either Walt Rostow or McGeorge Bundy (Kennedy's national security advisors)—or both—discussed "very early" in the Kennedy administration (i.e., within days of inauguration, if not before) the establishment of an "Executive Action Committee" to conduct assassinations.

Bissell's description of the group—"a small special unit highly compartmented from the rest of the [CIA]"—coincides with that of ZRRIFLE. As Bissell's tenure in office overlapped both presidential administrations, it is probable that Bissell was one of the moving forces—or perhaps *the* force—behind an assassination team. Bissell was fairly close to Kennedy and obviously had his approval, and he conceivably could have discussed such a plan with Rostow and Bundy (whom he already knew) at some point during the transition before Kennedy's inauguration. But whether or not he moved to establish an "executive action" capability without the knowledge of anyone in the Eisenhower administration remains unknown. It is certain, however, that Eisenhower and his director of central intelligence, Allen Dulles, were both in favor of assassinating Castro, as well as Lumumba and Trujillo. ZRRIFLE never became operational, however, probably a collateral victim of the Bay of Pigs.[42]

During his administration, Eisenhower was continually dealing with events in the Middle East. Although most of the United States policies and programs there were overt, including the landing of a Marine force in Lebanon in July 1958, Eisenhower did approve a covert action program intended to instigate a coup in Syria in 1956, code named "Straggle." This was to be a joint operation with the British Secret Intelligence Service (BSIS, otherwise known as SIS or MI-6), designed to thwart what was perceived to be Syrian alliance with the USSR by deposing a regime highly supportive of Egyptian leader Gamal Nasser, who was anathema to the British. Straggle was aborted when Israel, with British collusion, invaded Egypt, precipitating the Suez Crisis in October 1956 and seriously straining the U.S.–British relationship.[43]

The Eisenhower legacy of covert action was that it was (a) a means of halting the spread of Communism without risk of starting World War III, and (b) taken as a matter of faith to be a magic bullet capable of overthrowing governments with ease, on the cheap, and with little loss of life. When convenient, as with the failure in Indonesia, it was simpler to forget and move on rather than to look for lessons learned. Certainly, if Eisenhower could have had a third term he would have continued to rely on covert action, failures or not, for in his mind the positives would have outweighed the negatives. And like any president, he was far more concerned at that time with stopping the bad guys than he was with what the countries involved might become or experience four decades down the road. Many covert action programs that the Eisenhower administration had initiated continued into the Kennedy years. Like his predecessor, Kennedy would rely on covert action as a tool of statecraft, too, although his first program was to be an unmitigated disaster.

NINE

John F. Kennedy
and Lyndon B. Johnson

The CIA has often been called a "Rogue Elephant" by its critics, but I consider that to be a mischaracterization. During my seven years in the Defense Department (and I believe throughout the preceding and following administrations), all CIA "covert operations" (excluding spying operations) were subject to the approval of the president and the secretaries of state and defense, or their representatives. The CIA had no authority to act without that approval. So far as I know, it never did.[1]

Robert S. McNamara, Secretary of Defense

KENNEDY

Following his inauguration, John F. Kennedy dismantled the advisory group established in the NSC-5412 series and began permanently to chair meetings with his senior advisors (still loosely referred to as the "Special Group" or the "5412 Group," despite the official demise of that body). Kennedy's direct involvement, so different from Eisenhower's policy of remaining in the background, significantly eroded the concept of presidential plausible deniability. The only other oversight mechanism available to provide an independent review of covert action programs, the President's Board of Consultants on Foreign Intelligence, was also abolished by Kennedy shortly after he assumed office. With these actions, Kennedy "satisfied his desire for direct leadership" of covert action approval and review.[2]

According to former CIA director of operations Richard M. Bissell, while the Special Group's role "did not change greatly" at first under JFK, in the aftermath of the Bay of Pigs it became "much more conscious of its responsibility and reviewed proposed operations both more rigorously and more formally than before."[3] Partly due to the Bay of Pigs failure and partly as a result of the administration's review of U.S. paramilitary resources and capabilities occasioned by the growing conflict in Southeast Asia, in 1963 the "Special Group" was formally divided into two subcommittees, with the Special Group-Augmented (SG-A) focusing on covert action and Special Group-Insurgencies (SG-I) concerned with guerrilla warfare. The split was purely for administrative clarity, as the membership for both was the same: Attorney General Robert F. Kennedy, the president's primary advisor, confidant, and brother; the presidential military advisor and war hero General Maxwell Taylor; McGeorge Bundy, national security advisor; General Lyman Lymnitzer; deputy defense secretary and close Kennedy friend Roswell Gilpatrick; and the DCI (initially Allen Dulles, later John McCone).

The Kennedy inner circle was captivated by the allure of counterinsurgency operations as a method to contain Soviet expansionism in Southeast Asia and Africa; this was manifested in Special Group-I. Special Group-A was given responsibilities to review "important" covert action programs and operations, and to assume the oversight and planning for any other projects as assigned by the president.[4]

Following the Bay of Pigs in April 1961, covert action programs funded in excess of $3 million were required to navigate the

SG-A, while minor operations, usually defined as operations costing less than $250,000 and/or operations that were not highly sensitive, could still be approved and run with only the DCI's authority, so long as they were in congruence with general NSC guidance and directives. By then, SG-A had "developed general but informal criteria, including risk, possibility of success [or failure], potential for exposure, political sensitivity, and cost, for determining" which programs were submitted to group scrutiny.[5] Another change in policy, enacted in October 1962, required the DCI to begin vetting each of his programs with the Special Group-A.[6]

The use of the Special Group-Augmented, which not only reported to the president but also included him as an active participant, resulted in Kennedy's exercising concentrated authority over all major covert projects initiated by his administration. There can be little doubt that if Kennedy hadn't agreed with a program that came to his attention, that program would have been canceled. Thus, ultimate responsibility for approval and execution of these operations lay directly with Kennedy. That said, the criteria still permitted the CIA to originate and run numerous low-cost, low-level, low-risk operations, with the upper threshold set at $250,000 before the programs had to be taken to the SG-A.[7]

KENNEDY'S COVERT ACTION OPERATIONS

In the Truman and Eisenhower administrations, covert action was employed to deal with impending and genuine national security dangers, and was aimed either at halting the spread of Communism or weakening pro-Communist regimes. After 1962, however, these programs became more and more directed toward intervention in the domestic affairs of foreign nations, even without a concomitant high level of threat to core American interests. There was a "new doctrine" that seemingly justified "unlimited intervention to promote internal change in countries that [were] both friend and foe . . . directed against countries that [did] not threaten our national security [or were] allies of the United States."[8]

In a meeting in the White House on January 27, 1961, just days after inauguration, Kennedy ordered the CIA to conduct a number of covert operations against the Castro regime, to include sabotage and political action, and directed the State Department to generate an anti-Castro propaganda program for Latin America. Kennedy also ordered covert action programs in Africa, particularly in the former Belgian Congo. Concurrently, a paramilitary operation involving a force of Cuban exiles being trained in Guatemala with objectives of invading Cuba and overthrowing the Castro regime was in the final stages. This is the program that ultimately became known as the "Bay of Pigs." Assured by DCI Allen Dulles and his director of operations, Richard Bissell, that the invasion couldn't fail, Kennedy gave the go-ahead, even though experts in Cuban affairs at the State Department and CIA and amphibious warfare experts at the Defense Department—specialists who could have identified and explained the numerous flaws in the operation's concept and details—had been excluded from the planning.[9]

The invasion of Cuba by the CIA-trained exiles, Operation ZAPATA, has to be counted as among the worst CIA programs of any sort, ever. The long-classified report of the Agency's inspector general on the program, written in 1967, was finally published in 1994 and—combined with a large volume of other previously published materials on the Bay of Pigs disaster—renders superfluous yet another accounting now. One intelligence veteran and scholar summed up the Bay of Pigs fiasco as the "end of the golden age of covert action," demonstrating that "subversive warfare" was not the "complete answer to Soviet adventures around the globe."[10]

What remains little-known is that the few CIA career officers who were aware of the Bay of Pigs program argued against it to their politically appointed superiors; others, once they learned of the operation, were aghast at the mistakes made—mistakes that, had experts been consulted, could have been avoided. Indeed, such consultations probably would have convinced Kennedy not to allow planning for the invasion to go forward in the first place. Policy analyst David Isenberg has alleged that Director of Central Intelligence Allen Dulles "sought to steer Kennedy into a project he deeply mistrusted but that the CIA nevertheless wished him to carry out."[11] The truth of the matter is that it was not—and could not have been—the *institution* known as the CIA and its career staff who wanted the operation carried out, for they did not even know of it. Rather it was *individuals* within the CIA, Dulles, as DCI, and his head of operations, Bissell, who were so convinced of the Agency's infallibility that they persuaded the president that the plan could not fail. From then until William J. Casey's tenure as DCI, directors avoided being drawn into policy decisions.

Of course, no one will ever know what would have happened if Kennedy had decided to approve whatever measures would have been necessary to ensure success in the invasion, most notably by permitting air strikes from U.S. Navy and Marine squadrons on nearby aircraft carriers in support of invading exiles on the beaches. While he could not have canceled the invasion without incurring the wrath of the Republican Party, once the exiles stepped foot in the swamps of the Bay of Pigs, Kennedy was equally concerned over Soviet and world reaction to overt American intervention. Kennedy let the exiles go it alone, which meant going down in failure.

Taking personally the defeat at the Bay of Pigs and, perhaps, giving in to a personal hatred of Castro afterward, Kennedy became more determined to end Castro's regime in Cuba. To that end, he authorized the CIA to initiate and execute Operation Mongoose, a multifaceted covert action program to overthrow Castro through methods more subtle than invasion and war, predominantly economic sabotage. However, another important element of the program was to deter or prevent Castro from "exporting the revolution and Communism to other countries." Also included were at least eight assassination attempts on the life of the Cuban leader. (Former DCI Richard Helms, former DDCI Ray Cline, and former undersecretary of state U. Alexis Johnson all concur that the directive for the assassination of Castro was generated from within the White House.) Mongoose soon became the primary and most expensive foreign policy initiative of the Kennedy administration.[12]

Although Mongoose was cancelled near the end of 1962, the two Special Groups continued to oversee other covert operations in Cuba, as well as in Laos, Vietnam, and various African locales. According to Undersecretary of State U. Alexis Johnson, Kennedy took "a great deal of interest" in SG-A activities, which approved around 550 covert action projects of all kinds—political action, propaganda, and paramilitary—during the JFK years.[13]

The Cuban alliance with the Soviet Union also caused concern as the Castro regime, acting as a surrogate for the Soviets, began supporting subversive movements throughout Latin America. An additional concern in Chile were the Communists in the local trade unions who sought, like their political allies, close ties to Moscow.[14] Although CIA covert action undertaken in Chile is most readily identified with the Nixon administration, the CIA first began managing political action operations there in April 1962, in response to a diplomatic initiative by Kennedy known as the Alliance for Progress, which was intended "to promote the growth of democratic institutions" in Latin America. But there was also a covert element to the Alliance, via a presidential directive to strengthen the Chilean rightist party, the Christian Democrats (PDC), and support its leader, Eduardo Frei, who, Kennedy believed, both shared his political beliefs and possessed the organizational skills and structure to achieve their common objectives. In 1962 the Special Group approved an initial payment of $62,000 for the Alliance, followed by an additional $180,000 the same year. Interestingly, the next year, the administration also decided to aid the Chilean Radical Party (PR) in the April 1963 elections, to the tune of $50,000. As a result of the elections, the PR became the largest party in Chile.

Covert action in Chile continued through the Kennedy and Johnson administrations, with propaganda and political action operations involving "the press, radio, films, pamphlets, posters, graffiti, and direct mailings . . . and $3 million in 1962–64 for projects that ranged from organizing slum dwellers to funding political parties." Both the CIA and independent analysts have since concluded that these operations successfully kept the Socialists, or even Communists, out of power until 1970. It must be emphatically noted that CIA activities in Chile were *not* kept from Congress, at least until the Nixon administration, even though Chilean operations began a decade before Hughes-Ryan required that covert action programs be reported to the Hill. Former DCI Bill Colby has written that from 1964 until 1973 "at various times . . . the major steps in Chile were brought to the attention of the chairmen or appropriate members" of the cognizant committees, with "a series of discussions between the CIA and senior members of Congress which brought them up to date with the fact that this occurred and was occurring."[15]

In addition to the Chilean operations, the Kennedy administration also undertook, much to the astonishment of the British government, a "long, determined campaign, diplomatically and covertly, to prevent the Marxist Chedi Jagan from becoming the head of government in British Guyana after it achieved independence." Professor John Lewis Gaddis notes that Jagan, as a Marxist, made "no better impression than Castro and Kennedy ordered the CIA to get rid of him," believing that Jagan constituted "a major threat to the region." Despite political action operations involving bribery and instigating street disturbances, Jagan remained in power, leading the Brits to defer granting independence until Jagan's colonial government collapsed of its own accord. Ironically, once granted independence, Guyana voted Jagan in as its first freely elected president.[16]

Like Eisenhower, Kennedy was worried about events in the Dominican Republic under the iron rule of the cruel dictator Trujillo, and American patience with the regime was running thin both on the island and in Washington. The U.S. ambassador to the Dominican Republic recommended to the White House that its current policy of nonintervention be overturned, and to Richard Bissell at the CIA that the Agency provide weapons and munitions to an internal dissident group opposing Trujillo. It was obvious at the time to those in Washington that any arms supplied probably would be used to assassinate Trujillo. Bissell approved the arms transfer, but for one reason or another, it was soon put in abeyance. Then on January 12, 1961, with the Kennedy administration recently installed in power, the Special Group-Augmented met and approved the transfer of limited amounts of small arms and explosives, with the proviso that the handover of weapons take place outside the Dominican Republic.[17]

The SG-A membership understood the potential lethal consequences for Trujillo that this approval entailed; however, it was also clear to the committee that there would be no CIA involvement beyond the provision of the arms. Agency officers would neither train the dissidents, nor participate in mission planning, nor execute the operations. Although the president did not sit in on this SG-A meeting, there was a "White House representative" in the persona of Gordon Gray who was expected to brief the president on its results, permitting Kennedy the option of overriding the group's decision. He did not. Despite this, however, the dissidents were unable to devise a method for receiving the arms. Nevertheless, and without U.S. government assistance, the dissidents did kill Trujillo just a short time later, in May 1960.[18]

JFK continued the covert action program in Tibet in part because his secretary of state, Dean Rusk, had served as assistant secretary for Asian affairs during the Truman administration and was "thoroughly receptive" to sustaining the endeavor, despite the strenuous objections of the ambassador to India, John Kenneth Galbraith, who held a passionate liberal's intense dislike of these kinds of programs.[19] This split between an "Asian camp" and a "South-Asian camp" was reflected at CIA headquarters. There, the operations officers in the Far East Division favored harassing China anywhere possible, while those in the Near East Division (in whose jurisdiction India fell) were reluctant to "challenge China through their backdoor."[20]

Meanwhile, in Europe the CIA replayed its earlier successes in Italy by continuing to provide covert support to pro-democracy parties in order to undermine the Italian Communist Party (PCI).[21]

While there is no way of knowing what Kennedy would have done vis-à-vis Cuba, Indochina, and other critical regions had he lived to see a second term, nothing in the record indicates that he would have reduced his reliance on the CIA to achieve foreign policy objectives or to contain Communist expansionism, even after the Bay of Pigs. For JFK, the World War II veteran, war in the shadows was as much a tool of statecraft as diplomacy, and manifestly more preferable to an overt war that might trigger a reciprocal Soviet intervention.

JOHNSON

Assuming the presidency in 1963 after Kennedy's assassination, Lyndon Baines Johnson inherited growing foreign policy problems and the National Security Council mechanisms to deal with them, including the covert action committee familiarly, if incorrectly, referred to as the "5412 Group." Seven months after Johnson took office, a book appeared on the CIA that revealed the existence and name of Kennedy's "Special Group" committee. The publicity prompted the national security advisor, McGeorge Bundy, to issue National Security Action Memorandum 303, *Change in Name of Special Group 5412*, on June 2, 1964. Thereafter, this covert action approval and review group was known as the 303 Committee. However, despite the name change, the purpose, responsibilities, and membership of the group did not change. As one member stated, "all of the CIA's covert operations worldwide required clearance by the 303 Committee. The membership of the committee included the number twos at CIA, State, and Defense, and was chaired by national security advisor McGeorge Bundy."[22]

JOHNSON'S COVERT ACTION OPERATIONS

Covert action programs during the Johnson years included a continuation of the political programs in Italy to prevent the PCI from gaining ground and to counter Soviet activities supporting the PCI, and new or continuing programs in Indonesia, British Guyana, Pakistan, the Dominican Republic, Thailand, Israel-Jordan, Greece, Bolivia, and Chile.[23] However, very little has been declassified about these programs beyond an official acknowledgment of their existence, with a number of them running into the Nixon years. The assorted small-scale propaganda and political action programs infiltrating news, perspectives, cultural materials, and historical data into the USSR continued, as well, throughout the Johnson years. However, until more files from the LBJ administration are declassified, a fuller accounting of these covert action programs will have to wait.

The long-running Italian program was finally terminated by the Johnson administration in 1967, having run its course, although apparently not without some debate in the White House. The following material, texts from White House memos and State Department cablegrams, present a marvelous example of the back-and-forth that occurs at the policy levels in evaluating covert action programs.

Declassified minutes from a June 11, 1965, meeting of the 303 Committee explains the essentials of the Italian program at that point:

> The basic political problem to which the FY 1966 program is addressed is that Italy's four-party, center-left coalition Government, which was formed in December 1963 is faced with a profusion of problems which makes it a fragile working partnership. The Italian Communist Party has skillfully exploited the Government's vulnerabilities and has steadily increased its electoral appeal during this period when the vote of the two major coalition partners, the Christian Democrats (CD) and the Socialists (PSI), has declined. A basic premise of the FY 1966 program is that if the strength and unity of the Government coalition can be increased, thus permitting implementation of its program of basic social, economic and

administrative reforms, the democratic parties' appeal in the next national election should increase and that of the Communist Party should decline.

But a June 25, 1965, meeting of the 303 Committee recorded that a proposal to authorize funding for Fiscal Year 1966 was "generally viewed as a 'necessary evil' and approved with . . . National Security Advisor McGeorge Bundy deploring the chronic failure of the Italian democratic political parties to utilize their own bootstraps. . . . [Bundy] used the term 'annual shame' and felt obliged to advise [the president] of this continuing subsidy." The purpose of the program was declared to be the "strengthening of the [four-party] center-left government." The underlying premise was that if the coalition could be shored up, it would be able to make good on essential social, economic, and administrative reform programs.[24]

LBJ then asked Bundy to review the program, and he did so, transmitting his results to the president on August 4, 1965 (interestingly, the date of the alleged second attack on American naval vessels in the Gulf of Tonkin). In a highly classified memo to the president, Bundy wrote:

SUBJECT: Italian Covert Political Assistance
Some weeks ago you asked me to review this problem and bring you up to date on it more specifically. I have now done so, and the situation is as follows:
Over the years the U.S. has assisted the democratic Italian political parties and trade unions at a very high rate. Over the period 1955–1965, the total amount of assistance is just under [still classified]. In recent years we have been cutting this assistance back, primarily because the professionals closely related to the operation have concluded that we have not been getting our full money's worth and what the Italian political parties need is not so much U.S. money as energetic administrative leadership. President Kennedy had a personal feeling that

political subsidies at this level were excessive, and they were scaled down.

In the last two or three years, assistance has been running at a rate of about [still classified], except in the election year of 1963. The recommendation for next year runs to a total of [still classified]. The interdepartmental review committee for covert operations—Vance, Thompson, Raborn and myself—has approved this recommendation subject to your concurrence.

Meanwhile, by separate and somewhat unusual channels, [still classified] have let us know that they would like a lot more money. They have given no practical justification, and indeed have been at pains to suggest that our orthodox channels are stuffy and uncooperative. I have had a long interview with the [still classified] man most familiar with this subject (he was in Rome for 8 years), and he persuades me that this end run is as unjustified in fact as it appears to be on the surface. Having begun with a sympathetic view that money might beat the Communists, I have been entirely converted by his detailed account of the efforts we have made to get the Italian parties to do better with the money we have already given them.

In this situation, I believe that we should approve the recommended budget for this year and go back to [still classified] by appropriate quiet channels to say that we cannot do more unless and until there is evidence that additional money is what is really needed, and that such money can be used really effectively. This would put the responsibility with them, where it belongs, while leaving us free to do more if and when a really good opportunity presents itself. It remains true that the anti-Communist battle in Italy is one of politics and resources; but simple hand-outs and intelligently applied resources are two entirely different things. McG. B.

The program carried on into FY 1966 and when it was being considered for FY 1967, the American ambassador to Rome wrote a confidential cablegram to Undersecretary of State U. Alexis Johnson on September 12, 1966:

> SUBJECT: 303 Committee Consideration of the Italian Covert Action Program
>
> I want to elaborate further on our discussion on Tuesday about the Italian covert program. The coming months may represent a critical period for political stability in Italy. Decisive steps to reunify the Socialist and Social Democratic parties are anticipated this fall. This prospect, in conjunction with the strong rivalries within the Christian Democratic party, could put new strains on Moro's center-left coalition. An additional unsettling factor is the approaching general elections. They must take place not later than April 1968.
>
> Since my assignment to Rome I have consistently recommended the gradual reduction of covert activities in Italy. The record in fact shows sharp year-to-year cuts in expenditures. The level of funds has dropped from [still classified] in FY 1964 to a recommended [still classified] in FY 1967. The latter figure represents a cut of 35% from FY 1966. It is also significant that in recent years we have progressively discontinued direct subsidies to political parties—the last was the small program in FY 1966 for [still classified]. All other support to political parties has been contingent on approved action programs in support of U.S. policy objectives, in the absence of which no funds have been made available. The [still classified] is now on notice that any support for FY 1967 would be on such a basis. Accordingly the pro-￾posed program contains no unstructured contributions to any political party's finances.
>
> In the circumstances, I recommend that the program

proposed for FY 1967 be approved. An abrupt discontinuance of the program at this time would be interpreted by some of our friends, on whom we must depend for achievement of our policy objectives in Italy, as a change in our long-standing support for them and for what they are attempting to achieve. I am particularly concerned that we avoid any action which might disturb the Moro-Nenni-Saragat leadership, which is relatively strong by post-war Italian standards and which seems to offer the best chance of strengthening political stability and democracy in Italy. At the same time, I feel that we should continue the gradual reduction of the covert program in Italy with the general objective of a final phase-out in connection with the 1968 elections.

The program was to be ended, at last, before the beginning of FY 1968. A National Security Council position paper, finalized on August 4, 1967, concluded that:

The point has been approaching rapidly in recent years where the continuation of a large-scale covert action program in Italy would no longer have pertinence. Currently, socialist unification has been achieved and the Christian Democratic Party (DC) . . . despite continuing financial problems, is at least for the time being well united behind its incumbent political secretary. Domestic funds are available if . . . political groups make sufficient efforts to tap them. In addition, the amount of covert assistance the United States is prepared to offer in light of other more pressing commitments no longer equates with the amounts needed to have other than peripheral impact on the Italian political scene.

And so at the August 22, 1967, meeting of the 303 Committee it was recorded: "Italy—Covert Action Program for FY-1968: The wind-down of covert political support to Italian parties ahead of schedule was enthusiastically welcomed by the committee."

Although the Italian program was winding down, it is known, thanks mostly to the Church Committee, that in April 1964 Johnson approved $3 million to bolster Eduardo Frei in the Chilean elections, and, later, a modest $160,000 to Frei's Christian Democrat Party (PDC) as aid to peasants and the poverty-stricken to build goodwill for the PDC. That September, Frei was elected with 55.7 percent of the vote. In 1964 the 303 Committee authorized another $175,000 to support favored candidates for the Chilean legislature, with the PDC winning an absolute majority in the lower house and control of the upper house. This election was an example of the limits of plausibility deniability, with those affected—in this case the losing Socialist party under Salvador Allende—strongly suspecting (if not "knowing," in their heart of hearts) that the United States influenced their elections despite the absence of any probative evidence of such. In the final years of LBJ's administration, the U.S. government retained its support of both the Chilean Radical Party and the PDC, including the establishment of a "propaganda mechanism for making placements in radio and news media."[25] More, and worse, was to come under Nixon.

TEN

Richard M. Nixon
and Gerald R. Ford

It is tragic that it was necessary to establish this committee to inquire into the activities of agencies on which we depend so heavily for our security. But it would be even more tragic if the results of our investigation were now to be ignored.[1]

Congressman Robert Kasten (R-Wisconsin),
Pike Committee Member

NIXON

Richard M. Nixon had acquired a broad understanding of and appreciation for covert action while serving as Eisenhower's vice president, and as president he held no reservations about its use. Indeed, one can reasonably speculate that covert action greatly appealed to the secretive, suspicious chief executive who kept tight control of all aspects of American foreign policy, and to his equally secretive national security advisor, Henry Kissinger, as well. The principal proof of Nixon's personal involvement in covert action lies within four thousand hours of White House tapes showing that he "made excessive and sometimes self-defeating use of covert operations."[2]

Nixon retained the 303 Committee as a covert action oversight mechanism until its exposure in the press in 1969. As a consequence of that publicity, on February 17, 1970, Nixon signed *Responsibility for the Conduct, Supervision, and Coordination of Covert Action Operations*, National Security Decision Memorandum-40, rescinding and replacing NSC-5412/2 and concurrently superceding the 303 Committee.[3] NSDM-40 substituted the anti-Soviet language of its predecessor memos with a more general global perspective, stating that covert action programs were to be employed as supporting adjuncts to established overt foreign policy programs—proving collaterally that Nixon fully understood the role and function of covert action in the execution of foreign policy. The directive mandated that the DCI "obtain policy approval for all major and/or politically sensitive covert action operations" and required an annual review of programs already authorized. And, as with the earlier memos, NSDM-40 directed that a committee be established with the specific responsibility to review all major and/or politically sensitive covert action programs. The new group naturally assumed the title "40 Committee," although in-house it often continued to be referred to as the "Special Group."[4]

Nixon's national security advisor, Henry Kissinger, chaired the committee and continued to do so after he was elevated to secretary of state while retaining the security advisor position. At that point, Kissinger was at once secretary of state, a full member of the National Security Council, the president's most important foreign policy advisor, and chairman of the committee that oversaw the administration's most secret intelligence activities—a combination that, it may fairly be claimed, "corrupted the foreign policy decision-making process."[5]

Membership in the 40 Committee was, according to Kissinger, composed of the attorney general, the deputy secretaries of state and defense, the DCI, and the chairman of the Joint Chiefs of Staff, with Kissinger chairing the committee and assisted by a staff of one, an officer seconded from the CIA. As with the 303 Committee, this group was directed to "supervise" covert intelligence activities, although in reality the 40 Committee only authorized and funded covert action programs, with the president subverting his own White House process. It was Nixon's intent that Kissinger would manage the intelligence end of White House policy formulation and that the NSC under Kissinger would control the intelligence community. The reality, however, was that the committee was far more form than function. Also, Nixon distrusted the Agency at least as much as he did the State Department, in no small part because he believed that the Agency as an entity had somehow involved itself in the 1960 elections, contributing to his loss to John Kennedy. And Kissinger personally distrusted the DCI, Richard Helms, suspecting him of being part of a "liberal Georgetown set" that was anti-Nixon.[6]

It is doubtful that the inclusion in the 40 Committee membership of Attorney General John Mitchell, a longtime Nixon friend, former law partner, and political advisor, was to ensure that constitutional, legal, or procedural requirements were applied. In fact, one searches in vain for signs of any substantive role for Mitchell. As if to say that there was nothing unusual about the attorney general meeting with the president's foreign policy team, Kissinger notes that Robert Kennedy as attorney general sat with similar groups in his brother's administration.[7]

But Kissinger is too kind to John Mitchell. First, Robert Kennedy was his brother's closet policy advisor on every issue across the board, and would have been so regardless of his position in or out of the cabinet. Second, in the 1960s and 1970s the Justice Department was not extensively involved in foreign policy issues, as it today. Third, in Nixon's time congressional oversight of and legislative requirements for covert action did not exist to any significant extent. Indeed, this extensive oversight is one primary reason why, since the 1980s, the attorney general has been a full member of similar panels in every administration.

Unlike the closeness between the two Kennedys, the relationship between Nixon and Mitchell was not such that Nixon would have included the attorney general to play a substantive role in policy formation. Nixon's documented distrust of Kissinger (which included tapping Kissinger's phones), the State Department, the CIA, and just about everyone else working in the White House leads to the conclusion that Nixon placed Mitchell at the table simply to have a confidant reporting back on the actions of the president's own staff.[8]

Through Kissinger, Nixon established several other groups to review various clandestine or sensitive activities and programs. The Washington Special Action Group (WSAG) served as a planning and crisis management organ, and the Senior Review Group (SRG) provided the final scrub of sensitive programs and plans. The composition of these groups was the same as the 40 Committee, save that the attorney general did not sit with either and that the SRG had no staff members.[9]

In concept the 40 Committee was to oversee all covert action programs that were either sufficiently large or politically sensitive to merit White House consideration. Most of the covert actions proposed to the committee were from the CIA or the ambassador in the country at issue; only in the "rarest of cases" did the White House propose a program.[10] But Nixon and Kissinger ignored the 40 Committee and kept control, and even knowledge, of the majority of covert action programs to themselves. Virtually all major and many minor programs, perhaps as much as 75 percent, were never brought to the committee's attention. As a Senate investigation later found, "Criteria by which covert operations [were] brought before the 40 Committee appear to be fuzzy . . . the real degree of accountability for covert actions remains to be determined." Moreover, once a program was approved by the committee there was no provision for any review of the program, either on a one-time or a continuing basis. This no doubt suited Nixon and Kissinger perfectly, as it allowed them to exercise complete control without discussion or dissention.[11]

There were few actual meetings of the 40 Committee, with Kissinger often conducting the committee's business individually by telephone, thereby eliminating a written record. One-on-one conversations also precluded the animated give-and-take of debate which occurs in multiparty meetings, as well as any opportunity for genuine dissent. In one thirty-two-month period, over three dozen "sensitive" covert action operations were approved, even though the committee held not a single meeting on any of these operations. With respect to Chile, both the CIA and the State Department were, officially and on the record, "cool" to the idea of interfering in the Chilean elections; but realistically the feelings are more accurately described as hostile—which only gave Nixon and Kissinger more reason to restrict control and knowledge of the program to themselves alone. Out of literally dozens of covert action operations in Chile from 1963 to 1974, only eight were briefed, in whole or in part, to Congress.[12]

COVERT ACTION PROGRAMS UNDER NIXON

Informed by U.S. intelligence in 1969 that the Soviets were secretly attempting to influence the Chilean elections, Nixon believed that similar activities were appropriate to forestall a government with potentially pro-Communist sympathies. In this, he was of course only continuing and expanding a covert action program already in existence. While the objectives of Kennedy and Johnson had been only to support the Christian Democratic Party and, to a lesser degree, the Radical Party, Nixon intended to do much more: specifically, he sought to keep the Socialists out of power. In this program, however, the president was directly contradicting his own officially announced U.S. policy, which was to accept whatever government the people of Chile chose, engage in fully reciprocal relations, and allow the Chilean "problems to be settled by Chile."[13]

By late June 1969, the 40 Committee had approved almost $500,000 in propaganda and political action activities, first to prevent an Allende win in the election, and, when that failed, to undermine or reverse the Chilean elections.[14] The committee also included in its plans an economic destabilization program to "disrupt the Chilean economy," believing that the civil unrest created by the worsening economy would propel the Chilean military to remove Allende from office. Thus it was that the Chilean program ultimately became part of a complex diplomatic and covert pas de deux to bring about a military coup against the democratically elected president. This program, which would haunt the president, Kissinger, one DCI, and the Agency in future years, was personally ordered by the president despite serious resistance to it by Agency officers. Agency antagonism was no surprise even at the time, as Nixon's penchant for covert action operations far exceeded that of his DCI, Richard Helms, and many within the Agency's Directorate of Operations.[15]

Moreover, in keeping with Nixon and Kissinger's predilection for ordering covert activities without the knowledge of the 40 Committee, information on clandestine operations in support of a Chilean military coup against Allende was concealed from the committee, whose knowledge was limited only to the propaganda and political action programs intended to weaken support for Allende and obstruct Communist influence. While the Nixon administration acknowledged that Allende was openly and fairly elected through acceptable democratic processes, as well as understanding that he was neither a Communist nor under the influence of Communists, the administration was determined to oust him nonetheless. As justification, albeit specious, Kissinger claimed that there was "no reason why the United States should stand aside and let the country go Communist through the irresponsibility of its own people."[16]

Chile was an inexpensive program, relatively speaking. In the period from 1967 to 1973, the following expenditures were made: $8 million for election campaign material and support to favored political parties; $4.3 million for mass media to disseminate political messages; $900,000 to influence Chilean "institutions" (labor, students, peasants, trade unions, women, and private sector organizations); and a mere $200,000 to promote a coup against Allende.[17]

It must be emphasized that neither the Church Committee in 1976 nor the Hinchey Report in 2000 found any evidence—contrary to one of the favored allegations of CIA critics—that anyone in the CIA or U.S. intelligence community was involved in the death of Allende. Likewise, charges that any element of the U.S. government assisted General Augusto Pinochet to accede to the presidency of Chile have been refuted. Finally, while CIA contacts in the Chilean military and security forces were involved in "systematic and widespread human rights abuses," the Agency reported this to headquarters repeatedly and in line with the standing guidance at the time, and "admonished its Chilean agents against such behavior"; Agency personnel were in no circumstances supporters of these human rights tragedies.[18]

Nixon and Kissinger also ordered the CIA to conduct, against all advice from the intelligence organization and the State Department, another covert action program involving the Iranians, the Iraqis, and the Kurds, an ethnic group composed of several dozen loosely amalgamated tribes residing in the mountain region where Iran, Iraq, Turkey, and Syria intersect, known as Kurdistan. The president and his national security advisor must have been aware of the resistance the bureaucracy would mount, for they hid this program from the scrutiny of the 40 Committee.

The Kurdish program ordered by President Nixon yields yet another prime example of how the CIA can be wrongly saddled with blame for a failed program. As one intelligence scholar and former Agency analyst wrote in 2000, the "CIA established covert relations with the Kurds in northern Iraq [in 1972] . . . only to abandon them when U.S. policy changed."[19] Unfortunately, this language leads the reader to believe that the relationship began at Agency initiative and that the relationship was congruent with established U.S. foreign policy. Both implications are erroneous, however, and so contribute to a perpetuation of unmerited criticism and misinformation about the Agency and covert action. The records of the Pike Committee hearings bring forth the correct story as a matter of record.[20]

During the last week of May 1972, President Nixon and National Security Advisor Kissinger were guests of the Kremlin on a state visit to burnish an arms limitation treaty agreement with the Soviets. In the spirit of international friendship and East-West cooperation, Nixon and the Soviets signed a document entitled *Basic Principles of Relations*, which stated the United States's express willingness to work with the Soviets for stability and peace in the Middle East. Among the measures to be implemented to achieve those goals was a pledge to reduce arms sales by both parties. This gesture of goodwill played well to the world press. It also lasted less than a week.[21]

The president and his entourage departed Moscow on May 30, flying directly to Tehran to meet with the shah of Iran. At the first of two sessions, one topic on the shah's (not Nixon's) agenda was the rebellion of sorts being waged in Kurdistan. The shah asked Nixon—purely as a personal favor—to provide arms and supplies to the Kurdish rebels who were fighting the Iraqi army with the objective of establishing an independent nation of Kurdistan. But of course the situation was not that straightforward.

The Kurds' goal of independence had almost nothing in common with the individual objectives of the shah and the president. In point of fact, neither Nixon nor the shah cared one whit whether the Kurds ever achieved independence, which was, in any case, contrary to long-established U.S. policy vis-à-vis Turkey. Nixon was attracted to the idea simply as a means to "weaken and harass" the pro-Soviet regime in Baghdad; he had no interest much less desire in seeing the Kurds actually prevail. Not surprisingly, Nixon neglected to let the Kurds in on this secret. And the shah decidedly did not want an independent Kurdistan; he feared the Kurds, if successful, would detach the Kurdish region of Iran and incorporate it into the new Kurdish state. Rather, the shah was seeking only to precipitate disintegration within or an overthrow of the Iraqi regime, a traditional enemy made more dangerous now that it was a client state of the Soviet Union. The shah sought also to distract the Iraqi leadership from the continuing dispute with Iran over the Shatt-al-Arab border.[22]

But that wasn't all. The shah also had a collateral motivation of assisting his good friends, the Israelis. The latter, always alert for opportunities to weaken or divide their Arab enemies, wished to keep the Iraqi leadership and military focused on northern and eastern Iraq with the Kurdish problem so that they would be less likely to foment or join any Arab mischief against the Jewish state. In short, the Kurds were merely pawns in several larger games, games in which they had no inkling that they were even players. The Kurds were merely tools to be manipulated rather than a cause to be supported.

Details of the Kurdish covert action program were leaked to the *Village Voice* in February 1975 just days after they were revealed to the House Select Committee investigating the CIA under the chairmanship of Representative Otis Pike, a Democrat from New York. It was disclosed that the program ran for almost three years at a total cost of $16 million, despite heated objections from those who knew of it at the CIA. The Agency tried three times to stop the program before it commenced, fearing that thousands of Kurds would die. Nixon ordered the Agency to undertake the operations anyway, despite the fact that doing so was distinctly counter to U.S. policy in the region and that the United States had no interest at stake there. Nixon did not tell Secretary of State William P. Rogers of the Kurdish program for some time after its commencement, apparently presuming—correctly—that there would be objections from that quarter, as well, when the State Department finally learned of the program.[23]

During three years of vicious fighting in which the United States provided weapons, training, and other supplies, Nixon and Kissinger "discouraged the Kurds from negotiating a measure of autonomy with the Iraqi government but also restrained them from undertaking an all-out offensive." Then in 1975 the shah concluded a secret treaty with Iraq over the Shatt-al-Arab. When the CIA learned of the settlement, Nixon ordered Agency officers "not to inform the Kurdish command and to keep the Kurds fighting, thus providing the shah with a 'card to play' in his negotiations with Saddam." As partial payment for settling the border dispute, Saddam demanded that Iranian (i.e., United States) support for the Iraqi Kurds cease. The shah agreed and so informed President Ford, who was now in office after Nixon's resignation. The Kurds were dropped cold—*not* because of a change in U.S. policy, but rather because of a change in *Iranian* policy! And this despite promises to the Kurds from the U.S. government at the commencement of the program that they would not be "summarily dropped by the shah." Ultimately, "at least 35,000 Iraqi Kurds were killed and 200,000 made refugees as a direct result of U.S. policy."[24]

In 1975, while the Church Committee was investigating CIA abuses, a similar panel in the House of Representatives, the House Select Committee on Intelligence (known as the Pike Committee after its chairman, Congressman Otis Pike), was investigating Agency processes and procedures. Testifying before the Pike Committee, Kissinger maintained that "covert action should not be confused with missionary work." The final report of the Pike Committee stated in response to Kissinger that:

> [t]he president, Dr. Kissinger, and the foreign heads of state hoped that our clients would not prevail. They preferred instead that the insurgents simply continue a level of hostilities that would sap the resources of our ally's neighboring country. This policy was not imparted to our clients, who were encouraged to continue fighting. . . . Even in the context of covert action, ours was a cynical enterprise.[25]

If there was any one program that exemplified the accusations that covert action had turned from a tool applied strictly in the national interest during the Truman-Eisenhower years to one used by later presidents (especially Nixon) simply because it existed, this is it. Moreover, allegations that Nixon and Kissinger conducted a morally sterile foreign policy program devoid of any concern for loss of life or human rights were given great credence because of the callousness that underlay the Kurdish program.

FORD

Gerald R. Ford came into the presidency having developed and enunciated neither foreign nor domestic policy initiatives, but those who criticize him for this are highly unfair. Presidential candidates spend years pondering about where they want to take the country and how they intend to do it; and then they refine these plans as they navigate the electoral shoals and reefs. Ford, however, was a man who aspired only to become speaker of the House of Representatives but almost overnight found himself president only by dint of the most bizarre of circumstances. That he had to learn and devise as he went should have surprised no one. One result, though, was that Ford did not have great awareness of covert action programs or theory when taking office.

It wasn't until he had been in office for eighteen months and experienced the fallout from the Church and Pike Committee investigations into Agency abuses that Ford instituted changes in the covert action process. In February 1976 through Executive Order 11905, Ford replaced the 40 Committee with a new mechanism, the Operations Advisory Group (OAG), which was to serve as the president's advisory body on covert action programs and policies. Membership included the national security advisor, the secretaries of state and defense, chairman of the Joint Chiefs, and the DCI. The attorney general and the director of the Office of Management and Budget continued in an observer status, as before. The order elevated the review of these programs and operations to cabinet level, rather than the deputy level, and removed the DCI from direct responsibility for covert action programs. This in effect ensured that the DCI would have to consult with the president's most senior foreign and national security advisors more closely than before. Most important, the OAG ensured that policy decisions were made at the presidential level. This Executive Order was the first public document to describe intelligence functions and to place formal restrictions on them. The document also explicitly forbade assassinations, which had already been proscribed in internal CIA regulations under DCI William Colby.[26]

Ford was the first chief executive to face the need for Presidential Findings for covert action programs, thanks to Hughes-Ryan, but as the legislation provided no guidance as to form, the administration decided upon broadly targeted "Worldwide" Findings. These Findings were written for what would become known in later years as "transnational issues," threats emanating from multiple countries or geographic regions rather than from just one locus. Included in these Worldwide Findings were operations against terrorism, narcotics traffickers, counterintelligence targets, and, in the 1990s, the proliferation of weapons of mass destruction.[27]

COVERT ACTION UNDER FORD

The record of covert action programs under Ford is paltry, for several reasons. First, the Church and Pike investigations made the administration and the Agency reluctant to do much. However, the low-risk, low-cost political action programs aimed at the Soviet Union did continue, for they were not controversial. And second, there has been little declassified about covert action programs in the Ford years, again, no doubt, because they were minimal in scope. The above notwithstanding, there was one large program initiated in Angola, where, according to former DCI Robert Gates, Cuban military forces were acting as Soviet surrogates in a three-way civil war.[28] Begun in 1975, the covert action program generated sufficient congressional controversy that it became the genesis of the Presidential Finding. (The program has been dissected in *Covert Action* by Gregory Treverton, an intelligence historian who was a staff member for both the NSC and the Church Committee.)[29] On January 22, 1975, the Ford administration authorized a modest $300,000 for IAFEATURE, the covert action program that supported two of the three Angolian factions competing for power: the National Front for the Liberation of Angola (FNLA) under Holden Roberto and the UNITA (National Union for the Total Independence of Angola) Party of Jonas Savimbi. Interestingly, both groups also had relations with the Communist government of the Peoples' Republic of China! The third force was the Popular Movement for the Liberation of Angola (MPLA), a Marxist group in thrall to Cuba and the Soviet Union. There were eventually more than twenty thousand Cuban troops in Angola serving as Soviet proxies, a situation that provided "perhaps the first clear-cut and dramatic demonstration" of Soviet willingness to exercise power in the post-Vietnam and post-Watergate period when they perceived they possessed an improved "strategic strength." The late Cord Meyer, a former CIA senior officer and covert action specialist, said that the Soviet-Cuban intervention:

> In one strategic stroke . . . fundamentally succeeded in changing the balance of power in southern Africa to their advantage. In doing so, they gained effective political influence in a huge slice of the Dark Continent, obtained access to new strategic ports and airfields, and secured a political base from which to operate against the remaining non-Communist countries in Africa.[30]

Complicating the situation was the fact that all three groups, besides being competing political movements, were distinct ethnic tribes: the Mbundu (MPLA), the Bakongo (FNLA) and the Ovimbundu (UNITA).[31]

Secretary of State Henry Kissinger was again the driving force for this covert action program, arguing that the takeover of Angola by Soviet proxies would seriously damage U.S. interests. Yet, apparently all three warring parties laid modest claim to being Marxists of some ilk. In short, there was no genuine pro-democracy movement and there was no rational reason to think that whoever won in Angola would be pro-West, democratic, or progressive. Thus,

Kissinger moved the United States into a covert war in which the U.S. government could expect little positive in return. For these reasons, and no doubt others, career officers at the CIA as well as the Department of State's Bureau of African Affairs were solidly against any covert action in the former colony. The program's initial funding was to Holden Roberto for only $300,000, not to buy arms or to fight, but merely to "show resolve" on the part of the United States. An additional $15 million was authorized in July 1975 and $10 million more in September to Roberto and Jonas Savimbi's UNITA movement.[32] Congress legislated an end to U.S. assistance in December 1975, by which time the Communist proxy forces of the MPLA had driven Roberto and Savimbi out of the capital and into the wilds. Angola's was to become one of the world's longest-running civil wars, lasting into the twenty-first century.[33]

The stated goal of the administration—the prevention of a Soviet proxy taking power in Angola—was clearly articulated, but how that was to be attained was not obvious. According to Church Committee staff member Dr. Angelo Codevilla, the administration was unwilling to confront the Soviets by direct intervention, but it was equally unwilling to stand aside. Therefore it chose to apply covert action, the "third option," although this phase of U.S. intervention in Angola accomplished little, nor could it have given the limited amount of assistance allocated. It was argued that since the Soviets and the Cubans were providing significant aid overtly to the MPLA, similar U.S. aid could and should have also been sent overtly. This was especially so since the entire world knew that Roberto and Savimbi were being supported by the Americans, thus rendering the "covert" program manifestly overt in the first place.[34]

There was one other important covert action program in the Ford years that is still classified (although the government and citizens of the country itself undoubtedly know of it). This continuing classification is unfortunate in that it involved the removal of a dictatorship and the establishment of a full constitutional democracy that continues to this day. In essence, a nation and its people were brought into the family of democratic nations through the actions of the Central Intelligence Agency, acting on the explicit direction of the president of the United States. Beyond any doubt, this program is one in which the bad guys lost, the good guys won, and a democracy arose out of a dictatorship. And arguably only American citizens remain in the dark about it.

ELEVEN

Jimmy Carter

The CIA is a uniquely presidential organization. Virtually every time it has gotten in trouble, it has been for carrying out some action ordered by a president . . . [y]et few presidents have anything good to say about CIA or the intelligence they received.[1]

Robert M. Gates, DCI

James Earl Carter possessed a liberal's visceral dislike of the CIA, all that it stood for, all that it did, and how it did it—especially in regard to covert action. Carter and others in his administration had "accepted at face value allegations of CIA's role in plotting murder and other crimes," a belief that was possibly abetted, consciously or otherwise, by the fact that Vice President Walter Mondale, also more liberal than centrist in political philosophy, had been a member of the Church Committee investigating Agency abuses. Thus Carter professed to be "deeply troubled" by much of what the CIA did. Yet by the end of his administration Carter had instituted a dozen covert action programs "after overt responses to Third World trouble spots had proven ineffective or impracticable," and especially after the Soviet invasion of Afghanistan in 1979 shocked him to the core.[2]

Most, if not all, of the covert programs begun by Carter were continued and expanded by the Reagan administration. For this, however, Carter has received little credit, remembered more often instead for preelection comments such as his referral to the CIA as a "national disgrace."[3] But Carter must have changed his opinion, at least a little, with the CIA's successful covert extraction of six U.S. diplomats in Tehran who had escaped capture by Iranian militants and were being hidden by the Canadian ambassador to Iran. CIA officers also performed with heroism and ingenuity in preparations for the (later failed) rescue attempt of the Iranian hostages at Desert One, which could only have made another positive impression on the president.

Once inaugurated, Carter established in Executive Order 12036 two separate committees to help with foreign policy and national security issues, including intelligence matters. The lower level group, the Policy Review Committee (PRC), created and monitored policy, programs, and resources for the intelligence collection mission; the Special Coordination Committee (SCC), the highest-level White House committee, was given the responsibility to approve new and review current covert action programs, with the president exercising the final say. Membership in the SCC consisted of the usual suspects: secretaries of state and defense, chairman of the Joint Chiefs, the national security advisor, and the DCI. However, in a reflection of the increased congressional oversight and passage of federal statutes that in effect regulated covert action, Carter gave the attorney general and the director of the Office of Management and Budget full membership in the committee for the supervision of covert action operations.[4]

In response to congressional concerns over what the legislators probably saw as overly generous language in the Ford administration's Worldwide Findings, Carter merged the several Findings into just one "Omnibus Finding" covering all issues, albeit with the scope and limits of permissible operations more narrowly described. University of Georgia professor Loch Johnson's research found that Carter's Omnibus Finding "combined the first worldwide findings approved by the President into a single, somewhat more detailed finding. In his initially limited use of covert action, President Carter relied chiefly on this generic finding, which he augmented later with a few overarching propaganda themes and selected specific findings focused on individual countries."[5]

Still, the oversight committees remained worried about the nature of the language. As explained by Carter's DCI, Admiral Stansfield Turner, "Under a broad Finding, an operation can be expanded considerably; with a narrow one, the CIA has to go back to the president to obtain a revised Finding if there is any change in scope. The Congress is wary of broad Findings: they can easily be abused."[6] While the admiral is basically correct, changes to Findings (Memoranda of Notification, or MON) are less likely to be generated by the CIA than by the White House, which may seek to modify program objectives. MON are written documents that are reported to Congress exactly as original Findings are, keeping the integrity of the oversight process sound. As Carter began approving more Findings in 1978 and later, the president acknowledged congressional concerns by drafting discrete Findings for individual countries or specific issues. By the end of his tenure, there were three generic types of Findings—the Omnibus Finding, Worldwide Findings on transnational issues (modified from time to time by MON), and an increasing number of "single country/single issue" Findings whenever possible. Thus, it is accurate to say that "the Finding process under the Carter Administration . . . was quite exhaustive in its consideration of covert action recommendations."[7]

COVERT ACTION PROGRAMS UNDER CARTER

Just three months into his administration, Jimmy Carter, who as a presidential candidate had thought the CIA and covert action to be corrupt and undemocratic, initiated covert action programs targeted at the internal political situation in the Soviet Union. He followed these programs with a propaganda and political action campaign in Western Europe to counter a massive Soviet active measures program in the same region. The Soviets' goal was to prevent the NATO deployment of the neutron bomb on the continent.

Although the Nixon administration had found it convenient to accept the supposedly absolute right of the Soviet Union, as a sovereign political state, to conduct its internal affairs as it saw fit without outside interference, Carter took a new path. The president's concern for human rights impelled him to insist that the Soviet Union abide by all international agreements it was a party to, including those with provisions for respecting and adhering to international standards of humans rights. Carter saw this as a matter of the Soviets meeting their obligations and not as interference with the internal affairs of the USSR, an interpretation that the Soviets did not share. At the urging of National Security Advisor Zbigniew Brzezinski, Carter "approved an unprecedented White House effort to attack the internal legitimacy of the Soviet government."[8]

The president gave initial approval for "covert propaganda" to be infiltrated into the USSR proper, as opposed to merely the Eastern European satellite countries, as early as March 1977, but CIA and State Department bureaucratic accession didn't come through until later in the spring. Within the CIA, one reason for the delay was that the proposals first went to the Soviet/East European Division (SE) in the Operations Directorate, which was populated by "non-believers"—operations officers who had spent their careers handling agents reporting on the Soviet Union. These officers had little or no faith in the possibility that mere propaganda or even more ambitious political action programs, no matter how imaginative or how lengthy in duration, could ever make one iota of difference in changing the behavior of the Soviet regime. But, of course, changing the behavior of the Soviet government was only one objective of these programs, and a lesser one at that. That White House officials, including Brzezinski, didn't understand that SE was not the DO component to run these covert action programs delayed CIA action. It was only when White House officials sought out the Covert Action Staff—populated not by agent recruiters and intelligence collectors but by covert action specialists who, as "true believers," possessed an unlimited faith in the ability of the written word and subtle influences eventually to make a difference, even if only at the margins—that the right folks were finally in the loop.

CIA operations included support for the printing and underground distribution of political writings, known as *samizdat* by dissidents living in "internal exile" inside the Soviet Union. Samizdat was vitally important to the dissident movement, but it was illegal in the Soviet Union for anyone to make a copy of anything without permission of the state authorities—access to photocopiers, printing presses, and even typewriters was strictly limited and controlled. CIA assistance enabled the dissidents to circumvent the authorities. The CIA also provided Soviet and Eastern European émigrés living in self-imposed exile in Western Europe the means to publish books and academic journals for distribution within émigré circles; but a good portion of these products would also eventually find their way behind the Iron Curtain and into the hands of those living under the Communist boot.[9]

White House officials, especially Brzezinski, and the covert action specialists at the CIA believed that it was vital to continue the Nationalities programs, keeping alive the culture, history, religions, and traditions of the oppressed non-Russian minorities in the republics east of the Urals as well as the huge Ukraine Republic. And there were proposals to provide support, covertly through cut-outs (i.e., a third party functioning as a go-between for two principals so that there would be no evidence that the two principals were connected in any manner), funding, and other means, to Western European human rights and pro-democracy groups to counter Soviet propaganda. However, these proposals met with surprisingly intense opposition from the Departments of State and Defense, as well as elements within the CIA, because of the sensitivity that always accompanies the idea of conducting covert action operations intended to influence audiences in allied nations. It wasn't until more than a year later that many, but not all, of the proposals received final approval by nature of inclusion in the Omnibus Finding.

Just a month before leaving office, Brzezinski briefed a senior emissary from Pope John Paul II about these Nationalities programs to inform the Vatican that the United States had the covert mechanisms, resources, and dedicated personnel to come to the aid of the Solidarity labor movement in an increasingly troubled Poland. Topping the list of threats in Eastern Europe at that time was the potential for the Soviet Union to invade Poland militarily, as they did in Hungary in 1956 and Czechoslovakia in 1968. Aware of the reluctance of European governments to confront the Soviets for a variety of reasons, not the least of which was lucrative trade agreements, Brzezinski eventually asked the pope directly if he would be willing to "use his bishops [in European countries with] large Catholic populations to support an ultimatum threatening the Soviets with economic, political, and cultural isolation if they intervened in Poland." The pope was. But with the end of the Carter administration looming, the Polish program, as well as the enhancement and expansion of all of the Nationalities programs, would have to wait until the Reagan administration and the unrelenting pressure by DCI William J. Casey for a more active CIA role in the covert action arena.[10]

Although many observers think that the Afghan covert action program was initiated by Carter in the immediate aftermath of the Soviet invasion of that country on December 26, 1979, in fact it began months prior. As early as January 1979 the Carter administration began reflecting on the possibilities and opportunities presented by opposing the Marxist government in Kabul. The governments of Pakistan and Saudi Arabia each had strong interest in opposing the pro-Soviet regime, and their support was a factor in the eventual covert action program that Carter approved. Initial proposals were for "a small scale propaganda campaign publicizing Soviet activities in Afghanistan; indirect financial assistance to the insurgents; direct financial assistance to Afghan émigré groups to support their anti-Soviet, anti-regime activities; non-lethal material assistance; weapons support; and a range of training and support options." President Carter signed the original Afghan Finding on July 3, 1979, authorizing the provision of aid to the Mujahedin, an element opposing the pro-Soviet regime, which had taken control of the country in a coup the year before.[11]

Brzezinski realized that this covert aid might push the Soviet government to take a more active role in Afghanistan, or even invade it (which, of course, they ultimately did). However, he did not see this as a negative; when the Soviet army did invade the country, Brzezinski wrote a memo to the president saying that "We now have the opportunity of giving to the USSR its Vietnam," recognizing the difficulties an "unsustainable" war would entail for Moscow.[12]

While Carter's Afghan program was initially funded at a minimal level, with the invasion of Afghanistan by Soviet forces on December 26, the funding increased dramatically. By the time Carter left office, he had authorized the provision of large numbers and varieties of weaponry and other support for the Mujahedin, while funding rose to nearly $100 million.[13] This program was ultimately "approved by three U.S. presidents [Carter, Reagan, and Bush] and reviewed throughout the 1980–1992 period" by the House and Senate Intelligence Committees; it saw more than $2 billion in military supplies going to the anti-Soviet resistance, with as much as $250 million a year allocated for each of the last two years. And it contributed no small amount to the final downfall of the Soviet Union.[14]

In another region of the world, aggression on the part of the Marxist government of the Peoples' Democratic Republic of Yemen against its northern neighbor, the Yemen Arab Republic (YAR), in February 1979 led the Carter administration to suspect that either the Soviets or Soviet proxies in the form of Cubans or Ethiopians were at least participants, if not instigators. The proximity of the Yemens to Saudi Arabia was also of concern to the administration. After a series of discussions at the SCC, the administration decided it was necessary to shore up the YAR government and to enhance its ability to secure its borders. To this end, the president signed another Finding on July 3, 1979, authorizing covert assistance to the YAR.[15] National Security Advisor Brzezinski was said to have "pushed for a covert mission in part because he felt that the United States had been too passive in responding to Cuban activities [in] 1977 and 1978 in Zaire and Somalia." This program continued into the Reagan years.[16]

But after the Yemen program was terminated, there were numerous questions about the initial wisdom and logic of the program's goals. According to a senior CIA official quoted in a *Washington Post* article, "There were unrealistic grand strategic goals that the White House thought could be accomplished through covert action. And they were trying to fix a lot of things: many, too many, that had nothing to do with South Yemen." Still, there were also some in the administration who thought that it was necessary to show Saudi Arabia that the Carter team could be "tough," including Vice President Walter Mondale. Feelings in this regard were not as strong in the CIA (with the possible exception of the Near East Division in the DO and its Arabian Peninsula Branch); DCI Stan Turner was later quoted as calling the scheme "harebrained."[17]

In the summer of 1979, within two weeks of the Sandinistas' rise to power in Nicaragua, President Carter signed two Findings authorizing covert operations in the Central American region. Carter sought to:

> encourage democratic elements in Nicaragua rather than to risk a new totalitarian regime allied with Moscow in Latin America. One sub-component of this Finding was propaganda operations to inform and sensitize the world to the nature of the Marxist-oriented Sandinista regime and the covert supply of weaponry and other materials that they were receiving from Cuba's leader, Fidel Castro. This was not a lethal Finding, but rather one intended [to] "strengthen democratic elements."[18]

A concurrent Finding was signed for El Salvador, where the pro-West, right-wing government was under attack by leftist insurgents supported directly by the neighboring Sandinistas and indirectly by Cuba (Cuban arms and munitions flowed through Nicaragua to the Salvadoran rebels). Interestingly, at this juncture the State Department was highly supportive of these programs and, in October 1979, urged the president to expand and intensify them. The problems of Nicaragua and El Salvador were yoked with Cuban-instigated actions in Grenada and a hostile Marxist government in Jamaica, leading the Carter administration to sign a "broader Finding to counter the Soviets and Cubans throughout Latin America."[19] However, despite these programs Cuban and Soviet support to the Sandinistas and the Salvadoran rebels continued to the end of Carter's tenure, leaving a major policy problem to be inherited by the Reagan team.

A Soviet-supported regime in Ethiopia, having attained power by coup, was another cause for concern to the Carter foreign policy team. This was especially so after the Soviet Union and the new Ethiopian regime inked a military assistance pact in May 1977, paving the way for the arrival of some thousands of Cuban troops meant to aid the regime in its disputes with a rebellion in the Ogaden province and a separatist movement in Eritrea. Brzezinski believed that (a) Soviet activities were a test of the new American president and (b) U.S policy should be to link Soviet behavior in Africa with the overall U.S.–USSR relationship. In the end, however, the Carter administration made no response, taking no action against the Soviet and Cuban activities around the Horn; any covert action program for Ethiopia would have to wait. Brzezinski would come to believe that the administration's ultimate lack of response to those events emboldened the Soviets to invade Afghanistan in 1979.[20]

A coup in Grenada by a "pro-Cuban Marxist" named Maurice Bishop alarmed President Carter to the point that he requested options for a "covert effort to focus international attention" on the Bishop regime. After discussions with the CIA, the president signed a Finding on July 19, 1979, that "authorized a covert effort to promote the democratic process in Grenada and also to support resistance to the Marxist government there." However, the Senate oversight committee differed with the president as to the significance of the Bishop regime to U.S. interests, while also pointing out the dichotomy between the intent of the Finding and the administration's policy of "non-interference" in the affairs of other countries. Upon receiving a letter from the SSCI stating that the members would not support the covert program targeted against Grenada, Carter dropped the program, leaving the problem to "fester until President Reagan's use of military force" there in late October 1983.[21]

The Carter experience with covert action is instructive for those who call for it to be banned, either by executive order or though congressional statute. Jimmy Carter was as philosophically and morally opposed to the concept of covert action as any president in the nation's history. And yet, when confronted with issues in which diplomacy and sanctions wouldn't work, and in which the use of military force was inappropriate or would have been excessive, this president repeatedly relied on covert action to achieve his foreign policy goals.

TWELVE

Ronald W. Reagan

The [Nicaraguan] operation was totally different from what had been previously presented by the CIA briefers [to Congress] in Washington. It was obvious that covert policy was frequently out ahead of or overriding stated or implied U.S. foreign policy. A regional war was getting off the ground, and much of the planning was unspoken and subtle.[1]

Bob Woodward, Washington Post

For Ronald W. Reagan and his DCI, William J. Casey, covert action was not an adjunct endeavor but a fundamental component of an activist foreign policy and a means of thwarting Marxist regimes outside of the Warsaw Pact. Reagan expanded all of Carter's Findings and added numerous Findings of his own. The years 1981–1989 saw the CIA managing presidentially directed and congressionally approved covert action programs around the globe. Among the numerous covert action programs conducted during the Reagan administration, those that have been officially acknowledged by the U.S. government as of fall 2003 include operations for Afghanistan, Angola, Cambodia, Central America, Eastern Europe and the

USSR, Poland, Yemen, Ethiopia, and Lebanon, as well as operations for counterterrorism.[2] Reagan also authorized operations to counter or subvert the illegal transfer of banned technologies to the Soviet Union, a program that enjoyed great congressional support and approval. And Reagan approved covert support for the Polish labor movement Solidarity, which had gone underground once outlawed by the martial law regime. This proved to be one of the most successful covert action programs ever conducted and was certainly one that virtually all Americans, had they known of it at the time, would have resoundingly supported.[3]

To develop, implement, and monitor foreign and national security policy, Ronald Reagan continued with the aggregation of committees used by his predecessor. In National Security Decision Directive-2, *National Security Council Structure*, of January 12, 1982, (interestingly, signed a full year after inauguration), he created several "Senior Interagency Groups," one for foreign policy, another for defense policy, and a third for "intelligence policies and matters," charged to "advise and assist the NSC in exercising its authority and discharging its responsibilities." The composition of these groups was primarily at the deputy secretary or undersecretary level. But covert action was not under the umbrella of any of the three committees.[4]

At the urging of DCI William J. Casey, Reagan created a separate, high-level covert action screening committee which was, in effect, a restricted subcommittee of the National Security Council. Called the National Security Planning Group (NSPG), membership included the vice president, the secretaries of state and defense, the president's national security advisor (initially Richard Allen, although Reagan would eventually go through six advisors before the end of his second term), the DCI, and, remarkably, several purely political aides including the president's chief of staff, the presidential counselor, and the deputy chief of staff.[5] The director of the Office of Management and Budget, the attorney general, and the chairman of the Joint Chiefs were relegated to the status of occasional invitees. Reagan himself often chaired the NSPG, a forum in which many decisions were made right at the table—a fact that should not be surprising given that the NSPG membership included within it the statutory members of the National Security Council. As such, NSPG meetings negated the need to call formal NSC meetings. A level below the NSPG was an interagency review group, composed of deputy heads of the relevant agencies and supported by an active staff, called the Policy Coordination Group (PCG).[6]

The NSPG was the locus of foreign policy initiatives in the Reagan White House, and—at William J. Casey's insistence to ensure secrecy—it was the only group that was authorized to consider covert action programs. The group was determined to prevent leaks when covert action programs were on the NSPG agenda; no advance papers were prepared, no aides sat in on the meetings, all papers were collected at the ends of the meetings, and decisions were made by the principals without staff support. Despite this formalized structure, however, Reagan occasionally made key decisions—including those of supporting the Polish trade union Solidarity and the Afghan resistance—without convening the group, meeting instead only with William J. Casey and his longtime, close advisor and friend William Clark (who also had brief tenures as deputy secretary of state and national security advisor despite possessing not one whit of foreign policy experience).[7]

In revamping the White House's national security mechanism, Ronald Reagan promulgated Executive Order 12333, designating the National Security Council as "the highest Executive Branch entity that provides a review of, guidance for, and direction to" covert action programs.[8] The order further expanded the concept of covert action, employing the term "special activities" for generic, classic covert action, and gave authority for all special activity missions exclusively to the CIA unless the president designated in writing another agency to conduct a mission or program. (As of 2002, EO 12333 remains in effect, and so far no other agency has ever been so designated.) For the first time in any written policy document, EO 12333 also stated that special activities could be conducted from inside the United States so long as the intended target audience was foreign and such activities did not influence American domestic politics, media, or public opinion.[9] This provision reflected the reality of modern worldwide communications and media capabilities, both as a tool of covert propaganda and political action and as a potential drawback. And in a gesture to the increasing intensity of congressional oversight and ramifications from Hughes-Ryan, EO 12333 directed that covert action programs be reviewed by the attorney general for consonance with pertinent laws and rules.[10]

Just prior to his second term, President Reagan signed a directive that in effect codified the covert action review and approval process that had been in place since the beginning of his administration. National Security Decision Directive-159, *Covert Action Policy Approval and Coordination Procedures*, of January 18, 1985, reached beyond the scope of the NSC and its staff and out to the various agencies having a role in any covert action program. It detailed step-by-step what was to be done and when. And when the Iran-Contra scandal highlighted weaknesses in the covert action process, Reagan signed NSDD-286, *Approval and Review of Special Activities*, on October 15, 1987, eliminating loopholes.[11] The key difference between NSDD-159 and 286 was that the latter mandated that all covert action operations had to be conducted pursuant to a Finding and banned retroactive Findings. Most important, it also ordered that the "National Security Advisor and the NSC staff . . . shall not undertake the conduct of any special activities." NSDD-286 also required that all special activities had to be "consistent with national defense and foreign policies and applicable law."

NSDD-286 was further strengthened by the Intelligence Authorization Act of 1991, which required a Finding regardless of which agency had been assigned to manage the covert action program. Of equal significance, NSDD-286 required that a Finding be written and submitted to the Congress for "all CIA activities abroad, other than those activities that are intended solely for obtaining necessary intelligence."[12]

COVERT ACTION UNDER REAGAN AND CASEY

One of the first covert action programs considered by the Reagan administration after inauguration was a response to a perceived crisis in Surinam, generated by a bloody coup against the elected government led by an army noncommissioned officer. Afraid the left-leaning rebels would institute a Communist state, or at least move closer to the hemisphere's designated nemesis Fidel Castro, the Reagan National Security Council first reviewed possible actions in concert with the government of Netherlands, Surinam's former colonial suzerain. During a succession of meetings of the NSPG's subordinate element, the Crisis Pre-Planning Group, various options were analyzed, discussed, and rejected. When the program was briefed to Congress, the legislators were incredulous, questioning why the United States would waste time, money, and resources on a small, impoverished, barely populated country of absolutely no national interest to the United States. Ultimately, on January 4, 1983, the NSPG, chaired by the president, decided to forgo covert action in Surinam in favor of limited and (as it turned out) ineffective overt measures.[13]

Five months after taking office, in May 1982, Reagan signed NSDD-32, *U.S. National Security Strategy* (drafted by White House advisor Richard Pipes), which authorized a broad-ranging political action and propaganda covert action program to "'neutralize' Soviet control over Eastern Europe and authorized the use of covert action and other means to support anti-Soviet organizations in the region." Included were such classic propaganda and political action techniques as covertly "sponsoring many demonstrations, protests, meetings, conferences, press articles, television shows, exhibitions, and the like to focus attention" on nefarious Soviet activities.[14] The NSDD specifically noted that overt economic and diplomatic pressures were also to be brought to bear, with financial aid to Eastern European states "calibrated to their willingness to protect human rights and undertake political and free-market reforms."[15] This document also had a covert action element to it, which although still classified, clearly limns the all-important linkage of a covert action program to established overt policies and measures. It is important to emphasize that much of the impetus for these operations was to serve as a counter to massive Soviet KGB active measures operations being conducted throughout the European continent. According to former DCI Robert M. Gates:

> The Soviets were all over the place secretly supporting opponents of continuing INF [Intermediate Nuclear Forces] deployments and then SDI [Strategic Defense Initiative], which they sought to discredit in all possible ways. They created forgeries of documents purportedly signed by [Secretary of State George] Schultz, [DCI William J.] Casey, and senior U.S. military leaders in hopes of scaring the bejesus out of our friends and allies.[16]

With these instances of Soviet mischief, as well as KGB activities in Africa (accusing the CIA of creating AIDS), in South Asia (attempting to pin the assassination of the Indian prime minister on the United States), and the Third World (proliferating the "Baby Parts" story), the Reagan administration was not about to sit idly on the sidelines.[17]

Four months later, on September 2, 1982, Reagan authorized NSDD-54, *United States Policy Towards Eastern Europe*, which was the product of an interagency analysis of policies directed at the Warsaw Pact countries. Reagan's long-term goal was to "loosen the Soviet hold on the region and thereby facilitate its eventual reintegration into the European community of nations." The NSDD proposed to achieve this ambitious goal in Eastern Europe by "encouraging liberal trends in the region, furthering human and civil rights . . . reinforcing the pro-Western orientation of their peoples, lessening their political and economic dependence on the USSR . . . , undermining the military capabilities of the Warsaw Pact, and encouraging more private market-oriented development of their economies." The policy was to "discriminate" in favor of those countries that were able to show movement away from the yoke of the USSR (or which had at least not obstructed Western policies) and demonstrate greater "internal liberalization," including advances in human rights and a more market-oriented economy. The United States was to "employ commercial, financial, exchange, informational, and diplomatic instruments" to implement the policy toward states that evinced some degree of reciprocation, however limited. The precise measures included offering Most Favored Nation status, extensions of credit, and membership in the International Monetary Fund, as well as rescheduling debt payments, increasing cultural and educational exchanges, and providing "increased interactions" with scientific and technical "elites" and high-level "visits" from dignitaries and naval vessels.[18]

NSDD-54 was followed on November 12 of the same year by NSDD-66, *Protracted Economic Warfare Against the USSR*, which established new strategies for increasing the economic hardship in the Soviet Union by co-opting European governments as partners. The administration next adopted National Security Decision Directive-75, *U.S. Relations with the USSR*, on January 17, 1983, as its lodestar, a document stating that it was U.S. policy to "contain and over time reverse Soviet expansionism by competing effectively . . . in all international arenas—particularly in the overall military balance and in geographical regions" important to the United States; "promote . . . the process of change in the Soviet Union towards [a] more pluralistic political and economic system" while reducing the power of the "privileged elite"; and "engage the Soviet Union in negotiations to attempt to reach agreements which protect and enhance U.S. interests." The implementation of these objectives required that the United States "convey to Moscow that unacceptable behavior will incur costs that would outweigh any gains," while positive steps would likewise be rewarded.

NSDD-75 intended to "shape the environment in which Soviet decisions are made . . . in a wide variety of functional and geopolitical arenas and in the US–Soviet bilateral relationship." The U.S. military was to be modernized, NATO to be "reinvigorated," and Soviet adventurism in the Third World confronted with "U.S. military countermeasures." The economic facet of the policy was to make sure that "East-West economic relations [did] not facilitate the Soviet military buildup," and did not "subsidize" the Soviet domestic economy, while simultaneously permitting "mutual beneficial trade . . . in non-strategic areas, such as grains." In efforts to disrupt the Soviet economy, intelligence analysts developed a list of manufacturing equipment, raw materials, computers, and other technologies to determine what the Soviets needed to obtain from abroad. Of critical import to the Soviets was the requirement for imported supercomputers, for the USSR (according to its own experts) was fifteen years behind the West in this regard and lacked any domestically produced supercomputer.[19]

Seeking to deter or prevent the Soviets from using Western (and especially American) high-tech materials to improve their economic situation, the Reagan administration initiated a comprehensive covert action program that involved the sabotaging of important materials sent legally or otherwise to the Soviet Union. Among these items were "doctored" blueprints or inaccurately printed operating/technical/repair instructions for Western-made civilian manufacturing equipment; damaged or degraded computer chips used in manufacturing tools; specially designed computer hardware with well-hidden flaws embedded inside; distorted information on off-shore oil drilling and other means of oil extraction (seriously damaging the Soviets' efforts to increase their domestic production for their own use as well as to earn hard currency); and "advanced designs" of computers and equipment that had already been discarded by American engineers.[20] In some operations, "contrived computer chips were inserted into Soviet military equipment, flawed turbines were installed on a gas pipeline, and defective plans disrupted the output of chemical plants and a tractor factory . . . [;] the Pentagon introduced misleading information pertinent to stealth aircraft, space defense, and tactical aircraft . . . [and] the Soviet space shuttle was a rejected NASA design. . . . The program had great success and was never detected." The Soviet–East European covert action programs contributed to undermining the legitimacy of the Soviet government in the eyes of its own citizens, thus accomplishing one of the programs' collateral goals.[21]

The imposition of martial law in Poland, the outlawing of the Solidarity labor movement, and the ever-present threat of Soviet invasion (in circumstances similar to the Soviet invasions of Hungary in 1956 and Czechoslovakia in 1968) brought about what must be considered as the CIA's finest hour in terms of covert action programs. Interestingly, critics of covert action somehow always manage to overlook the outstanding successes of this program; and those who crucify covert action as "immoral" seem unable to grasp that these programs supported right against wrong, democracy over Communism, freedom over oppression.

Covert action in Poland during the 1990s prevented Soviet invasion and occupation, and brought democracy to more nations than just Poland. The Reagan administration believed strongly that a "free, non-Communist Poland . . . would be a dagger in the heart of the Soviet empire; and if Poland became democratic, other East European states would follow."[22] In the spring of 1989, Poland did indeed become the first of the Soviet satellite states to hold free elections as a newly democratized state, and in less than a year, all of Eastern Europe was free to determine their own futures. While the CIA's covert action program cannot take full credit for this, without the covert action operations the end result may well have been longer in coming and, perhaps, not nearly as peaceful.

According to journalist Carl Bernstein of Watergate reporting fame, President Reagan met alone with Pope John Paul II in the Vatican on June 17, 1982, barely a month after signing NSDD-32. Bernstein writes that during the meeting the president asked the Holy Father to join with the United States to support covertly the now-underground Solidarity movement and, of even greater import, "a clandestine campaign to hasten the dissolution of the Communist empire."[23] Advising Reagan on the Polish program in the early years of the administration were Carter's national security advisor Zbigniew Brzezinski (who also served in an advisory capacity to the CIA's propaganda and political action specialists), DCI William J. Casey, current national security advisor Richard Allen, longtime Reagan advisor William Clark, Secretary of State Alexander Haig, former DDCI Lieutenant General Vernon Walters, and U.S. Ambassador to the Vatican William Wilson—devout Catholics all.[24]

The extensive research by Carl Bernstein on the Reagan administration's support to Solidarity indicates that the circumstances surrounding the program were the best possible to achieve success, in that the U.S. government had only to provide covert support at the margins, thus merely permitting "the natural forces already in place to play this out."[25] Never was the United States commitment to Solidarity in doubt. Both Bernstein and author Peter Schweizer (who has chronicled the Reagan policies directed at the collapsing of the Soviet Union) have detailed some of the covert assistance to Solidarity and the Polish underground, to include the provision of funds to sustain Solidarity; infiltration of a variety of communications equipment for the underground to maintain contact with the West; the receipt of information inside and the reporting of intelligence to the outside; provision of personal computers, fax machines (the first in Poland), and other means of desktop publishing to allow Solidarity to publish newsletters and other informative tracts; and the training of members in communications, computer skills, and other essential skills allowing them to survive while on the run.[26] And as the martial law regime became more repressive, it became concomitantly more important for accurate news to be disseminated to the Polish citizenry; Solidarity would thus become the underground "town crier" with U.S. government assistance.

NSDD-32, the Reagan administration's commitment to undermine Soviet power in Eastern Europe, was also directly relevant to the Polish program. NSDD-32 initially allocated a modest $2 million going to the Polish underground, but Reagan and Casey— who both believed that Poland was "the weakest link in the Soviet bloc" (an assessment shared by the KGB)—soon thereafter sought an increase in funds and materials for the underground.[27] By 1985 infiltration mechanisms were established and functioning, allowing, for example: "the printing and smuggling into Poland [of] forty thousand postcards" bearing the image and pro-Solidarity sermons of a popular Polish priest, Father Popielusko, who was viciously murdered by Polish security policemen; and the smuggling into Poland of copies of a map and supporting documents used by Nazi and Soviet officials in 1939 in planning for the dismemberment of Poland.[28]

But of course the Soviet Union and Eastern Europe weren't the only concern for Reagan and Casey. Early in the administration Casey proposed a sizeable expansion of the covert action programs initiated by the Carter administration to counter Cuban-sponsored subversive activities in Central America; the president signed two Findings to this effect on March 9, 1981, barely two weeks after Casey's proposal. Included in the Findings were programs to deter Sandinista activities in the region in general, and to cripple, if not stop completely, the flow of Cuban arms from the Nicaraguan Sandinistas to the rebels in El Salvador. Of course, the Cubans weren't the only ones aiding the Salvadoran rebels—the Soviets were also intensively involved. In July 1980, Shafik Jandal, the head of the Communist party of El Salvador, wrote the Communist Party of the Soviet Union (CPSU) asking to send to the USSR thirty Salvadoran party members for training in various military skills. The CPSU was concurrently sending non-Communist manufactured weaponry, captured at the end of the Vietnam War, to the rebels. And there were similar Soviet ties to the Sandinistas in Managua. On December 1, 1981, in an NSPG meeting with the foreign policy principals plus political advisors Edwin Meese, Michael Deaver, and James Baker present, Reagan signed a Finding which authorized covert funding and assistance for the anti-Sandinista rebels who came to be called the "Contras."[29]

At first, the assistance was via provision of funds to Argentina sufficient to organize and train a five-hundred–man anti-Sandinista unit for deployment in the Central American region. In the first year, funding to the Contras was about $20 million, with a like amount the next year but with the proviso that the funds could not be utilized to overthrow the Nicaraguan government. By the mid-1980s the Central American program and the separate Nicaraguan program were each costing close to $100 million per year, and the five-hundred-member Argentine unit was transformed into a multi-thousand Nicaraguan rebel force.[30]

The mining of the harbors in Nicaragua was one of the most controversial operations of the Reagan years, with questions arising over how much Congress knew of the program in advance. It appears certain that oversight committee staff was briefed, and there is good reason to think that at least some of the representatives and senators had also been informed, although probably not in great detail. (Of course it must be noted that the presence of a representative or senator in a briefing does not guarantee that he or she knows or retains what was being said; these officials may have been thinking about some other matter more important to them at the time, they may have been nodding off, or they may have been otherwise distracted. California representative "B-1 Bob" Dornan, self-proclaimed patriot and staunch supporter of national defense, was not a faithful attendee of HPSCI while on the committee, but when he did show he was more apt to read the *Los Angeles Times* than to listen to the briefers.)[31] Besides the harbor operations, CIA's recruited paramilitary assets also blew up power lines, although this never seemed to bother Congress. An example of the president's personal involvement in these activities was a May 31, 1983, meeting of the NSPG, which Reagan himself chaired to review the CIA's plan.[32]

The operations were highly controversial, especially the Nicaraguan program, and in part contained the seeds of the Iran-Contra scandal. There are many who believe that any covert action program should be such that, if it ever becomes public knowledge (which is more and more likely in the Information/Internet Age), the majority of the public will support it. This was not the case with Nicaragua, leaving one expert to opine that it "may have been a mistake for the Reagan administration to depend so heavily on covert action when its [overt] policies failed to generate sufficient public and congressional support. And too, the program had grown so large that it was not covert by anyone's definition." And, one hastens to add, still did not garner the public's support.[33]

Obviating any chance of objective appraisals within the White House and the CIA over the effectiveness and political wisdom of these Central American programs were the intense personal feelings on the part of the most senior officials, especially including DCI Casey. One insider, Robert M. Gates, described them as "zealots" who sustained a sense of self-righteousness and absolute moral certitude over the program, thus foreclosing any opportunity to overcome congressional antagonism through serious negotiation. Worse, those in and out of government who questioned the programs were criticized by the true believers as being lacking in American patriotism, insufficiently anti-Communist, and disloyal to the president. Dedication to the Contras would inexorably lead to the scandal known as Iran-Contra, nurtured by contempt for Congress, for federal law, and even for the Constitution.[34]

Regardless, the administration pursued its Central American policy with determination. One element of the Central American program was a Finding signed by Reagan toward the end of his first term authorizing the interdiction of Soviet and Cuban-supplied arms crossing that country's border into Nicaragua for the Sandinistas. A memo written by William J. Casey (as cited by his DDCI, Bob Gates, in his authoritative history of the times) told the president that the "Soviets care about perpetuating instability in the region south of the United States border and distracting the United States from its threats in Europe, Africa, and Asia . . . [i]f Central America is lost, our credibility in Asia, Europe and in NATO will go with it." The Finding was signed in September 1983.[35]

The largest, and arguably most important, covert action program in the Reagan administration was the one mounted to force the Soviets to withdraw from Afghanistan. In light of the criticisms that befell the Afghan program years after it ended, particularly by those who blame the CIA for any failures, shortcomings, or problems, it is important to emphasize that the program was, as recorded by former DDCI Ray Cline, in complete accord with U.S. policy and had strong backing in Congress.[36] Support to the Mujahedin initiated under Carter rapidly grew under Reagan and Casey who saw it as a way to deeply, if not fatally, wound the Soviet Union. Indeed, Robert Gates comments that it was in NSDD-166, *U.S. Policy, Programs, and Strategy in Afghanistan*, of March 27, 1985, that the Carter administration's limited objective of merely harassing the Soviets was greatly expanded to that of defeating and expelling the Soviets from Afghanistan—a much broader, more difficult, and far more expensive proposition. Gates references the program under NSDD-166 in citing "large increases in weapons," and an "improved logistics base," that allowed "weapons, ammunition, clothing, and food" to flow to the Mujahedin, paid for by an increase of $125 million over the previous year's funding.

Milt Bearden, the CIA's chief in Islamabad, Pakistan, at the time, recalls that Reagan's escalation of covert operations in Afghanistan was due both to congressional pressures and Soviet escalations; by "upping the ante," Reagan was signaling that he believed it possible to inflict a major defeat on the Soviets. On the most basic level, the goal was to "hurt" the Soviets as badly as possible (read: kill as many as possible) to exact a heavy political and personal price for the invasion.[37] NSDD-166 was the "turning point" of the war, as it enabled the administration to greatly increase the amount and types of aid going to the Mujahedin. Funding rapidly increased, from under $100 million in 1981 to $120 million in 1983, then jumped to about $250 million in 1984 to a staggering sum of almost $700 million in 1988, the final year of the program. In contrast, the majority of the individual propaganda and political action programs aimed at the Soviet Union and Eastern Europe cost considerably less.[38]

During this period, supply lines were improved; high-tech weapons were given to the Mujahedin, including the Stinger shoulder-fired antiaircraft missiles that proved to be a silver bullet; more attention was paid to the Soviet high command and to Soviet political and military plans; pressure was placed on other countries either to support the United States or at least not to aid the Soviets; and the status of normal U.S.–USSR relations was linked to the Soviet occupation of Afghanistan. In the end, the Soviets packed their bags and went home. The Soviet defeat in Afghanistan was also a defeat for the "Brezhnev Doctrine," which had declared that "no socialist country would ever be 'lost' to the West."[39] While the total funds spent in Afghanistan for the better part of a decade (well over $1 billion) seems to be—and indeed is—an enormous amount of money, what it essentially purchased was the demise of the Soviet Union. Perhaps that billion dollars was not an unreasonable price at all to pay for an end to the cold war.[40]

Terrorism was also, but belatedly, a target of covert action in the Reagan years. On January 27, 1981, at the ceremony for the returning fifty-two Americans who had been held hostage in Iran, the president's welcoming remarks also included a warning to future perpetrators of terrorism against Americans. Terrorists, the president vowed, would suffer "swift and effective retribution" for their heinous activities. Despite this warning, the administration failed to retaliate when, two years later, sixty-three people—seventeen of them American officials—were slaughtered at the hands of the Iranian-sponsored terrorist group Hezbollah, which blew up the U.S. Embassy in Beirut on April 18, 1983. The White House knew of Hezbollah's culpability and knew the location of Hezbollah's headquarters and training camps in Lebanon's Biq'a Valley. Calls for strikes at the terrorist facilities were rejected by the president, however, because Reagan's secretary of defense, Caspar Weinberger, argued successfully that attacking the terrorist facilities would lead to "innocent" casualties in terms of the women and children among them. There was no retribution, "swift and effective" or otherwise. The terrorists won.

Emboldened by their escape from retaliation, the same group then truck-bombed the barracks of the U.S. Marine forces ashore near Beirut's airport six months later, on October 23. The toll was staggering, with 241 of America's best dead and hundreds more injured.[41] Again, there was no serious retaliation or retribution, only a token, limited, and highly ineffective show of force that of course did nothing to deter terrorism. The terrorists won big this time, as Reagan soon reversed his initial post-attack pledge not to be driven out of Lebanon and ordered the remaining forces to leave. Then, in 1984, a newly constructed U.S. Embassy "Annex" in Beirut, which had replaced the original embassy destroyed a year earlier, was damaged in a car bombing. Only quick action by an alert bodyguard of the visiting British ambassador saved the United States from having its second embassy in Beirut totally destroyed in less than two years.[42]

Hezbollah then began kidnapping American civilians and diplomats in Beirut, certain that the United States would do little more than "condemn" these acts as "despicable" in State Department briefings. The absence of any meaningful United States response only encouraged the terrorists. As this is being written in 2003, Hezbollah is still one of the most dangerous terrorist groups in the world, and every bombing it conducts in Israel holds the possibility of killing more Americans who might be visiting or living in that county.

By 1984 the Reagan administration was considering a counter-terrorism Finding in response to numerous terrorist actions against U.S. and Western interests in the Middle East (especially Lebanon) and in Western Europe. On April 3, 1984, almost a year after the Beirut Embassy bombing, Reagan signed NSDD-138, *Combating Terrorism*, intended to establish an effective counterterrorism policy. Initially intended to authorize the "pre-emptive neutralization" of terrorists, it was eventually watered down in response to opponents who thought it sounded too much like sanctioning assassinations, which of course had been prohibited since the Ford administration.[43]

In 1986 William J. Casey authorized the establishment of the Counterterrorism Center under Duane "Dewey" Clarridge. The Center was a merger of specialists from across the four Agency directorates, along with representatives from the FBI, FAA, Secret Service, Customs, and other government agencies with a role in or responsibility for countering terrorism directed at the United States and its allies. Shortly after starting up the Center, Clarridge related that the president—finally—signed a Finding that allowed the Agency to "undertake covert action to counteract terrorism—with or without the help of foreign governments." The actions permitted by the Finding were then bolstered by the Omnibus Crime Act of 1986, "establishing the legal right to capture abroad terrorists who had committed acts against American citizens and to return them to the United States for prosecution." A separate Finding also permitted Clarridge to establish "counterterrorist action teams" composed both of U.S. citizens and foreign nationals to locate, track, and assist in the capture of terrorists. The Reagan administration was finally getting serious about terrorism.[44]

Reagan also looked to Africa as a region where covert action might be useful. Reagan entered office intent on restoring to the United States the respect he believed the country had lost under the Carter administration. An early target was the Libyan dictator Muammar Qaddafi, who was spending his country's oil wealth supporting terrorist groups as well as using his own intelligence service to commit acts of terrorism. One locale on which the administration could confront Qaddafi was the desolate Saharan country of Chad, where Libyan proxies were in a civil war with forces led by Hissène Habré, who was supported by the French. Although Habré initially took the capital of N'djamena, the Libyan forces regrouped and eventually recaptured the city and, in effect, the country. But as the purpose of the U.S. covert action program was merely to "bleed" Qaddafi and not to place Habré in power, the ultimate winner of the civil war made little difference to the administration. Nonetheless, the program carried with it an element of success for the administration, in that Qaddafi now had to be concerned with a "hostile" (i.e., French and U.S.–supported) force on his southern frontier.[45]

Covert action plans for Angola were the subject of another

presidentially chaired NSPG on November 12, 1985. Congress repealed the legislation from 1975 prohibiting aid to Savimbi's UNITA movement in Angola and ultimately authorized $50 million a year through the end of the administration.[46] This was arguably a program that should not have been covert, as the president and others in his administration made repeated public references to supporting Savimbi and even "received UNITA leadership in the White House." It remains debatable how much good the program actually did, however, as the citizens of oil-rich Angola still lived in poverty and civil war through the end of the century.[47]

Nor was Asia missing from Reagan and Casey's covert action constellation. In a questionable program, justified by its anticommunist orientation, the Reagan administration agreed to provide financial support to two non-Communist factions in Cambodia who were opposing the Soviet-supported Communist regime in power. The problem was that one of the most odious and evil political movements in world history, the Khmer Rouge (KR), was also in league with the non-Communist elements. The KR was, conservatively, responsible for the slaughter of more than two million Cambodians during the interval when it was seeking and then exercising power in that small kingdom. The atrocities the KR committed against all Cambodians were almost beyond description and almost beyond belief. The concern over this program was that funds sent to the two non-Communist factions would find their way to the KR. There was significant antagonism toward the program from the Department of State and from CIA careerists, but Casey prevailed. The administration provided only $5 million, although Casey envisioned perhaps another $12 million in the future. Eventually, and perhaps inevitably, the program became mired in controversy over both purpose and financial mismanagement, and was eventually terminated, leaving nothing positive and productive in its wake.[48]

A number of other covert action programs from the Reagan years have yet to be officially declassified or acknowledged by the U.S. government. Some were successful, some find the jury still out, and a few were disastrous—at least in terms of evading success and in their consequences to the foreign national agents in the program. The last not withstanding, the Reagan years relied on covert action as much as any previous administration had, and more than most. The covert action successes, at least based on what has been reported so far, measurably outweigh any failures. Covert action significantly contributed to the end of the cold war and aided in bringing democracy and freedom to the former Eastern European nations. The program in Poland in particular must be regarded, even by the CIA's most ardent critics, as one of the greatest intelligence successes ever.

THIRTEEN

George H.W. Bush and William J. Clinton

Rule one is that in planning and carrying out a covert operation the law has to be followed to the letter. . . . Don't look for shortcuts and don't try to circumvent the process.[1]

President George H.W. Bush

GEORGE H.W. BUSH

George H.W. Bush is the only president to have also served as intelligence chief (save, perhaps, George Washington). As such, he understood the value and processes of not only intelligence but, particularly, covert action. This was of enormous help to President Reagan when Bush was his vice president, with the thirty-five-plus covert action Findings extant during that administration. Although the first year of Bush's administration saw him managing a full plate of covert action programs, the fall of the Berlin Wall along with the collapse of the Soviet Union and the Communist threat changed that. By early January 1990, the type of assistance governments and citizens needed in Poland, the Czech Republic, Slovakia, Hungary, Romania, and Bulgaria—specifically, the creation of commercial and labor laws so free enterprise and capitalism could flourish, instruction in the workings of democratic institutions, demonstration of the need and value of subordinating a nation's military to civilian authority, and development of police forces sensitive to human and civil rights—were precisely the types of missions that should be and were being done openly by government officials, corporate executives, labor unions, and law enforcement groups. In Eastern European cities, reading materials that were banned just months before were now being openly sold in street corner kiosks and shops. Simply put, after 1990 there was no mission for CIA covert action in any of the former Eastern European nations. As for circumstances in the Soviet Union (which would continue to exist for another year), one story sums it up: diplomatic officers at the American Embassy were now openly able to take books and journals to Soviet citizens that previously had to be smuggled in—and Soviet government officials were the most eager of all recipients!

With the end of the cold war, covert action under Bush was transformed from operations against countries and political systems into operations against "transnational" issues: terrorism, narcotics, proliferation of weapons of mass destruction, and international organized crime.[2] Indeed, National Security Review-29 (signed by the president on November 15, 1991) began by stating, "The end of the Cold War and collapse of Soviet Communism have already radically altered the international landscape"; it continued with an assessment that "[m]any new non-Soviet issues have assumed greater importance for the Intelligence Community in recent years, issues such as terrorism, narcotics, proliferation, economic intelligence, technology transfer, and others."[3]

Upon taking office, George H.W. Bush retained the basic covert action oversight structure and processes of the Reagan administration, but he gave the committees different names. In National Security Directive-1, *Organization of the National Security Coun-*

cil System, signed on January 30, 1989, Bush established his White House policy hierarchy, first by adding his chief of staff and his national security advisor, retired Air Force Lieutenant General Brent Scowcroft, as attendees of all meetings of the statutory National Security Council. The Treasury secretary was also to attend NSC meetings unless the subject was such that his presence would be inappropriate, and the attorney general was to "attend meetings pertaining to his jurisdiction, including covert action."

The primary policy element was named the Principals Committee (PC), "the senior interagency forum," composed of the same individuals expected to attend the NSC meetings and chaired by the national security advisor. The "senior sub-Cabinet interagency forum" (i.e., the group just below the Principals) was called the Deputies Committee (DC), but the only "deputies" included were the DDCI and the vice chairman of the Joint Chiefs. The State Department was to be represented by the undersecretary for political affairs and the Defense Department by the undersecretary for policy. However, at the discretion of the national security assistant and with the concurrence of the secretaries of state and defense, the undersecretaries could be replaced by the deputy secretaries of each department. The committee was chaired by the deputy national security advisor, Robert M. Gates, a former DDCI. Below this, as the first-tier interagency coordinating committees, the president created Policy Coordination Committees (PCC) for the "development and implementation of national security policy for that regional or functional area." PCCs were to have a representative at the assistant secretary level for each of the agencies represented on the DC.[4]

The interesting part of NSD-1 is that the responsibilities of each committee were not specifically delineated, including that of covert action. The charge for the Principals Committee was merely to serve as "the senior interagency forum for consideration of policy issues affecting national security [to review, coordinate, and monitor the development and implementation of national security policy]." Obviously, covert action programs fall under this rubric and so were a key element in the review and approval process for the president. The Deputies Committee was to "review and monitor the work of the NSC interagency process . . . and make recommendations concerning the development and implementation of national security policy." The sherpas were the interagency PCCs.

BUSH AND COVERT ACTION

The majority of covert action programs run during the Bush administration remain classified, and while some programs, or elements thereof, have been discussed in the media, they have not been declassified or otherwise officially acknowledged. Thus, while this author is permitted to say little about the Bush years, the salient point is that the end of the cold war permitted President Bush to terminate a great majority of covert action operations, with Findings dropping in number from more than thirty to less than ten. The terror of global destruction through nuclear war with the Soviet Union was replaced with the serious (but not so deadly) menaces of terrorism, narcotics, and weapons proliferation. So for the Bush administration, as with all of his post–World War II predecessors, covert action remained a tool of statecraft for the dangers that still lurked in the shadows.

WILLIAM J. CLINTON

President Bill Clinton continued with his predecessor's system when he signed Presidential Decision Directive-2, *Organization of the National Security Council,* on January 20, 1993. As before, the Principals Committee was composed of cabinet and agency heads from the foreign policy and national security community, while the Deputies Committee was composed of the number-two officials in the same agencies.[5] Further, Clinton established a third, lower-echelon committee, the Interagency Working Committee for Covert Action (IWG), composed of senior (GS-15 to SES-2 grade and military equivalent) officers with responsibility for coordinating covert action programs in their respective departments. The group would meet as required in the Old Executive Office Building under the chairmanship of the National Security Council's director for intelligence programs (initially George Tenet and, after his elevation to DDCI, E. Rand Beers, a detailee from the State Department). Once options for a covert action program were thoroughly explored at Langley and submitted by the DCI to the National Security Council, the IWG would meet to provide the initial interagency coordination for the program. If changes were required, the Agency would rework the options in line with the needs, criticisms, and/or suggestions of the IWG, and the proposal would again navigate its way through the Agency process and back to the IWG.

In the IWG, the Department of State was represented by officers from the Bureau of Intelligence and Research (INR), joined by officers from the operational line bureau(s) in which the programs would take place (e.g., Near East and South Asian Affairs, Office for Combating Terrorism, etc.); the Defense Department was represented by "suits" from the Office of the Secretary of Defense (OSD) and "uniforms" from the staff of the Joint Chiefs. The CIA's permanent representative (this author) was a staff officer from the Directorate of Operation's Special Activities Division, who served as liaison to the NSC's director of intelligence programs and coordinated IWG meetings for the operational components executing the programs. The CIA line operations officers actually running the program and affiliated operations would brief the IWG on programs details, respond to questions, and modify the program as necessary.

CLINTON AND COVERT ACTION

Clinton had several characteristics in common with Jimmy Carter: both were governors of small southern states who came to Washington as outsiders, both placed in senior White House positions their "small state" political advisors who had no understanding of national-level politics, both were inexperienced in national security intelligence matters, and both were intrinsically hostile to covert action. Complicating the overall mission of the CIA, and covert action programs in particular, was Presidential Decision Directive-35, *Intelligence Requirements/National Needs Process,* of March 2, 1995, in which the intelligence requirements for the administration were arranged in five "tiers" of priority. Although the contents of PDD-35 remain classified, this seemingly straightforward document in actuality created confusion in the foreign policy and national security community. The requirements of PDD-35 impelled the CIA to undertake actions that the Agency knew in advance would cause problems almost immediately, while laying the foundation for more significant difficulties down the road.

Exacerbating the confusion over the priorities laid forth in PDD-35 was the downsizing of the CIA, with large numbers of experienced operations officers leaving and replacement hiring at low ebb. To accommodate this loss of personnel, the Agency began to close stations in small, usually Third World countries where there was little policy interest. These stations had originally been opened to recruit Soviet and other "hard" (i.e., difficult to recruit) targets because they were more accessible in these countries than in their home countries. Over the years, the record of hard target recruitments in these back-water capitals was slim, yet these stations expended increasing amounts of resources collecting intelligence reports on their countries' internal political situations, which were of marginal interest, if that, to policymakers. (This situation had existed for years and reflected the DO's chronic inability to forego the "numbers game" to focus instead on the quality of operations as opposed to the quantity of intelligence reports.) The Congress also had a major role in reducing the Agency's overseas presence, although that didn't stop members from hollering "intelligence failure" when something happened in a locale where the Agency had been forced to terminate its presence.

Because of the relative recency of the Clinton administration, there is an even greater paucity of officially acknowledged covert action programs than with his predecessor's administration. To be sure, however, at least through 1996 there was little in the broad requirements of American foreign policy that covert action programs could facilitate. But there were exceptions to this generality.

Clinton entered office with three "transnational" covert action programs covered by Presidential Findings already underway—counternarcotics, counterterrorism, and operations to disrupt or otherwise thwart weapons proliferation programs. As his administration progressed, he expanded and added to each of these programs. In the mid-1990s the counternarcotics programs were highly successful in bringing down several Colombian narco-cartels or their leaders.[6] The counterterrorism program was greatly expanded in response to PDD-35, in which terrorism was a "Tier 1B" issue. Per PDD-35, the intelligence requirements for terrorism included "collection [of] information on plans/intentions inside terrorist circles, [an] increase [in] Near East/South Asia and Islamic cultural and language expertise, [and an] expansion of analytic cadre."[7] Three months later, the president inked another Presidential Decision Directive, PDD-39, that mandated operations to reduce terrorist capabilities via an aggressive covert action program.[8] And, according to testimony by Clinton's second national security advisor, Samuel Berger, to a joint congressional committee investigating the terrorist attacks of September 11, 2001, the president, beginning in August 1998, authorized a series of both "overt and covert measures" targeting Saudi extremist Osama bin-Ladin. (Importantly, Berger also informed the joint committee that "we do not have a rogue CIA.") Of note, this authority was signed by the president after the American embassies in Kenya and Tanzania were car-bombed by bin-Ladin's Al-Qaeda international terrorist organization.[9]

While "disrupting terrorist plans . . . and narcotics shipments" was nothing new, Clinton did chart new territory by authorizing the Agency to begin "fouling up financial transactions" of weapons proliferators—in effect, Clinton's administration began the utilization of information warfare as a covert action tool. Other operations included use of developing technologies to sabotage "imports to and exports from rogue countries . . . to create dissatisfaction [and, hence, internal political unrest]" as well as clandestinely inserting "faulty parts" into equipment sold to "military research and development operations of hostile governments."[10] Collaterally, some of these operations also highlight the difference between classic covert action operations and special activities in what are seen as "representing [a] new type of clandestine activity"; in the words of the chairman of the House intelligence oversight committee at the time, "There are a large number of hidden activities going on to meet transnational threats, but I'm reluctant to call them covert action."[11] But whether covert action or "special activity," they all required a Presidential Finding.

The record of the Clinton administration's application of covert action for the most part was dismal. The only programs that were genuinely productive were those that had begun under other presidents; Clinton's attempts to develop his own covert action programs were absolute failures. The counternarcotics program was perhaps the most effective of all of Clinton's programs, when one looks at the damage inflicted on the most important Colombian cartels and the deaths of their leaders, but, again, this was a program begun under Reagan. Arguably, Clinton missed his opportunity to increase the effectiveness and scope of the counterterrorism program in the wake of the African embassy bombings and the attack on the USS *Cole* at port in Yemen. While he did sign the directive to "disrupt" bin-Ladin's organization, in point of fact the CIA had already been disrupting terrorist attacks for a quarter-century; Clinton's policy added little to the Agency's capabilities. When George W. Bush was inaugurated on January 20, 2001, no one at the CIA shed any tears for the outgoing president.

CONCLUSION

Covert action is likely to remain an instrument of U.S. national security policy for the foreseeable future . . . covert action is an option that U.S. officials must be prepared to use in at least some situations, but only in an acceptable manner.[1]

Twentieth Century Fund

If nothing else, this work should prove beyond question that there is a great deal of misunderstanding about covert action, even by so-called intelligence and foreign policy "experts." Likewise, the reasons underlying this degree of misunderstanding should be equally clear: (a) critics who don't like covert action, for whatever reason, continue to write materials that are wrong, deliberately distorting facts or ignoring data that are contradictory to their personal opinions; (b) misinformed writers continue to assert that presidents use covert action because it avoids congressional oversight; (c) critics continue to cite programs that were conducted nearly a half-century ago as current examples of presidential abuse and ignore the significant reforms of 1974, 1981, and 1991; and (d) individuals continue to ignore successful covert action programs after 1981 and the history of covert action in early America.

And certainly it should now be clear that post–World War II

presidents were the final approving authority for all covert action programs of any magnitude or significance undertaken by the U.S. government, often personally instigating large programs. And through it all, the CIA has been a faithful servant of the president, even when its professional staff disagreed with the programs and even when it was unfairly saddled with the blame for programs that became compromised or failed.

Beyond this, there can be no doubt that presidents will continue to use covert action, although the methodology it entails is changing because of modern technology. Concomitantly, much of what used to be done covertly can and should now be done overtly. To cite one example, support by the U.S. government to Boris Yeltsin and the Russian government during the 1991 coup was done with "telephones, televisions, and fax machines . . . [w]orking in broad daylight, the United States and its allies were able to do things that would have been unthinkably dangerous had they been done in the shadows."[2]

Since presidents will continue to rely on covert action, the "objective" for the future "must not be to ban covert action but so far as possible to bring it within a democratic framework."[3] That Congress will continue to support covert action programs that are well conceived, well managed, and productive is without question, and the strict oversight it conducts of covert action programs will ensure that these programs remain within the requisite "democratic framework." Congressional oversight should be viewed by the executive branch, and by the CIA, as a positive force in preventing bad ideas from becoming programs and in preventing bad programs from becoming disasters.

With respect to future operational factors, the Internet and satellite communications will have a major effect on covert action. For example, there may be less need for print propaganda because of international satellite TV broadcasting; propaganda disseminated on satellite TV will reach a larger audience, increasing both effectiveness and potential for unwanted replay back into the United States. Too, the Internet and information warfare will become highly useful tools, which will be used more and more frequently in covert action against our nation's enemies.

Lastly, despite the justifications for and value of covert action outlined in this work, covert action will probably continue to be controversial, with detractors offering legitimate as well as contrived criticisms. But just as we know that all post–World War II presidents, whether avidly or reluctantly, relied on covert action as part of their foreign and national security policies, so too we can be confident that future presidents will do the same.

NOTES

PREFACE

1. The opening epigraph is lifted from the Introduction to National Security Decision Directive-286. The declassified text may be found in Twentieth Century, *Need to Know*, at 87, or at www.fas.org/irp/offdocs, the Web site for the Federation of American Scientists.

2. Godson, *Tricks*, xxxi. Hulnick asserts that "many observers of United States Intelligence came to believe that the CIA . . . was an independent actor in selecting and running covert actions, without any oversight or control, either by the president or the Congress" ("Covert Action," 145–57).

3. Hulnick, "Covert Action," 145.

4. Ibid.; Godson, *Tricks*, 40.

5. See Andrew, Gordievsky, and Mitrokhin, *Sword*, 225–46, for compelling and convincing details of these KGB active measures and others. The United States government worked diligently in the mid-to-late 1980s to defeat the AIDS and "Baby Parts" disinformation, but it met with only partial success—even among sophisticated populations in Western Europe—so strong was the inclination to believe anything negative about American policies and government. Hulnick, "Covert Action," at 153, clarifies this "distorted view."

6. Melvin Goodman, in Eisendrath, *National Insecurity*, 28. The quotations are from Warner, "Origins," 1 (the version used here is found on the *Studies In Intelligence* Web site, and the page numbers correspond to that version). See Saunders, *Cultural*, for a detailed history of the Congress for Cultural Freedom.

7. Johnson, *Bombs*, 6.

8. On January 15, 2000, the author conducted a Lexis-Nexis search for newspaper articles and editorials, dating from January 1, 1950, to January 1, 2000, using "covert action" as a keyword in either the title or in the text. The result was 815 stories, of which fewer than 10 percent were favorably disposed to covert action. While empirical in nature, this evidence highlights an ample prejudice against covert action in general on the part of the media. Not coincidentally, a 1992 survey of 1,400 journalists found 44 percent claiming membership in the Democratic Party, and presumably a corresponding preference for liberal ideals, as opposed to 16 percent belonging to the Republican Party; an "overwhelming majority" of these journalists admitted that they had voted for Democratic presidential candidates in the six elections between 1964 and 1980. (Janda, *Challenge,* 201). See also Hulnick, "Covert Action," 153.

9. Among the operations that professional CIA officers argued against as being unwise, illegal, or high-risk/low-gain were the overthrow of the Arbenz government in Guatemala; the Bay of Pigs invasion and assassination plots against Castro during the Kennedy years; support of the Kurds at the behest of the shah of Iran and political action in Chile, both during the Nixon administration; and Angola during the Ford years. And let us not forget that the Iran-Contra scandal occurred in part because DCI Bill Casey, realizing that the majority of the career professionals in the CIA would oppose his plans, turned instead to members of the National Security Council staff and a few handpicked senior Agency officers whose actions exceeded their legitimate Agency roles.

INTRODUCTION

1. Opening epigraph is from the Twentieth Century, *Need to Know,* at 5.

2. Godson, "Focus." Virtually all (90 percent) of the gunpowder used by the American forces in the initial twenty-four months of the Revolutionary War were acquired through covert relationships with France and other European nations who were foes of the British. Turner, "Constitution," 101, n67. Carter, in *Covert,* passim, identifies fourteen out of the first twenty-eight American presidents as practitioners of classic covert action programs, from 1787 until 1920.

3. See: Wise, "CIA," A35; Wicker, "Fiasco," A29; Editorial, "Change," 10A; Hoagland, "Costs," A27; Goodman, "CIA," 18; Halperin, "Prohibiting," 85; Kennedy, "History," A21; Kennedy, "Outlaw," A22. These comments and sources do not even begin to include those who call for the demise of the CIA and *all* of its duties. Those who

do so are generally less informed about intelligence matters, and their writings frequently are so laden with falsehoods, inaccuracies, distortions, and other things that are the product of an antagonistic imagination as opposed to research and knowledge that it's amazing anyone publishes them. For a sterling example of this, see Baker, "CIA."

4. Berkowitz and Goodman, "Logic," 38.

5. Hitchens, "Unlawful," 60. Hitchens makes numerous damning allegations, some of which (to the knowledgeable reader) are ludicrous at face value. Moreover, he provides absolutely no references or support for these serious allegations.

6. Melvin Goodman, quoted in Eisendrath, *National Insecurity*, 28.

7. Lowenthal, *Intelligence*, 118.

8. Codevilla, *Statecraft*, 241.

ONE: THE ROLE OF COVERT ACTION IN INTELLIGENCE AND FOREIGN POLICY

1. The opening epigraph is found in Twentieth Century, *Need to Know*, at 41.

2. The percentage of content from the different source categories will of course vary with the nature of the issue or topic being analyzed. "Open source" intelligence may imply to some that the information is known and readily available, but that is not the case. The sources may or may not be readily available, depending upon where they are published. What turns information into intelligence is the ability of the analyst to collate and correlate diverse bits of information from various sources to produce a coherent picture of what has happened, is happening, or may happen in the future. In many cases, it is the clandestinely acquired information that puts the rest of the material into final context, rather than providing the meat of the analysis.

3. Godson sees covert action as "influencing conditions and behavior in ways that cannot be attributed to the sponsor . . . [i]t seeks to influence values, mostly through overt institutions and instruments," in *Tricks*, at xxxi and 19. Johnson has defined covert action, in "Accountability," at 81, as "the pursuit of American foreign policy objectives through secret intervention into the affairs of other nations." True enough, but this definition overlooks programs and operations in which transnational groups (e.g., drug cartels, terrorist elements) and individuals may be targeted. Covert Action: it's not just for countries anymore.

4. Executive Order 12333, *United States Intelligence Activities*, 4

December 1981, 3 CFR 200 (1981, 46 FR 59955 [as amended by Executive Order 12701, 14 February 1990, 55 FR 5933]).

5. Strong, "Covert," 64.

6. Intelligence Authorization Act of 1991, Pub. L. 102–88, 105 Stat, 429 (1991), Section 503 [c][4][e].

7. Simply put, all covert action programs are special activities, but not all special activities are covert action. See inter alia Tuttle, "Secrecy," 530–52, where he states that special activities is a "generally accepted euphemism for covert action"; and Strong, "Covert," 64–65, who calls special activities a "euphemistic term" that has been "substituted" for covert action. Johnson states the same in "Accountability" at 82, and in *Bombs* at 2 and 48, where he refers to "disruptive economic covert action" as "special activities." In point of fact, "disruptive economic covert action" is one element of classic covert action, that of political action operations, and has no relation to "special activities"—the use of the covert action infrastructure to perform non-covert action operations. Johnson errs further (*Bombs,* at 101–2) when he talks of the DO's "Covert Action Staff" as the propaganda and political action component, and "Special Activities Division" (referred to simply as "SA" by DO officers) as the home of the paramilitary unit. Actually, SA is the home division of all covert action elements in the DO and manages the assets in the covert action infrastructure; the Covert Action Staff per se was disbanded some years after Vietnam.

8. Godson, in *Tricks* at 3, refers to "intelligence assistance" as a category of covert action; however, the particular actions that he lists fit nicely under the rubric of "special activities." See also Woodward, *VEIL,* 1 307–8.

9. This same segment of society is loath for America to exercise any act of power, whether military, economic, or political, in foreign policy, as though it is ashamed or embarrassed by the very idea that America may have interests that could require defending or merely that it is possessed with such power. See also Godson, *Tricks,* 8; Twentieth Century, *Need to Know,* 16–17, 45–47.

10. Berkowitz and Goodman discuss the first two points in "Logic," at 41, and again in *Truth,* at 129; the requirement of foreign governments who might be beneficiaries of or participants in these programs should be self-evident.

11. Meyer, *Reality,* 66.

12. Codevilla, *Statecraft,* 41.

13. Felix, *Short Course,* 137.

14. Godson, *Tricks,* 21–24; Codevilla, *Statecraft,* 38. See Mahl,

Desperate Deception, for perhaps the definitive study to date of British covert action against the United States during the 1939–1941 period.

15. Twentieth Century, *Need to Know*, 5.

16. Ibid.; Laqueur, "Future," 304.

17. Johnson, "Accountability," 82, and *Bombs*, 28; Laqueur, *Uses*, 333; Berkowitz and Goodman in "Logic," at 38, and in *Truth*, at 126; Twentieth Century, *Need to Know*, 41–43; Lowenthal, *Intelligence*, 113. The Newsom quotation is found in Twentieth Century, *Need to Know*, 37.

18. Cline, "Prerogative," 360.

19. Colby, "CIA's," 74.

20. In covert action programs in Chile from 1967 to 1973, the following was spent: election campaign material and support to parties—$8 million; use of mass media to disseminate political messages—$4.3 million; influencing Chilean "institutions"—$900,000; promoting a coup against Allende—$200,000. Cited in Smist, *Congress*, 77, from the Church Committee hearings (page 95 of that document).

TWO: THE "ROMANCES"
OF COVERT ACTION

1. The definition of Romances may be found in the *American Heritage Dictionary of the English Language*. "Romances" as myth or misconception was coined by Theodore A. Dodge in an 1886 paper written for the Massachusetts Historical Society on the battle of Chancellorsville (as explained in Stephen W. Sears's outstanding work, *Chancellorsville* [Boston: Houghton Mifflin, 1996], 502).

2. For detailed examples of early covert action and deception operations run by American presidents, see Andrew, *Eyes Only*, 6–13; John Carter, *Covert*, 15–52; Knott, *Secret*, 13–115.

3. The reader can find concise histories of both the Church Committee and the Pike Committee in Loch Johnson, *Inquiry*, and Olmsted, *Challenging*, both of which present a balanced view of the hearings and faithfully report the findings of the committees.

4. Hitchens, "Unlawful," 60.

5. In this, the author can speak from personal experience. Assigned for seven months to a country ruled by one of the absolute worst dictators in the hemisphere, it was a psychological ordeal just to live in the capital, much less to represent the United States government to officials of that odious regime.

6. See Hitchens, "Unlawful," passim, which manages to capture, in one article, the majority of criticisms aimed at the CIA. While many others have made the same condemnations, Hitchens presents them as succinctly, completely, and erroneously as any. In this article, he makes a number of spurious allegations, none of which received the comfort or support of references.

7. Related to the author by a senior Agency officer who attended the meeting.

8. Johnson, *Bombs*, 211. The DCI was George Tenet.

9. Twentieth Century, *Need to Know*, 61.

10. Colby, "CIA's," 72; Halperin, "Prohibiting," 13; Damrosch, "Covert," 795. The Hughes-Ryan Amendment is found at 22 USC 2422, section 662.

11. Nutter, *Black*, 38. However, Nutter cites no examples to make his case, possibly because there haven't been any since 1974.

12. Hitchens, "Unlawful," 60. He also ignores the scrutiny the Agency receives from leaks to the press and the information provided to both the public and the media through the Freedom of Information Act. And see Halperin, "Prohibiting," 13. Whether a law limiting a policy element of a president's general ability to conduct foreign policy would be compatible with the Constitution is problematic. Halperin also advances the interesting proposition that intelligence officers who lie in the line of their work become so corrupted that they lose the ability to tell the truth to anyone, especially to Congress. But this is merely Halperin's supposition, which he conveniently leaves unsupported by any statistics or factual data.

13. Hitchens, "Unlawful," 61; Johnson, "Bright Line," 300–301.

14. See the bibliography for the writings of Halperin, Baker, Goodman, Kennedy, and Schorr, as well as selected editorials.

15. See John Carter, *Covert*, 15–42, for enlightenment on the ultimate democrat's employment of covert action during his two administrations. See both Carter, *Covert*, and Knott, *Secret*, for enlightening histories of our early presidents and their resort to covert action.

16. The National Security Act of 1947 is found at 50 USC 403. See Houston, "Hillenkoetter," 14; and inter alia Berkowitz and Goodman, *Truth*, 124.

17. Intelligence Oversight Act of 1980, adopted as part of the Intelligence Authorization Act of 1991 50 USC 413; Damrosch, "Covert," at 797.

18. Damrosch, "Covert," at 802. Readers should not confuse United States domestic law with international law and the United Nations char-

ter, nor for that matter, with the domestic laws of foreign nations. Virtually all nations prohibit espionage operations of any type being conducted against them by foreign governments; and many nations further prohibit foreign governments from simply running espionage operations on their territory even though another, "third party" government is the actual target. This is, of course, why intelligence officers, whether American or other nationalities, are posted abroad "under cover," so as to hide activities that are illegal in the host country but which are legal under the laws of their own nation.

19. In a demonstration of why inaccurate myths about covert action persist, critic Morton H. Halperin wrote in 1975 ("Decision-Making," at 51) that the CIA "has been dominated by officials whose primary concerns and interest was covert operations over intelligence operations." Although arguably correct during the 1950s and 1960s, by the time Halperin wrote this statement in 1975 it was manifestly untrue. Halperin, who worked in both the White House and the Pentagon as recently as the Clinton administration, and who no doubt maintained contacts in the national security arena (as "in and out and in again" political appointees are wont to do) either knew this wasn't accurate or should have known.

20. During the late 1940s and early 1950s, when the covert action element, OPC, and the intelligence collection element, OSO, were separate institutions, circumstances allowed OPC officers to advance to higher grades more quickly at a younger age. When the two organizations were merged in 1952 into the CIA's Directorate of Plans, OPC officers held a disproportionate number of senior positions (Godson, *Tricks*, 35). This may be one reason why the CIA as an institution looked more favorably on covert action in those years than it did after the 1970s.

21. See Godson, *Tricks*, 35–36 and 61–63, for additional detail. Woodward's *VEIL* is replete with comments pointing to the CIA's and the DO's reluctance about and distaste for covert action.

22. Horton, "Reflections," 84. One assumes, however, that with the expanded authorities granted to the CIA after the terrorist attacks of September 11, 2001, that the ranks of covert action specialists have increased, particularly those of the paramilitary operators.

23. Agency officers are fond of noting that while covert action programs are less than 5 percent of the Agency's budget, they constitute about 95 percent of the Agency's problems and bad publicity. Codevilla, *Statecraft*, 240; Johnson, "Accountability," 88; Pike, "CIA Budget," 1 (the entire document, printed out from the Federation of American Scientists Web site, is fourteen pages; page numbers in this and subsequent endnotes correlate to the pages of the printout).

24. See Editorial, "Restricting," A25, for a cogent explanation of why Iran-Contra was an "aberration" and not a genuine covert action. Also, Stone, "Loophole," 5.

25. The White House directives were NSDD-2, *National Security Council Structure* (12 January 1982) and NSDD-159, *Covert Action Policy Approval and Coordination Procedures* (18 January 1985). The Iran-Contra conspirators violated both of these directives.

26. See Draper, *Thin Line*, and Walsh, *Firewall*, for a fulsome accounting of this scandal; Berkowitz and Goodman, in *Truth*, present a useful summary at 133–36. See also Johnson, "Accountability," at 83.

27. In discussing Iran-Contra with numerous colleagues, the author personally heard dozens of comments about what was, to them, an obvious illegality, as well as expressions of wonder that it was never mentioned to Congress. The quotation comes from Nutter who is no Agency admirer (*Black*, at 37–38).

28. See Clarridge and Diehl, *Spy*, for an example of a "woe is me, I did nothing wrong, I was a victim" proclamation.

29. Godson, *Tricks*, 36–37.

30. See for example, Isenberg, "Pitfalls," 1, where he describes paramilitary operations as "secret wars" that resulted in "countless deaths and immense destruction," an exaggeration of several magnitudes.

31. As the final draft of this book was being readied for Agency review and publication, the administration of George W. Bush has received congressional authority to initiate war against Iraq, with the ultimate goal of regime change. The administration not only has no way of controlling who might come to power in such an event, but is even clueless as to who might actually possess the ability to seize and hold power. These two questions accompany a frightening number of unknowns with respect to a postwar Iraq, but likewise have not engendered any hesitation or doubt in the administration about the wisdom of its policies.

32. Godson, *Tricks*, 3.

33. Since the demise of the Soviet Union, much has been written by former intelligence officers, including those of the Soviet Union, on Soviet intelligence activities against the West and the United States. The most thorough of these works has also relied on files from the archives of the KGB. See inter alia: Andrew and Gordievsky, *KGB*, and Andrew, Gordievsky, and Mitrokhin, *Sword*.

34. The official is George Carver, Jr., cited in Bittman, "Use," 245.

35. Bittman, "Use," 246. Bittman notes that, during the period of supposed détente in the 1970s, the Soviets were particularly successful in achieving dominating influence (i.e., a pro-Communist regime) in nine

countries in Africa, Central America, and Southeast Asia (247). See also Turner, "Coercive," 429n10. The evidence for this is "overwhelming," 435. Perhaps the most authoritative source is the KGB's own highly secret files, published in Andrew, Gordievsky, and Mitrokhin, *Sword*, passim.

36. Weber, *Spymasters*, 296.

37. Church Committee, "Alleged Assassination Plots Involving Foreign Leaders." And Ranelagh, *The Agency*, where he states, at 383, that "there is no evidence . . . that the CIA ever succeeded in assassinating anyone. However, as William Colby remarked, it was not for want of trying."

38. Damrosch, "Covert," 800.

39. Church Committee, "Alleged Assassination Plots Involving Foreign Leaders."

40. See inter alia: Prados, *Blood Road*; Logevall, *Choosing War*; Kimball, *Nixon's Vietnam War*. The reference to the White House tapes is from John Prados, *The White House Tapes: Eavesdropping on the President* (New York: The New Press, 2003), which was published just as this manuscript was being completed. The National Security Archives at George Washington University prepared a summary of the book, and the quotation in the text is lifted from its first paragraph; the summary and supporting document abstracts are at (www.gwu.edu/~nsarchiv/NSAEBB/NSAEBB101/index2.htm). On ABC-TV *Evening News* with Carole Simpson, Sunday, November 3, 2002, Kennedy administration official Theodore Sorenson emphatically stated that, while the White House knew of the coup, the United States government neither initiated nor participated in it.

41. Church Committee, "Covert Action in Chile 1963–1973." The quotation is lifted from Olmsted, *Challenging*, 217n109.

42. McClory, "Covert," 23.

THREE: COVERT ACTION POLICY AND PITFALLS

1. Opening epigraph from Colby, "CIA's," 73.

2. Berkowitz, "Backfire," B1.

3. The author was present at a meeting in the DDO's office when the DDO related the story to gathered officers.

4. Samuel Halpern, cited in Weber, *Spymasters*, at 124.

5. Roy Godson calls this the "essential principle" of covert action (*Tricks*, 121).

6. Godson, "Focus," 32. See also Lowenthal, *Intelligence*, 109.

7. Godson, *Tricks*, 121 and 132; Berkowitz and Goodman, *Truth*, 136–37; Lowenthal, *Intelligence*, 109; Statement from George Tenet's

Senate confirmation hearings for the position of Director of Central Intelligence, May 1977; Berkowitz and Goodman, "Logic," 43; Berkowitz, "Backfire," B1. Twentieth Century, *Need to Know*, lists its own similar desiderata at 8–9.

8. Barry, "Managing," 21; Mathias and Leahy, "Covert," 14; Phillips, "CIA," 3; Newsom, "Successful," 24. These criteria were deemed "critical" by DCI George Tenet at his Senate confirmation hearing, May 1997. Other DCIs and intelligence professionals would undoubtedly agree.

9. Horton, "Reflections," 87.

10. The insider was Robert M. Gates; see *Shadows*, at 294.

11. Tuner, in "Coercive," at 446n110, writes from personal knowledge that a SSCI staffer took notes during a briefing of the SSCI in which the mining of the harbors was discussed with the senators present. Tuner believes that senators did not later misrepresent (i.e., lie about) not being briefed, but rather opines that they "simply did not focus on the issue when it was reported and consequently could not recall it when it came under attack in the press." Andrew writes that in a two-and-a-half hour briefing by Casey of the SSCI, the mining was mentioned only in one sentence and in a manner that implied it was a Contra operation without CIA participation (*Eyes Only*, 478). Woodward, in *VEIL*, at 322–23, writes that Casey told the SSCI about the mining in two briefings, although the CIA connection wasn't noted, and also notes (at 327) that Senator Patrick Leahy later told aides that he did indeed remember Casey informing the committee of the harbor minings.

12. Related to the author by the senior Agency officer who received the information directly from the officer who provided the briefing.

13. Woodward, *VEIL*, 226–27; Godson, *Tricks*, 56–57.

14. Nor was Central America and Nicaragua the only case in which Congress confused the issue with contradictory legislation. The Angola program also saw a series of contradictory legislation between 1976 and 1986.

15. Chomeau, "Role," 408.

16. See Chomeau, "Role," 408–10, for a cogent discussion of this and related issues.

FOUR: THE MILITARY AND PEACETIME COVERT ACTION

1. Opening epigraph was a favorite observation of the late John Millis, former staff director, House Permanent Select Committee on Intelligence, which was spoken several times in the presence of the author.

2. Lowenthal, *Intelligence*, 116.

3. Ibid., 116.

4. As mentioned in chapter 2, many observers consider the Iranian hostage rescue operation to be a covert action operation. Given the scale of the operation, the resources required, and the purely military nature of the mission, however, it is inappropriate to consider it an example of peacetime covert action. It was in fact a secret military operation (as many military operations are), which was supported by CIA intelligence collection and support assets.

5. 10 USC 167 (g): the establishment of a unified special operations command "does not constitute authority to conduct any activity which, if carried out as an intelligence activity by the Department of Defense," would require a Presidential Finding under Hughes-Ryan.

6. Lowenthal, *Intelligence*, 116.

7. Related to the author by an officer who was personally involved in the program.

8. Author's personal knowledge from his last assignment at the CIA in covert action policy.

9. For one example among the many who advocate such foolishness, see Isenberg, "Pitfalls," 22 and 26. Isenberg's monograph is replete with errors of fact and misjudgments based on those errors; one reason may be found in his bibliography: his sources are almost all authored by critics, whose allegations and negative perspectives he parrots.

10. Related to the author by a member of the HPSCI staff who was present when they talked with Blair after the press conference. Blair was a Rhodes Scholar and shared the characteristics of arrogance and absolute certitude of other Rhodes Scholars in the Clinton administration, even in areas of which they knew little or nothing.

11. This, of course, resulted in an enormous amount of distrust between the operations folks and Deutch. This antagonism was exacerbated when, in an exercise of supremely poor judgment, Deutch gave a speech in the CIA auditorium to Agency personnel, praising military officers while concurrently denigrating the Agency and officers in the Directorate of Operations. Deutch's idea of raising morale at the Agency was to build a field house and swimming pool—similar to the facilities at the Pentagon. Agency personnel were outraged: they had no desire for such facilities, mostly because there simply wasn't the time available during the day to use them, but also because they'd rather have had the money to conduct more operations and because they didn't *want* to be like DoD employees. Deutch never did realize the vast difference in staffing levels between the Agency and the Pentagon.

12. Related in confidence to the author by an Agency officer who was present at the briefing.

13. My position directly supported the executive director (ExDir) in the review and approval process of covert action programs. Prior to the arrival of the sycophantic Slatkin, there were three people supporting the ExDir in this manner. As I was leaving my position, Slatkin had directed the creation of a minor bureaucracy, with an anticipated twelve officers, to do the same work for just a small handful of programs. These officers, for the most part, were to be taken from field operations and turned into staff officers, even though Agency downsizing was creating serious shortages of experienced officers overseas and in operational management positions at headquarters. Slatkin was totally unmoved by any pleas for reconsideration—being served by staff was much more important to her than accomplishing the core mission.

14. Several officers in the Directorate of Science and Technology who worked with this author's component on newly emerging technologies related instances in which very sensitive technologies, developed by the CIA for a range of CIA missions and paid for by CIA funds, were in effect "hijacked" by Deutch and turned over to the military. Because of this, and Deutch's clear desire to become SecDef, there was consternation about this conflict of interest in which he acted in ways inimical to the best interests of the CIA and for the benefit of DoD. Of course, there were and no doubt still are numerous "black" technologies developed by DoD which were or are not shared with the CIA. This is justified as "need to know" but can also be highly counterproductive.

15. Related to the author by a senior DO officer who was involved in the dénouement of the fiasco.

16. Thomas, "Shadow Struggle," 31; Arkin, "Secret War," 1 (page number references Web site version of this article).

17. Shanker and Schmitt, "Pentagon," 1 (page number references Web site version); Editorial, "Propaganda," A12.

FIVE: THE DISCIPLINE OF COVERT ACTION

1. The opening epigraph is from Gates, *Shadows*, 292.

2. Intelligence scholar Loch K. Johnson has analyzed a range of possible covert action operations and constructed a "ladder of escalation," with thirty-eight steps ascending in relation to the intensity of the program. The lowest three levels, which he labels "Routine Operations," are really intelligence collection. Covert action operations, labeled "Modest Intrusion," begin at step four and climb to step nine, and include "truth-

ful benign information in autocracies," "truthful benign information in democracies," and "low-level funding of friendly groups." The next "threshold" is "High Risk Options," ascending from rung ten through rung twenty-six and encompassing most of the remaining non-lethal or highly visible covert action options, such as "truthful but contentious information," "disinformation," "economic disruption," and "limited supply of arms." The last echelon are the "Extreme Options," from rung twenty-seven to thirty-eight, covering "sophisticated arms supply," "environmental alterations," "major economic dislocations," and "major secret wars." See Johnson's *Agencies*, 60–88, and "Bright Line," 284–300.

3. Johnson, "Accountability," 84. Johnson claims that propaganda is the equivalent of psychological warfare, but that's not exactly correct.

4. The Office of International Information Programs (IIP) describes itself as "the principal international strategic communications service for the foreign affairs community." IIP designs, develops, and implements a variety of information initiatives and strategic communications programs, including Internet and print publications, traveling and electronically transmitted speaker programs, and information resource services. These reach (and are created strictly for) key international audiences, such as the media, government officials, opinion leaders, and the general public in more than 140 countries around the world.

5. Gates, *Shadows*, 91; Johnson, "Accountability," 84. See also Gates, 90–94, for additional insights.

6. Godson, *Tricks*, 151.

7. Johnson, in *Bombs* at 29, gives an example of an editorial encouraging a nation not to pursue a weapons proliferation program.

8. Godson, *Tricks*, 145.

9. Ritchie, "Covert," 2 (page number coincides with Web version).

10. Gates, *Shadows*, 357–58; Ritchie, "Covert," 1.

11. Holland, "Disinformation," 5–17.

12. Godson, *Tricks*, 157.

13. Definition found in Polmar and Allen, *Spy Book*, 158.

14. Godson and Wirtz, "Deception," 427; Codevilla, *Statecraft*, 31–32.

15. Godson and Wirtz, "Deception," 426.

16. Godson and Wirtz, "Deception," 426, cited from Godson, *Tricks*, 236.

17. Godson and Wirtz, "Deception," 427. During World War II, Operation Mincemeat called for a corpse dressed as a Royal Marine major with false plans for the invasion of Sicily handcuffed to his wrist to be placed by submarine off the coast of Spain. As planned, the "major" washed ashore and pro-Nazi Spanish authorities passed the false documents to their German counterparts.

18. Godson, *Tricks*, 16. For a fuller discussion of the Trust operation, see inter alia: Andrew and Gordievsky, *KGB*; Lockhart, *Reilly*; and Epstein, *Deception*. What makes the Trust special, in addition to its overwhelming success, was that it was a deception program with a counterintelligence goal.

19. Johnson, "Accountability," 85; O'Brien, "Interfering," 432; Isenberg, "Pitfalls," 4, 7.

20. Roger Hilsman was director of the Department of State's Bureau of Intelligence and Research in the Kennedy years, and Lyndon Johnson's assistant secretary of state for Asian affairs. The ambassador was U. Alexis Johnson, who held numerous high-level State Department positions in the 1960s and 1970s. Details of the Italian covert action program from its inception until its termination in the 1960s is related by former DCI Bill Colby in Colby and Forbath, *Honorable Men*, at 136–40.

21. The Italian program was carried through the 1960s, phased out only in FY 1968. See Minutes of the 303 Committee for June 25, 1965, and August 22, 1967, and relevant State Department correspondence of January 24, 1964, and September 12, 1966, on the same topic in FRUS/WE Volume XII, Western Europe 1964–1968. The particular documents may be found on the Federation of American Scientists Web site as www.fas.org/sgp/advisory/state/italy.html; and the entire *FRUS* volume is available on the State Department's Web site. For additional information on support to Solidarity see inter alia: Gates, *Shadows*, passim; West, *Third Secret*; and Bernstein and Politi, *His Holiness*.

22. Weiss, "Farewell."

23. For an interesting, if somewhat biased, account of CIA "grunts" training the anti-Sandinista forces in Nicaragua, see Garvey, *Gringo*. For accounts of the CIA's war in Laos, see: Holm, *American Agent*; Parker, *Mule*; Warner, *Shooting the Moon*; Conboy and Morrison, *Shadow War*; Hamilton-Merritt, *Tragic Mountains*; Robbins, *Air America* and *Ravens*; and Lert, *Wings of the CIA*.

24. Love, "Cyberthreat," 205.

25. Johnson gives the examples of inserting a virus to destroy data or providing "faulty" computer components to an opposing power as types of information warfare (IW) covert action in *Bombs*, 29. See also Berkowitz and Goodman, *Truth*, 142, where they define IW in part as "attacks on an adversary's information systems" (at 142); see also Berkowitz and Goodman, "Logic," 45–46.

26. Love, "Cyberthreat," 198.

27. Love, "Cyberthreat," 201–2.

28. The clandestine intrusion into computer systems merely to "read"

or collect the data while leaving no sign of entry is simply one more method of intelligence collection, not covert action, and so is beyond the scope of this work. A wonderful primer for novices (among literally hundreds of books and other writings available) on how computers and the information contained therein may be remotely entered and either manipulated, damaged, or destroyed is found in Schwartau, *Information Warfare*.

29. Johnson, *Bombs*, 181, provides the example of "emptying out" the funds held in a bank by a terrorist group as one use for CIA computer hacking.

30. Were the Agency to clandestinely and remotely enter a computer system only to read or acquire data without the "owner" realizing it, this would fall under the rubric of either foreign intelligence collection or counterintelligence.

31. Among others, President Clinton's national security advisor Anthony Lake raises precisely this specter in *Six Nightmares*, 38–65. Lake calls this use of hacking "cyber-terrorism."

32. Pincus, "Boutique," A-06.

SIX: APPROVAL AND REVIEW OF COVERT ACTION PROGRAMS IN THE MODERN ERA

1. Opening epigraph is from Walter F. Murphy, Ph.D, McCormack Professor of Jurisprudence Emeritous at Princeton University, and cited in Twentieth Century, *Need to Know,* at 18.

2. See Smist, *Congress,* at 5, for Clark and Pforzheimer; Johnson, *Bombs,* at 202, for Stennis; and Treverton, *Covert Action,* 232, for Saltonstall. See also Fein, "Constitution," 55, and Twentieth Century, *Need to Know,* 62–63.

3. Twentieth Century, *Need to Know,* 62–63.

4. Cinquegrana, "Dancing," at 183. The other obvious attempt to exert control over the executive branch at the time was the War Powers Act of 1973.

5. Rindskopf, "Intelligence," 23.

6. Smist, *Congress,* 263.

7. Cinquegrana, "Dancing," 183. The text of the Hughes-Ryan Amendment may be found in Pub. L. No. 187-195, para. 662 (1974) (codified as amended at 22 USC 2422 [1988]).

8. Twentieth Century, *Need to Know,* 62.

9. Barry, "Managing," 26. The January 17, 1986, Finding for Iran is reprinted in Twentieth Century, *Need to Know,* 95–96, but is missing the Supporting Document. See also Richelson, *Community,* 430, for an exemplar of a Finding.

10. Intelligence Oversight Act of 1980, as amended by the Intelligence Authorization Act of 1991, at Title V of the National Security Act, 50 USC 413.

11. Colby, "CIA's," 76.

12. Johnson, "Accountability," 90. Johnson notes (at 91) that the importance of accountability, in lieu of deniability, was lost on John Poindexter during the Iran-Contra scandal.

13. See Cohen, "Oversight," 157. Representative Lee Hamilton, chairman of former HPSCI, from a speech, "The Role of Intelligence in the Foreign Policy Process," delivered on December 16, 1986, at the University of Virginia. Hamilton noted that the withholding of funds for covert action programs by Congress is very rare, in that "CIA activities enjoy strong bi-partisan support" in HPSCI. See Simmons, "Intelligence," 15.

14. See Getler, "Hill," A1; Hoffman and Goshko, "Administration," A1; Gordon, "Bush, A12; Schorr, "Sad," 19; Associated Press, "Grab," A1; Wicker, "Not Covert," A19; Gerstenzang, "Reagan," 5.

15. Johnson, "Accountability," 100–101.

16. During the 1980s counterterrorism training programs were conducted for intelligence, military, and security services in "dozens" of countries around the world, including Sudan, Egypt, Bolivia, Venezuela, South Korea, Lebanon, Greece, and Peru. When the CIA conducted the training, it was under the authority of a Presidential Finding. See Wright and Broder, "Secretly Aids."

17. PL 102-88; Twentieth Century, *Need to Know*, 57; Cohen, "Oversight," 157.

18. See Daugherty, *Ayatollah*, 184–91, for a succinct explanation of this mission. For further reading, see Beckwith and Knox, *Delta*; Haney, *Inside*; Earl, "Principle"; Kyle and Eidson, *Guts*; and Ryan, *Rescue*.

19. Brzezinski, *Power*, 59–63; Johnson, "Accountability," 97–98. This process was incorporated in NSDD-159 (see chapter 11).

20. NSDD-286 of October 15, 1987, is reprinted in full in Twentieth Century, *Need to Know*, 87–93. See also Reisman and Baker, *Regulating*, at 213; and Richelson, *Community*, at 431. NSDD-159 required that all senior members of Reagan's National Security Planning Group review and approve draft Findings prior to their being sent forward to the president for signature.

21. National Security Presidential Directive-1, *Organization of the National Security System*, signed by President George W. Bush on February 13, 2001, retained the system set up under Clinton, including the Principals and Deputies Committees. The Interagency Working Groups were abolished,

and in their place a network of Policy Coordinating Committees (PCC) was created. See inter alia: Johnson, *Agencies*, 133, and "Accountability," 94-95; Gates, *Shadows*, 379; and Twentieth Century, *Need to Know*, 53–59.

22. See inter alia Chomeau, "Role," 412; Strong, "Covert," 71; Meyer, *Reality*, 382. Johnson, in "Accountability" at 94, cites a "senior DDO" officer as telling him in 1980 that "roughly 85 percent" of covert action proposals originate in the CIA field stations. This number is manifestly wrong for the period after 1980 and very questionable, for several reasons, for the era prior to 1980. First, as discussed earlier, CIA officers, whether in the field or at headquarters, are not enamored of covert action programs, preferring for multiple reasons to run collection operations instead. Second, there were few programs running after the Nixon administration and early in the Carter years, and most of those were low-key propaganda/political action programs for the USSR and Eastern Europe that had been in existence for years. Third, there were but few covert action specialists at the CIA to run such programs after Carter's DCI, Stansfield Turner, cut 880 positions from the DO, most of them in the covert action area. Fourth, when Carter did start to ramp up covert action programs, it was much more at the insistence of National Security Advisor Zbigniew Brzezinski than anyone else. DCI Turner has written (*Secrecy*, at 88) that at times he would relate to covert action specialists the "problems the policymakers were facing" and these officers would generate ideas that the DCI would then take back to Brzezinski and the NSC. But Turner goes on to say that others, including the secretaries of state and defense, would offer suggestions for covert action programs.

23. Twentieth Century, *Need To Know*, 53. It is possible that the Twentieth Century Panel was in fact referring to specific operational methodology, which of course is the responsibility of Agency officers, and not the overall policy, but that's not the sense one acquires from a first reading. See also Nutter, *Black*, at 293, stating that "sometimes the impetus" flows down from the president, as though this is an aberration in normal procedures. It is not: it is the way things are done. While Bill Casey may well have pushed (vice merely suggested) covert action programs to the president while he was DCI, in seeming contravention of my point, it must also be remembered that Casey held cabinet rank and, as such, was "dual-hatted" as a presidential policy advisor. Nutter also states that the DCI possesses the authority to order "minor" covert action programs on his own authority (270n5). While this was the case prior to the Nixon years, it has not been so since the advent of the Presidential Finding. All covert action programs must, as a matter of federal law, be approved by

the president and reported to Congress. Nutter, while presenting a fairly wide range of legitimate issues about covert action, loses credibility for several reasons. First, he tends to draw broad, very general conclusions from single, isolated events (which he may or may not have described accurately); second, he often does not provide any further sources of support or evidence for his conclusions; and finally, he simply repeats or elaborates on (without providing additional information) many ancient allegations of Agency behavior.

24. Aspin, "Covert," 10.

25. Richelson, *Community*, 431.

26. Richelson identifies the CARG only as "the top echelon of CIA management." See *Community* at 431.

27. Laqueur, "Future," 309.

28. The forty-eight-hour requirement was added to the Intelligence Oversight Act of 1988 in response to the Iran-Contra scandal.

29. Richelson, *Community*, 431.

SEVEN: HARRY S TRUMAN

1. Opening epigraph is found in Twentieth Century, *Need To Know*, 36.

2. Anderson, "Security," 407. The fate of the postwar intelligence community and the creation of the CIA are beyond the scope of this work. Among the copious volumes on this subject are: Darling, *Central Intelligence Agency*, chapters 1 and 2; Ranelagh, *The Agency*, chapters 3 through 7; Andrew, *Eyes Only*, chapter 5; O'Toole, *Treachery*, chapter 33. For personal accounts, see: Colby and Forbath, *Honorable Men*, chapters 2 and 3; Thomas, *Best Men*, chapters 1 through 5; Ralph E. Weber, ed., *Spymasters*, introduction, chapters 1 and 2.

3. Godson, *Tricks*, 24–25.

4. OPC/CIA, 2.

5. Rossitzke, *Operations*, 14–15.

6. Thomas, *Best Men*, 29; Ranelagh, *The Agency*, 133; O'Toole, *Treachery*, 434–35; Cline, *CIA*, 120.

7. CIG, *Review of the World Situation as it Relates to the Security of the United States*, 26 September 1946. Cited in Karabell, *Architects*, at 39n6.

8. O'Toole, *Treachery*, 435.

9. NSC-1/1, *The Position of the United States with Respect to Italy*, 14 November 1947. My copy of the original document was provided courtesy of the Harry S Truman presidential library, as were cop-

ies of NSC-1/2 and NSC-1/3. One may also find NSC-1/1 in *FRUS/BC*, 724–26.

10. Karabell, *Architects*, 46.

11. NSC-1/2, *The Position of the United States with Respect to Italy*, 12 March 1948, *FRUS/WE*, 1948, 756–69, although the CIA censors must have struck before clearing the document for publication as the statement in paragraph 9(e) about allowing the use of unvouchered funds has been deleted from the *FRUS* version. The same applies for NSC-1/1.

12. NSC-1/3 may be perused in *FRUS/WE*, 1948, Kennan's acknowledgment, which was made to the Church Committee, may be found in Twentieth Century, *Need to Know*, at 111n1.

13. NSC-1/2, *The Position of the United States with Respect to Italy*, 12 March 1948, in *FRUS/WE, 1948*; NSC-1/3, *Position of the United States with Respect to Italy in the Light of the Possibility of Communist Participation in the Government by Legal Means*, 12 March 1948, in *FRUS/WE, 1948*. Also see Cline, *CIA*, 122; Godson, *Tricks*, 30–32.

14. NSC-4 may be found in *FRUS/EIE*, "Psychological and Political Warfare," document 251.

15. Karabell, *Architects*, 47.

16. Andrew, *Eyes Only*, 172; Karabell, *Architects*, 40; Anderson, "Security," 411; Prados, *Presidents'*, 83; *FRUS/EIE*; Ranelagh, *The Agency*, 115, 118n; Powers, *Man*, 30; Peake, "Truman," 35. NSC-4A was signed on December 17, 1947. The text of NSC-4/A may be found in *FRUS/EIE*, 1945–1950, document 257.

17. Cline, *CIA*, 124; Ranelagh, *The Agency*, 115; Colby and Forbath, *Honorable*, 108–40; Richelson, *Community*, 343.

18. *Washington Post*, December 22, 1963; Andrew, *Eyes Only*, 171. While there has been some argument that Truman speech writer David Noyes wrote the article without the former president's knowledge, CIA official and intelligence historian Hayden B. Peake has established that Truman almost certainly had prior knowledge of the contents of the article and so must have approved it. See Peake, "Truman," 31.

19. Thomas, *Best Men*, 28–29; Ranelagh, *The Agency*, 115n; Peake, "Truman," 35. Colby and Forbath, in *Honorable* at 108–39, provides a detailed account from his perspective as one of the principal officers involved in the operations.

20. O'Toole, *Treachery*, 437. Concurrently, there was a similar program in France intended to reduce the influence of the French Communist Party and its supporters, while swaying public opinion against European

Communists. See Richelson, *Community*, 343; Aldrich, *Hidden*, 137–38; Pisani, *CIA*, 81–105.

21. Karabell, *Architects*, 42.

22. See *FRUS/WE*, documents 92, 113, 116, 125, 133.

23. Bukovsky, "Secrets," 5. See Aldrich, *Hidden*, 342–70; Meyer, *Reality*, 60–67; and Pisani, *CIA*, passim for more details of the European covert action programs.

24. Prados, *Presidents'*, 79, 472; Powers, *Man*, 31; OPC/CIA, 30.

25. *FRUS/EIE*, "Psychological and Political Warfare," documents 277 and 280.

26. Pforzheimer, "Remarks," 147.

27. OPC/CIA, 7.

28. *FRUS/MSA*, "Management of Covert Actions in the Truman Administration."

29. *FRUS/EIE*, "Psychological and Political Warfare," document 292. See also Ranelagh, *The Agency*, 118n; Andrew, *Eyes Only*, 172–73; Richelson, *Community*, 394; Peake, "Truman," 35; Cline, *CIA*, 126. The Office of Policy Coordination was officially established on September 1, 1948. OPC was not to operate completely independently, however; as with the Agency's covert action component in the 1980s, it was to receive thematic guidance from the Department of State in time of peace.

30. Cline, "Prerogative," 363.

31. Prados, *Presidents'*, 79, 81, 109.

32. Official CIA history of OPC, found at www.foia.ucia.gov, accessed on June 22, 2001.

33. The CIA's formerly secret official history of OPC may be found at the Agency's Web site, www.foia.ucia.gov. See also OPC/CIA, at 11, and Sayle, "Déjà Vu," 399–400, for a succinct account of this merger.

34. Prados, *Presidents'*, 83–84.

35. Weber, *Spymasters*, 44.

36. Godson, *Tricks*, 36–37.

37. Warner, "Origins," 1 (page number is consistent with Web-based version). The history of the Congress is explored in Saunders, *Cultural Cold War*.

38. Sullivan, "Review," 1 (page number corresponds to the Web version).

39. O'Brien, "Interfering," 437.

40. Andrew, *Eyes Only*, 172–73; Bowie and Immerman, *Waging*, 12–13.

41. NSC-20/4, *U.S. Objectives with Respect to the USSR to Counter Soviet Threats to U.S. Security*, November 24, 1948.

42. Godson, *Tricks*, 46–50; Nutter, *Black*, 51.

43. Bowie and Immerman, *Waging*, 27–28; Prados, *Presidents'*, 45–60; Dorril, *MI-6*, 360–403; Richelson, *Community*, 343; Codevilla, *Statecraft*, 246.

44. O'Toole, *Treachery*, 460; Ranelagh, *The Agency*, 265n; Pincus, "CIA," A4; Risen, "Documents," A11. O'Toole claims lower-level State Department officers were the driving force behind the cancellation.

45. Andrew, *Eyes Only*, 203. See also Gavin, "Politics," passim.

46. Rositzke, *Operations*, 173.

47. The full story may be enjoyed in Knaus, *Orphans*.

48. O'Toole, *Treachery*, 455–56. Lansdale would later apply the same tactics and strategies that worked so well in the Philippines in Vietnam, where they met with abject failure; the lessons of the Philippines were not transferable to Indochina.

EIGHT: DWIGHT D. EISENHOWER

1. Opening epigraph is from Cline, "Prerogative," 365.

2. Knaus, *Orphans*, 137. This is no doubt the most complete recounting of the Tibetan program in the public domain.

3. Ambrose, *Eisenhower*, 110–11.

4. Richelson, *Community*, 347. The two instances are Congolese prime minister Patrice Lumumba and Cuban revolutionary Fidel Castro.

5. Bowie and Immerman, *Waging*, 149–62; Cullather, *Guatemala*, 36. NSC-162/2 was further revised on January 7, 1955, making it clear that the administration's "Cold War strategy" was based on Kennan's doctrine of containment. Bowie and Immerman, 177.

6. Andrew, *Eyes Only*, 20; Prados, *Presidents'*, 105, 472; *FRUS/MSA*, "NSC-5412 Special Group; 5412 Special Group; 303 Committee."

7. National Security Council Directive 5412, *National Security Council Directive on Covert Operations*," 15 March 1954; FRUS/MEA, "5412"

8. NSC-5412, *National Security Council Directive on Covert Operations*, 15 March 1954; NSC-5412/1, *Note by the Executive Secretary to the National Security Council on Covert Actions*, 15 March 1954. See Peake, "Truman," 38–39; Karabell, *Architects*, 128; Prados, *Presidents'*, 109; Ranelagh, *The Agency*, 279; Richelson, *Community*, 394; FRUS/MEA, "5412"

9. National Security Council Directive (NSC) 5412/1, *National Security Council Directive On Covert Operations*, March 12, 1955, in FRUS/MEA; Treverton, *Covert Action*, 75.

10. Treverton, *Covert Action*, 75; Prados, *Presidents'*, 112.

11. Prados, *Presidents'*, 148.

12. NSCD-5412/2, "Directive On Covert Operations," 28 Decem-

ber 1955; Prados, *Presidents'*, 147; Ambrose, *Eisenhower*, 506–7; Cook, *Declassified*, 182; Treverton, *Covert Action*, 75; Ranelagh, *The Agency*, 279, 341, 346; Weber, *Spymasters*, 80; Karabell, *Architects*, 128; Peake, "Truman," 38; FRUS/MEA, "5412"; Andrew, *Eyes Only*, 212.

13. Recommended readings, among a host of materials, on this event include Gasiorowski, *Shah*; Gasiorowski, "Coup D'Etat"; Cottam, *Iran*; Bill, *Eagle*; Daugherty, *Ayatollah*; Roosevelt, *Countercoup*. The CIA's own history of the coup was obtained by *New York Times* reporter James Risen and published in the *Times* as "Secrets of History: The CIA in Iran," 16 April 2000, A1.

14. Karabell, *Architects*, 83.

15. Roosevelt, *Countercoup*, 210.

16. Draft NSC Policy Paper, August 19, 1953, cited in Cullather, *Guatemala*, 38.

17. Powers, *Man*, 85.

18. Ranelagh, *The Agency*, 266n; Karabell, *Architects*, 128; Prados, *Presidents'*, 105.

The whole story is recounted in Immerman, *Intervention*; Cullather, *Guatemala*; Schlesinger and Kinzer, *Bitter Fruit*, keeping in mind that the last is clearly prejudiced against the CIA and the intervention.

19. O'Toole, *Treachery*, 462.

20. Gaddis, *We Now Know*, 177–78.

21. Ibid., 178; Rabe, *Eisenhower*, 61.

22. Gaddis, *We Now Know*, 179–81.

23. Weiner, "Millions."

24. Bukovsky, "Secrets," 2 (page citations for this article relate to those of the Web version printout).

25. Collins and Tovar, "Sukarno," 338–39; Andrew, *Eyes Only*, 250.

26. Collins and Tovar, "Sukarno," 340–42.

27. Powers, *Man*, 88–89. See also Smith, *Portrait*, 205–48 for the personal account of one officer involved with Indonesian operations.

28. Collins and Tovar, "Sukarno," 340–42. Conboy and Morrison, *Feet*, at 12 and 176n22.

29. Conboy and Morrison, *Feet*, at 12.

30. Conboy and Morrison, *Feet*, at 12–13; Cline, *CIA*, 206.

31. Nutter, *Black*, 54, 56.

32. Samuel Halpern, cited in Weber, *Spymasters*, at 122.

33. Knaus, *Orphans*, 138, 139, 187.

34. Richard Bissell believed, based on meetings he attended in the Eisenhower White House, that Eisenhower's desire to see Lumumba's assassination is "one perfectly clear case." Bissell claimed that Ike regarded the

African as a "thorough scoundrel and a very dangerous one," and he wanted Lumumba "got rid of" by whatever means worked. See Weber, *Spymasters*, 104–6. See also Ranelagh, *The Agency*, 338; Trento, *Secret History*, 194; Nutter, *Black*, 58, citing US Senate, *Interim Report of the Select Committee to Study Governmental Operations with Respect to Intelligence Activities*, Book 6: "Alleged Assassination Plots Involving Foreign Leaders," 94th Congress, 1st Session, 1975, S. Rept. 94–465; Tuttle, "Secrecy," 528n38.

35. Andrew, *Eyes Only*, 253; Ranelagh, *The Agency*, 339–41. See De Witte, *Assassination*.

36. Prados, *Presidents'*, 176; Andrew, *Eyes Only*, 252; Nutter, *Black*, 15; Rabe, *Eisenhower*, 162.

37. Prados, *Presidents'*, 180.

38. Andrew, *Eyes Only*, 252. Andrew asserts that Eisenhower's words "strongly imply assassination" (252), and in light of Gray's comments, it is hard to think otherwise. Andrew believes any claim that the president was unaware of planning to assassinate Castro or that the planning was undertaken against Eisenhower's wishes is "barely conceivable" (253).

39: Rabe, *Eisenhower*, 152. See also Rabe, *Dangerous*, 35–40, for additional perspective on Trujillo, Eisenhower, and Kennedy.

40. Rabe, *Eisenhower*, 153–62; Weber, *Spymasters*, 83–90.

41. Nutter, *Black*, 71n37.

42. Weber, *Spymasters*, 73–74; Rabe, *Eisenhower*, 167.

43. Andrew, *Eyes Only*, 225, 233; Aldrich, *Hidden*, 482.

NINE: JOHN F. KENNEDY
AND LYNDON B. JOHNSON

1. Opening epigraph is from McNamara, *Retrospect*, 129–30.

2. Ranelagh, *The Agency*, 411; Prados, *Presidents'*, 197, 472. Some in the White House continued informally to refer to "5412," probably more out of habit than anything else. In an interview years afterward, Richard Bissell persistently used "5412" vice any of the other titles (Weber, *Spymasters*).

3. Weber, *Spymasters*, 71.

4. Prados, *Presidents'*, 211; Ranelagh, *The Agency*, 411; Andrew, *Eyes Only*, 272.

5. Ranelagh, *The Agency*, at 411; FRUS/MEA, "5412"

6. Andrew, *Eyes Only*, 272, 370; Ranelagh, *The Agency*, 411–12; FRUS/MEA, "5412." Treverton, in *Covert Action*, states that "some thousands of covert action projects between 1949 and 1968" were run by the

CIA with only "some six hundred" reviewed or approved by the extant NSC body, and that by 1970 only about "a fourth" of covert action programs were considered by the White House (at 230 and 234). However, it must be noted that those run by the DCI were under his appropriate delegated authority and constituted only very small, inexpensive, low-key ("routine," if any covert action programs can be considered such) operations with little or no ability to embarrass the president or the nation.

7. The threshold level was set at $25,000. FRUS/MEA, "5412" notes that while the Kennedy administration approved 163 covert action programs and the Johnson administration 142, these numbers represent only a fraction of the total programs run, in that the DCI through those years was still able to run minor programs without White House approval. It is also worth noting that many of Johnson's covert operations approved by the 303 Committee were in support of the war in Southeast Asia and, thus, outside the scope of this work.

8. Amazingly, the speaker was Henry Kissinger, who was architect of some of the programs that intervened directly in countries that manifestly did not present a genuine danger to American national interests (in *Twentieth Century, Need to Know*, at 39).

9. See Richelson, *Community*, 343–70, for a list of covert action programs in this era, not all of which have been officially acknowledged by the U.S. government.

10. O'Toole, *Treachery*, 483. Arguably, however, Bill Casey's tenure as DCI was a second "golden age of covert action."

11. Isenberg, "Pitfalls," 9.

12. Andrew, *Eyes Only*, 276; Dr. Ray S. Cline has remarked that both the president and his brother, Attorney General Bobby Kennedy, held "very bitter personal feelings" toward Castro, even referring to it as an "obsession." See Weber, *Spymasters*, 201–3.

13. Andrew, *Eyes Only*, 272, 275; Ranelagh, *The Agency*, 411; Richelson gives the operational dates for Mongoose as November 1961 to January 1963 in *Community*, 343.

14. Barry, "Managing," 22; Godson, *Tricks*, 45. As with Iran and Guatemala, analysis of the Chilean program has assumed a life of its own, and as such exceeds the scope of this work. Hence, just the basic policy elements will be mentioned. Much of the information in this section and in subsequent chapters comes from the findings of the Church Committee. See *Staff Report of the Select Committee to Study Governmental Operations with Respect to Intelligence Activities*, "Covert Action in Chile 1963–1973," 94th Cong., 1st Session, December 1975. The version used in the book is found at http://foia.state.gov/Church report.htm (the print-

out is seventy-eight pages, and page numbers will refer to this version, vice any published edition). A highly readable synopsis of the program may be found in Kristian C. Gustafson's "CIA Machinations in Chile in 1970: Reexamining the Record," *Studies in Intelligence* 47, no. 3 (2003, unclassified version).

15. Godson, *Tricks*, 45; Colby, "CIA's," 76–77.

16. Kaiser, *Tragedy*, 15; Gaddis, *We Now Know*, 186.

17. Rabe, *Eisenhower*, states that it was the assistant secretary of state for Latin America, R. Richard Rubottm, who approved the arms transfers, at 157.

18. Weber, *Spymasters*, 83–90

19. Knaus, *Orphans*, 245.

20. Ibid., 245–46.

21. Ibid., 296.

22. McNamara, *Retrospect*, 129; Weber, *Spymasters*, 254. DCI Richard Helms believed that the book revealing the Special Group was *The Invisible Government* by Thomas B. Ross and David Wise; however, another work by the same authors, *The Espionage Establishment*, references the 5412/Special Group at 169–70. Helms also states that he, as DCI, was a member of the group and not the DDCI (Weber, *Spymasters*, at 254). For some reason mythology has the 303 Committee taking its name from a room it supposedly convened in, either in the Old Executive Office Building or at Main State.

23. These programs were considered for acknowledgment (which is not synonymous with "declassification") by a "high level" panel of officers from the State Department, the CIA, and the NSC, for possible inclusion in the *FRUS* series.

24. Minutes, 303 Committee, Section 7, *Italy-Covert Action Program for Italy in FY 1966*, of 28 June 1965. The document may be found either in State's INR Historical Files or on the Web at www.fas.org/sgp/advisoryu/state/italy.html.

25. *Hinchey*, 3. This report was ordered in the FY 2000 Intelligence Authorization Act, which required the National Intelligence Council and the intelligence community to review documents relating to Chile. Page numbers for this source relate to the Web document printout.

TEN: RICHARD M. NIXON AND GERALD R. FORD

1. Opening epigraph quoted in Smist, *Congress*, 213.

2. Andrew, *Eyes Only*, 387; Prados, *Presidents'*, 298, 337.

3. Kissinger, *White House Years*, 660; Richelson, *Community*, 394. Prados is skeptical of the press exposure reason; see *Presidents'*, 322.

4. Treverton, *Covert Action*, 234; Richelson, *Community*, 394; Ranelagh, *The Agency*, 539.

5. See Smist, *Congress*, 191–94, for enlightenment as to how Kissinger (mis)used this confluence of power.

6. Kissinger, *White House Years*, 660, 465n, 661; Prados, *Presidents'*, 323; Ranelagh, *The Agency*, 500.

7. Kissinger, *White House Years*, 660.

8. According to Prados, Mitchell contributed almost nothing to the meetings he attended save for pipe smoke (*Presidents'*, 323).

9. Kissinger, *White House Years*, 660.

10. Ibid.

11. Prados, *Presidents'*, 322, 472, 516n; Treverton, *Covert Action*, 234; Church Report, 52, 64, 77. For examples of how this tightly controlled secrecy was hidden from CIA analysts, some of the issues involved, and the consequences, see Colby and Forbath, *Honorable*, 355–56.

12. Prados, *Presidents'*, 323, 516n; Smist, *Congress*, 195; Church Report, 53, 61.

13. Andrew, *Eyes Only*, 370; Church Report, 34. As with Iran and Guatemala, there has been much written on this particular program, and therefore, it shall not receive a fulsome account in this work.

14. Brewer and Teitelbaum, *Policy*, 263.

15. Johnson, "Accountability," 85; Ranelagh, *The Agency*, 539; Andrew, *Eyes Only*, 371–72.

16. Andrew, *Eyes Only*, 371–72; Prados, *Presidents'*, 317, citing Special Group minutes (not further specified).

17. Church Report, 11.

18. *Hinchey*, 2.

19. Melvin Goodman, in Eisendrath, *National Insecurity*, 32.

20. Pike Committee Report, 192–218. See also Lowenthal, *Intelligence*, 134; Treverton, *Covert Action*, 115; Codevilla, *Statecraft*, 262–63; Prados, *Presidents'*, 313–15; Nutter, *Black*, 155–56.

21. See Kissinger, *White House Years*, 1202–57, for his detailed account of the summit. Also Nixon, *RN*, 609–21.

22. Wicker, *One of Us*, 664; Kissinger, *White House Years*, 1265.

23. Pike Committee Report, 195 *et. Seq*; Pallister, "Abandoned," 2 (page numbers coincide with Lexis-Nexis printout).

24. Pallister, "Abandoned," 1; Codevilla, in *Statecraft*, gives similar figures at 263.

25. Pike Committee Report, 197. See inter alia Sick, *All Fall Down*,

13; Prados, *Presidents'*, 313–15; Codevilla, *Statecraft*, 263; Schorr, "Kissinger," at D3; Pallister, "Abandoned," 2; Nutter, *Black*, 155–56; Wise, "CIA," at A35.

26. Executive Order 11905, 18 February 1976, 41 FR 7703; Ranelagh, *The Agency*, 627 (text and note); Cline, *CIA*, 264; Andrew, *Eyes Only*, 419; Prados, *Presidents'*, 349.

27. Johnson, "Accountability," 96.

28. Gates, *Shadows*, 76.

29. Treverton, *Covert Action*, 26, 59, 148–60, 167–68, 173–74.

30. Meyer, *Reality*, 243.

31. Gates, *Shadows*, 66; Meyer, *Reality*, 249–53.

32. Gates, *Shadows*, 66. Codevilla claims in *Statecraft* that the July Finding was for $32 million in "food, arms, and other supplies," at 264.

33. Isenberg, "Pitfalls," 10.

34. Codevilla, *Statecraft*, 265.

ELEVEN: JIMMY CARTER

1. Opening epigraph is from Gates, *Shadows*, 567.

2. Twentieth Century, *Need to Know*, 50; Gates, *Shadows*, 136. A succinct recounting of this "180" transformation may be found in Crile, *Charlie Wilson's*, 14–15.

3. Tuttle, "Secrecy," 512. Tuttle mentions that Carter's first choice to head the CIA was Ted Sorenson, who had been a speech writer in the JFK administration and a conscientious objector during Vietnam, and who held "hostile views" toward the CIA (530n47).

4. Executive Order 12036, *United States Intelligence Activities*, 24 January 1978, 42 FR 4311. The national security advisor chaired SCC meetings. See also Brzezinski, *Power*, 59–63; Johnson, "Accountability," 96.

5. Johnson, "Accountability," 96.

6. Turner, *Secrecy*, 169; also cited in Johnson, "Accountability," at 96.

7. Johnson, "Accountability," 96–97.

8. Gates, *Shadows*, 85, 89–91, 142; Godson, *Tricks*, 18.

9. Gates, *Shadows*, 91; Meyer, *Reality*, 395.

10. Brzezinski, *Power*, 461; Bernstein and Politi, *His Holiness*, 258–59; Gates, *Shadows*, 90–95.

11. Gates, *Shadows*, 145–46; Blum and Gibbs, "Révélations," 1.

12. Blum and Gibbs, "Révélations," 2.

13. Gates, *Shadows*, 148–49.

14. Smist, *Congress*, 326.
15. Gates, *Shadows*, 149–50.
16. Woodward, "Carlucci," A1.
17. Ibid.
18. Godson, *Tricks*, 55.
19. Gates, *Shadows*, 150–51.
20. Ibid., 73–74; Brzezinski, *Power*, 429.
21. Gates, *Shadows*, 143.

TWELVE: RONALD W. REAGAN

1. Opening epigraph is from Woodward, *VEIL*, 233, and refers to differences between Casey's CIA and the U.S. Congress in December 1983.

2. See Gates, *Shadows*, 251, for the Afghan Finding and program; 346–48 for the Angola program; 242 for mention of the Findings on Central America, Cambodia, Ethiopia, and Lebanon; 73–74 for the Ethiopian program; 536 for the covert programs for the USSR and Eastern Europe; 358 for the Polish/pro-Solidarity program; 319–21, 322 for Cambodia; and 348–50 for Afghanistan. The unclassified *Joint Inquiry Into The Terrorist Attacks of September 11, 2001* cites the March 1986 Finding for Counterterrorism in the Appendix, "Evolution of the Terrorist Threat," at chart 2. See Bearden and Risen, *Main Enemy*, 205–368, for a fulsome accounting of the Afghan program.

3. See inter alia Gates, *Shadows*, passim; Godson, *Tricks*, 278n89; Bernstein and Politi, *His Holiness*; and West, *Third Secret*.

4. National Security Decision Directive-2, *National Security Council Structure*, 12 January 1982.

5. Woodward, *VEIL*, 173; Persico, *Casey*, 227.

6. Treverton, *Covert Action*, 251; Prados, *Presidents'*, 376; Persico, *Casey*, 227; Woodward, *VEIL*, 181.

7. Schewizer, *Victory*, xix and 19.

8. Executive Order 12333, *United States Intelligence Activities*.

9. Prados, *Presidents'*, 376.

10. Reisman and Baker, *Regulating*, 124; Bruemmer and Silverberg, "Impact," 235.

11. The first iteration of this document was NSDD-276, which Secretary of State George Schultz rejected over differences of chairmanships of the two review committees subordinate to the NSC. Reagan signed it, but it was soon replaced by NSDD-286. See Schultz, *Turmoil*, 903–9.

12. Intelligence Authorization Act, FY 1991, Pub. L. No. 102-88.

13. Schultz, *Triumph*, 292–97; Woodward, *VEIL*, 240.

14. Gates, *Shadows*, 358; West, *Third Secret*, 201.

15. Bernstein, "Alliance," 28; Andrew, *Eyes Only*, 168; Schewizer, *Victory*, xvi.

16. Gates, *Shadows*, 357. There is unapproved discussion of NSDD-32's alleged covert action content in Schweizer, *Victory*, at xviii–xix, 77, 228, 257; and in Bernstein, "Alliance," at 28.

17. Gates, *Shadows*, 357.

18. NSDD-54, *United States Policy Towards Eastern Europe*, 2 September 1982.

19. NSDD-75, *U.S. Relations with the USSR*, 17 January 1983.

20. Schweizer, *Victory*, 189, 249.

21. Gates, *Shadows*, 536; Weiss, "Farewell," 5.

22. Bernstein, "Alliance," 28.

23. Ibid. The administration had decided within two weeks of inauguration that it would "make a stand on Poland—not only to prevent a Soviet invasion but to seek ways to undermine [Communist] power" there; Bernstein and Politi, *His Holiness*, 262.

24. Bernstein, "Alliance," 28.

25. Ibid.

26. Schweizer, *Victory*, 75; Bernstein, "Alliance," 28.

27. Schweizer, *Victory*, 159; Andrew, *Eyes Only*, 468.

28. Gates, *Shadows*, 358; West, *Third Secret*, 206–9.

29. Bukovsky, "Secrets," 9–11; Gates, *Shadows*, 242, 297.

30. Woodward, *VEIL*, 173; Pike, "Budget," 7. Highlighting the difficulty that the administration would ultimately have in keeping covert operations in Central America secret, the *Christian Science Monitor* published detailed information about the Argentine unit and the costs associated with operations in Honduras and Nicaragua within a year of the administration's signing of the Finding ("Nicaragua," 24).

31. Related to the author by a staff member of HPSCI.

32. Johnson, *Bombs*, 48; Schultz, *Triumph*, 308; Persico, *Casey*, 373. The author was told by several senior Agency officers who briefed the NSPG in the Reagan years how surprised they were initially when the president personally showed up to chair these meetings.

33. Cline, "Prerogative," 367; Newsom, "Guerrillas," 14.

34. Gates, *Shadows*, 295. One shining example of zealotry passing as patriotism is the case of former assistant secretary of state for inter-American affairs Elliott Abrams, who was considered to be such a zealot that his trustworthiness was placed in question. Some members of Congress would let him testify only if he was placed under oath first. Indeed, Lawrence Walsh, the Iran-Contra special prosecutor, intended to indict

Abrams on a felony charge of lying to Congress but ultimately accepted a plea bargain of two misdemeanor counts of withholding information. While in office, Abrams was quick to label those who spoke in opposition to the Reagan administration's Central American policy as "Un-American," "unpatriotic," or worse. Yet after his sentencing, Abrams, while talking to the press and alluding to the criticism that he was subjected to, bemoaned how unfortunate it was that American citizens couldn't express their beliefs without becoming the target of personal attacks!

35. Gates, *Shadows*, 299–301. It has been alleged that the program leaked soon thereafter and the seizure of arms dwindled; Woodward, *VEIL*, 228–29.

36. Cline, "Prerogative," 367. The story of Congress's most ardent supporter of the Afghan program is told in George Crile's *Charlie Wilson's War*. See also Bearden and Risen, *Main Enemy*.

37. Richelson, *Community*, 363; Smist, *Congress*, 327.

38. Bearden and Risen, *Main Enemy*, 210; Gates, *Shadows*, 319–21; Pike, "Budget," 7; Grier, "Beefing Up," 20.

39. Schweizer, *Victory*, 283.

40. Ibid., 213–14.

41. The author has been told, but has also been unable to verify, that the death toll was even higher, as Marines listed as "missing in action" have never been redesignated as "killed in action," despite the passage of two decades.

42. This bomber was shot dead by the bodyguard before he could enter the embassy garage. The bombing never should have happened, but the American ambassador, Reginald Bartholomew, was so anxious to move from temporary quarters in the British Embassy to the new Annex that he insisted the move take place before all the antiterrorist devices were in place, including especially the "pop-up" barriers that would have stopped a vehicle well before it could get close to the building. As it was, only the good shooting by the bodyguard waiting outside the Annex kept the bomber from the underground garage. For this egregious act of poor judgment, Bartholomew went on to bigger and better assignments in the State Department and administration.

43. Schultz, *Triumph*, 645.

44. Clarridge and Diehl, *Spy*, 324–27. See Joint Inquiry at 279 for confirmation to Congress of the existence of the 1986 Finding.

45. Codevilla, *Statecraft*, 273; Woodward, *VEIL*, 157–58, 215.

46. Gates, *Shadows*, 336; Schultz, *Triumph*, 1119.

47. Mathias and Leahy, "Covert," 14.

48. Woodward, *VEIL*, 216, 373; Reisman and Baker, *Regulating*, 209, citing language in the vetoed version of the Intelligence Authorization Act of 1991.

THIRTEEN: GEORGE H.W. BUSH AND WILLIAM J. CLINTON

1. Opening epigraph may be found in Hoagland, "Costs," A27, citing George H.W. Bush's biography for the 1988 presidential campaign, *Looking Forward*.
2. Johnson, *Bombs*, 180.
3. National Security Review-29, *Intelligence Capabilities 1992–2005*, of 15 November 1991.
4. National Security Directive-1, *Organization of the National Security Council System*, 30 January 1989.
5. Presidential Decision Directive-2, *Organization of the National Security Council*, 20 January 1993.
6. *Killing Pablo*, by Mark Bowden, is an excellent account of how the most dangerous cartel and its leader were destroyed.
7. Joint Report, Appendix: "Evolution of the Terrorist Threat and the US Response," 8.
8. Joint Report, Appendix: "Evolution of the Terrorist Threat and the US Response," 9.
9. Joint Report at 281, 285.
10. Pincus, "Boutique," A-06.
11. Ibid.

CONCLUSION

1. Opening epigraph is found in Twentieth Century, *Need to Know*, at 75.
2. Ignatius, "Innocence," C1.
3. Johnson, "Accountability," 106.

BIBLIOGRAPHY

SOURCES AND IDENTIFICATION IN NOTES

Foreign Relations of the United States—FRUS
Foreign Relations of the United States, 1945–1950, Emergence of the Intelligence Establishment—FRUS/EIE
Foreign Relations of the United States, 1964–1968, Africa—FRUS/AF
Foreign Relations of the United States, 1964–1968, Mainland Southeast Asia; Regional Affairs—FRUS/MSA
Foreign Relations of the United States, 1964–1968, Western Europe— FRUS/WE
Foreign Relations of the United States, Vol. III, British Commonwealth; Western and Central Europe, 1947, FRUS/BC
The Hinchey Report: CIA Activities in Chile (18 September 2000)— Hinchey. (Located at www.foia.state.gov/HincheyReport.htm, accessed 25 November 2000.)
Office of Policy Coordination, 1948–1952 (CIA Official History)—OPC/CIA

GOVERNMENT DOCUMENTS

Central Intelligence Group, *Review of the World Situation as it Relates to the Security of the United States*, 26 September 1946.
Department of Defense Directive 3600.1, *Information Operations*, October 2001.
Executive Order 11905, *United States Foreign Intelligence Activities*, 18 February 1976, 41 FR 7703.
Executive Order 12036, *United States Foreign Intelligence Activities*, 24 January 1978, 43 CFR 3674 (revoked by Executive Order 12333).
Executive Order 12333, *United States Intelligence Activities*, 4 December

Bibliography

1981, 3 CFR 200 (1981, 46 FR 59955 (as amended by Executive Order 12701, 14 February 1990, 55 FR 5933).

Hughes-Ryan Amendment to the 1961 Foreign Assistance Act, Pub. L. No. 187-195, para. 662 (1974) codified as amended at 22 USC 2422 (1998), section 662.

Intelligence Authorization Act of 1991, Pub. L. 102–88, 105 Stat, 429 (1991), Section 503[c][4][e].

Intelligence Oversight Act of 1980, adopted as part of the Intelligence Authorization Act of 1991, as amended by the Intelligence Authorization Act of 1991, at Title V of the National Security Act, 50 USC 413.

National Security Act of 1947, 50 USC 403.

NSC-1/1, *The Position of the United States with Respect to Italy*, 14 November 1947.

NSC-1/2, *The Position of the United States with Respect to Italy*, 12 March 1948.

NSC-1/3, *Position of the United States with Respect to Italy in the Light of the Possibility of Communist Participation in the Government by Legal Means*, 12 March 1948.

NSC-4, *Coordination of Foreign Intelligence Information Measures*, 14 December 1947.

NSC-4A, *Annex to NSC-4*, 17 December 1947.

NSC-10/5, *Scope and Pace of Covert Operations*, 23 October 1951.

NSC-20/4, *U.S. Objectives with Respect to the USSR to Counter Soviet Threats to U.S. Security*, 24 November 1948.

NSC-162/2, *Basic National Security Policy*, 30 October 1953.

NSC-5412, *National Security Council Directive on Covert Operations*, 15 March 1954.

NSC-5412/1, *Note by the Executive Secretary to the National Security Council on Covert Actions*, 15 March 1954.

NSC-5412/2, *Directive on Covert Operations*, 28 December 1955.

National Security Decision Directive-2, *National Security Council Structure*, 12 January 1982.

National Security Decision Directive-32, *U.S. National Security Strategy*, 12 November 1982.

National Security Decision Directive-54, *United States Policy Toward Eastern Europe*, 2 September 1982.

National Security Decision Directive-75, *U.S. Relations with the USSR*, 17 January 1983.

National Security Decision Directive-159, *Covert Action Policy Approval and Coordination Procedures*, 18 January 1985.

National Security Decision Directive-286, *Approval and Review of Special Activities*, 15 October 1987.

Bibliography

National Security Decision Memorandum-40, *Responsibility for the Conduct, Supervision, and Coordination of Covert Action Operations*, 17 February 1970.

National Security Directive-1, *Organization of the National Security Council System*, 30 January 1989.

National Security Presidential Directive-1, *Organization of the National Security System*, 13 February 2001.

National Security Review-29, *Intelligence Capabilities 1992–2005*, of 15 November 1991.

Presidential Decision Directive-2, *Organization of the National Security Council*, 20 January 1993.

Presidential Decision Directive-35, *Intelligence Requirements / National Needs Process*, 2 March 1995.

Presidential Decision Directive-39, *Counterterrorism Policy*, 21 June 1995.

Special Operations Forces Command Authority, 10 USC 167.

Testimony of Warren Marik Before The Subcommittee on Technology, Terrorism, and Government Information, Senate Judiciary Committee.

United States House of Representatives, Select Committee on Intelligence, 94th Congress, 1st Sess. 1976. [Pike Committee Report]

United States House of Representatives Permanent Select Committee on Intelligence and the United States Senate Select Committee on Intelligence, *Joint Inquiry Into Intelligence Community Activities Before and After the Terrorist Acts of September 11, 2001*, December 2002, 107th Congress, S. Rept. No. 107-351 and H. Rept. 107-792. [Joint Report]

United States Senate, *Alleged Assassination Plots Involving Foreign Leaders: An Interim Report of the Select Committee to Study Governmental Operations with Respect to Intelligence Activities*, Book 6: 94th Congress, 1st Session, 1975, S. Rept. No. 94-465 (20 November 1975). [Church Committee Report]

United States Senate, *Final Report of the Select Committee to Study Governmental Operations with Respect to Intelligence Activities*, 94th Cong., 1st Session, S. Rept. No. 94-755 (26 April 1976). [Church Committee Report].

United States Senate, *Staff Report of the Select Committee to Study Governmental Operations with Respect to Intelligence Activities*, "Covert Action in Chile 1963–1973," 94th Cong., 1st Session, December 1975. [Church Committee Report].

BOOKS

Acheson, Dean. *Present at the Creation*. New York: W.W. Norton, 1969.

Bibliography

Aldrich, Richard J. *The Hidden Hand: Britain, America, and Cold War Secret Intelligence.* New York: Overlook Press, 2002.

Ambrose, Stephen E. *Eisenhower: The President.* New York: Simon & Schuster, 1989.

————. *Ike's Spies.* New York: Doubleday, 1981.

————. *Nixon: Volume Two: The Triumph of a Politician, 1962–1972.* New York: Simon & Schuster, 1989.

Andrew, Christopher. *For the President's Eyes Only.* New York: Harper-Collins, 1995.

————, and Oleg Gordievsky. *KGB: The Inside Story of Its Operations From Lenin to Gorbachev.* New York: HarperCollins, 1992.

————, Oleg Gordievsky, and Vasili Mitrokhin. *The Sword and the Shield: The Mitrokhin Archive and the Secret History of the KGB.* New York: Basic Books, 1999.

Baer, Robert. *See No Evil: The True Story of a Ground Soldier in the CIA's War on Terrorism.* New York: Crown, 2002.

Bearden, Milt, and James Risen. *The Main Enemy: The Inside Story of the CIA's Final Showdown with the KGB.* New York: Random House, 2003.

Beckwith, Charlie A., and Donald Knox. *Delta Force.* New York: Harcourt Brace Jovanovich, 1983.

Berkowitz, Bruce D., and Allen E. Goodman. *Best Truth: Intelligence in the Information Age.* New Haven: Yale University Press, 200.

Bernstein, Carl, and Marco Politi. *His Holiness: John Paul II and the History of Our Time.* New York: Penguin Books, 1997.

Bill, James. *The Eagle and the Lion: The Tragedy of American-Iranian Relations.* New Haven: Yale University Press, 1988.

Bittman, Ladislav. *The Deception Game: Czechoslovak Intelligence in Soviet Political Warfare.* Syracuse: Syracuse University Research Corp., 1972.

————. *The KGB and Soviet Disinformation: An Insider's View.* McLean, Virginia: Pergamon-Brassey's, 1985.

Bowden, Mark. *Killing Pablo: The Hunt for the World's Greatest Outlaw.* New York: Atlantic Monthly Press, 2001.

Bowie, Robert R., and Richard H. Immerman. *Waging Peace: How Eisenhower Shaped an Enduring Cold War Strategy.* New York: Oxford University Press, 1998.

Brewer, Thomas C., and Lorne Teitelbaum. *American Foreign Policy: A Contemporary Introduction (4th ed.).* Saddle River, N.J.: Prentice-Hall, 1999

Brzezinski, Zbigniew. *Power and Principle: Memoirs of the National Security Advisor, 1977–1981.* New York: Farrar Straus Giroux, 1983.

Bibliography

Carter, James Earl. *Keeping Faith: Memoirs of a President* (3rd ed.). Fayetteville: University of Arkansas Press, 1995.

Carter, John J. *Covert Operations as a Tool of Presidential Foreign Policy in American History from 1800 to 1920.* Lewiston, NY: Edwin Mellen Press, 2000.

Clarridge, Duane R., and Digby Diehl. *A Spy for All Seasons: My Life in the CIA.* New York: Scribner's, 1997.

Cline, Ray S. *The CIA Under Reagan, Bush, and Casey.* Washington, D.C.: Acropolis Books, Ltd., 1981.

Cochran, Burt. *Harry Truman and the Crisis Presidency.* New York: Funk & Wagnalls, 1973.

Codevilla, Angelo. *Informing Statecraft: Intelligence for a New Century.* New York: The Free Press, 1992.

Colby, William E., and Peter Forbath. *Honorable Men: My Life in the CIA.* New York: Simon & Schuster, 1971.

Conboy, Kenneth, and James Morrison. *Feet to the Fire: CIA Covert Operations in Indonesia, 1957–1958.* Annapolis: United States Naval Institute, 1999.

———. *Shadow War: The CIA's Secret War in Laos.* Boulder, CO: Paladin Press, 1995.

Cook, Blanche Wiesen. *The Declassified Eisenhower.* New York: Penguin, 1984.

Copeland, Miles. *The Game of Nations: The Amorality of Power Politics.* New York: Simon & Schuster, 1969.

Cottam, Richard W. *Iran and the United States: A Cold War Case Study.* Pittsburgh: University of Pittsburgh Press, 1988.

Crile, George. *Charlie Wilson's War: The Extraordinary Story of the Largest Covert Operation in History.* New York: Atlantic Monthly Press, 2003.

Cullather, Nick. *Secret History: The CIA's Classified Account of Its Operations in Guatemala, 1952–1954.* Stanford: Stanford University Press, 1999.

Darling, Arthur B. *The Central Intelligence Agency: An Instrument of Government, to 1950.* University Park, PA: Pennsylvania State University Press, 1990.

Daugherty, William J. *In the Shadow of the Ayatollah: A CIA Hostage in Iran.* Annapolis: United States Naval Institute Press, 2001.

De Witte, Ludo. *The Assassination of Lumumba.* New York: Verso, 2001.

Dorril, Stephen. *MI-6: Inside the Covert World of Her Majesty's Secret Intelligence Service.* New York: The Free Press, 2000.

Draper, Theodore. *A Very Thin Line: The Iran-Contra Affairs.* New York: Hill and Wang, 1991.

Bibliography

Eisendrath, Craig, ed. *National Insecurity: US Intelligence After the Cold War*. Philadelphia: Temple University Press, 2000.

Eisenhower, Dwight D. *Mandate for Change*. Garden City: Doubleday & Co., 1963.

Emerson, Steven. *The Secret Warriors: Inside the Covert Military Operations of the Reagan Era*. New York: G.P. Putnam's Sons, 1988.

Epstein, Edward Jay. *Deception: The Invisible War Between the CIA and KGB*. New York: Simon & Schuster, 1989.

Feis, Herbert. *From Trust to Terror: The Onset of the Cold War, 1945–1950*. New York: W.W. Norton, 1970.

Felix, Christopher. *A Short Course in the Secret War*. Lanham, MD: Madison Books, 1992.

Ferrell, Robert H. *The Eisenhower Diaries*. New York: W.W. Norton, 1981.

Gaddis, John Lewis. *We Now Know: Rethinking Cold War History*. New York: Oxford University Press, 1997.

Gasiorowski, Mark J. *U.S. Foreign Policy and the Shah: Building a Client State in Iran*. Ithaca: Cornell University Press, 1991.

Gates, Robert M. *From the Shadows: The Ultimate Insider's Story of Five Presidents and How They Won the Cold War*. New York: Simon & Schuster, 1996.

Garvey, Glenn. *Everybody Had His Own Gringo: The CIA and the Contras*. Washington, DC: Brassey's, 1992.

Godson, Roy. *Dirty Tricks or Trump Cards: US Covert Action and Counterintelligence*. New Brunswick, NJ: Transaction Publishers, 2001.

Gosnell, Harold F. *Truman's Crises*. Westport, CT.: Greenwood Press, 1980.

Grose, Peter. *Operation Rollback*. New York: Houghton-Mifflin, 2000.

Hamilton-Merritt, Jane. *Tragic Mountains: The Hmong, the Americans, and the Secret Wars for Laos, 1942–1992*. Bloomington: Indiana University Press, 1999.

Haney, Eric L. *Inside Delta Force: The Story of America's Elite Counterterrorist Unit*. New York: Delacorte Press, 2002.

Holm, Richard L. *The American Agent: My Life in the CIA*. London, England: St. Ermin's Press, 2002.

Holt, Pat M. *Secret Intelligence and Public Policy*. Washington, DC: CQ Press, 1995.

Immerman, Richard H. *The CIA in Guatemala: The Foreign Policy of Intervention*. Austin: University of Texas Press, 1982.

Janda, Kenneth, Jeffery M. Berry, and Jerry Goldman. *The Challenge of Democracy: Government in America* (5th ed.). Boston: Houghton Mifflin, 1997.

Bibliography

Jefferys-Jones, Rhodri, and Christopher Andrew, eds. *Eternal Vigilance? Fifty Years of the CIA.* London: Frank Cass, 1997.

Johnson, Loch. *America's Secret Power: The CIA in a Democratic Society.* New York: Oxford University Press, 1989.

———. *A Season of Inquiry: Congress and Intelligence.* Chicago: Dorsey Press, 1988.

———. *Bombs, Bugs, Drugs, and Thugs: Intelligence and America's Quest for Security.* New York: New York University Press, 2000.

———. *Secret Agencies: US Intelligence in a Hostile World.* New Haven: Yale University Press, 1996.

Kaiser, David. *American Tragedy: Kennedy, Johnson, and the Origins of the Vietnam War.* Cambridge, MA: Belknap Press, 2000.

Karabell, Zachary. *Architects of Intervention: The United States, the Third World, and the Cold War, 1946–1962.* Baton Rouge: Louisiana State University Press, 1999.

Kimball, Jeffery. *Nixon's Vietnam War.* Lawrence: University Press of Kansas, 1998.

Kissinger, Henry. *White House Years.* Boston: Little Brown, 1979.

———. *Years of Upheaval.* Boston: Little Brown, 1982.

Knaus, John Kenneth. *Orphans of the Cold War: America and the Tibetan Struggle for Survival.* New York: PublicAffairs/Perseus Books, 1999.

Knott, Stephen F. *Secret and Sanctioned: Covert Operations and the American Presidency.* New York: Oxford University Press, 1996.

Kuhns, Woodrow J., ed. *Assessing the Soviet Threat.* Washington, DC: Center for the Study of Intelligence, Central Intelligence Agency, 1997.

Kuzichkin, Vladimir. *My Life in Soviet Espionage.* New York: Ivy Books, 1990.

Kyle, James H., and John Robert Eidson. *The Guts to Try: The Untold Story of the Iran Hostage Rescue Mission by the On-Scene Desert One Commander.* New York: Orion Books, 1990.

Lake, Anthony. *Six Nightmares: Real Threats in a Dangerous World and How America Can Meet Them.* New York: Little Brown, 2000.

Laqueur, Walter. *The Uses and Limits of Intelligence.* Brunswick, NJ: Transaction Press, 1995.

Lert, Frédéric. *Wings of the CIA.* Paris, France: Histoire and Collections, 1999.

Lockhart, Robin Bruce. *Reilly, Ace of Spies.* New York: Viking Press, 1984.

Logevall, Fredrik. *Choosing War: The Lost Chance for Peace and the*

Bibliography

Escalation of War in Vietnam. Berkeley: University of California Press, 1999

Lowenthal, Mark M. *Intelligence: From Secrets to Policy* (2nd ed.). Washington, DC: CQ Press, 2003.

Mahl, Thomas E. *Desperate Deception: British Covert Operations in the United States, 1939–1941*. Washington, DC: Brassey's, 1998.

Martin, David C. and John Walcott. *Best Laid Plans: The Inside Story of America's War Against Terrorism*. New York: Harper & Row, 1988.

McNamara, Robert S. *In Retrospect: The Tragedy and Lessons of Vietnam*. New York: Vintage Books, 1996.

Meyer, Cord. *Facing Reality: From World Federalism to the CIA*. New York: Harper & Row, 1980.

Montague, Ewen. *The Man Who Never Was: World War Two's Boldest Counter-Intelligence Operation*. Annapolis: U.S. Naval Institute Press, 2000.

Nixon, Richard M. *RN: The Memoirs of Richard Nixon*. New York, Grosset & Dunlap, 1978.

Nutter, John Jacob. *The CIA's Black Ops: Covert Action, Foreign Policy, and Democracy*. Amherst, NY: Prometheus Books, 2000.

Olmsted, Kathryn S. *Challenging the Secret Government: The Post–Watergate Investigations of the CIA and FBI*. Chapel Hill: University of North Carolina Press, 1996.

O'Toole, G.J.A. *Honorable Treachery: A History of US Intelligence, Espionage, and Covert Action From the American Revolution to the CIA*. New York: Atlantic Monthly Press, 1991.

Parker, James E. *Code-Name Mule: The CIA's Secret War in Laos*. Annapolis: United States Naval Institute Press, 1992.

Persico, Joseph E. *Casey, From the OSS to the CIA*. New York: Viking, 1990.

Pisani, Sallie. *The CIA and the Marshall Plan*. Lawrence: University Press of Kansas, 1991.

Polmar, Norman, and Thomas B. Allen. *Spy Book: The Encyclopedia of Espionage*. New York: Random House, 1997.

Powers, Thomas. *The Man Who Kept the Secrets: Richard Helms and the CIA*. New York: Alfred A. Knopf, 1979.

Prados, John. *The Blood Road: The Ho Chi Minh Trail and the Vietnam War*. New York: John Wiley and Sons, 1999.

———. *Presidents' Secret Wars* (rev. ed.). Chicago: Ivan R. Dees, 1996.

Rabe, Stephen G. *Eisenhower and Latin America: The Foreign Policy of Anti-Communism*. Chapel Hill: University of North Carolina Press, 1988.

Bibliography

———. *The Most Dangerous Area in the World: John F. Kennedy Confronts Communist Revolution in Latin America.* Chapel Hill: University of North Carolina Press, 1999.

Ranelagh, John. *The Agency: The Rise and Decline of the CIA.* New York: Simon & Schuster, 1986.

Reisman, Michael W., and James E. Baker. *Regulating Covert Action: Practices, Contexts, and Policies of Covert Coercion Abroad in International and National American Law.* New Haven: Yale University Press, 1992.

Richelson, Jeffery T. *The U.S. Intelligence Community* (3rd ed.). Boulder, CO: Westview Press, 1995.

Robbins, Christopher. *Air America.* New York: Avon Books, 1979.

———. *The Ravens: The Story of the Men Who Flew in America's Secret War in Laos.* New York: Crown, 1987.

Roosevelt, Kermit. *Countercoup: The Struggle for Control of Iran.* New York: McGraw-Hill, 1979.

Rositzke, Harry. *The CIA's Secret Operations.* New York: Readers Digest, 1977.

Ryan, Paul B. *The Iranian Rescue Mission: Why it Failed.* Annapolis: U.S. Naval Institute Press, 1984.

Saunders, Frances Stoner. *The Cultural Cold War: The CIA and the World of Arts and Letters.* New York: The New Press, 1999.

Schewizer, Peter. *Victory: The Reagan Administration's Secret Strategy That Hastened the Collapse of the Soviet Union.* New York: Atlantic Monthly Press, 1994.

Schlesinger, Stephen, and Stephen Kinzer. *Bitter Fruit: The Untold Story of the American Coup in Guatemala.* Garden City: Doubleday/Anchor Press, 1983.

Schwartau, Winn. *Information Warfare: Chaos on the Electronic Superhighway.* New York: Thunder's Mouth Press, 1994.

Shultz, George P. *Triumph and Turmoil: My Years as Secretary of State.* New York: Scribner's, 1993.

Sick, Gary. *All Fall Down: America's Tragic Encounter with Iran.* New York: Random House, 1985.

Smist, Frank J., Jr. *Congress Oversees the United States Intelligence Community.* Knoxville: University of Tennessee Press, 1994.

Smith, Joseph Burkholder. *Portrait of a Cold Warrior.* New York: G.P. Putnam's, 1976.

Thomas, Evan. *The Very Best Men: Four Who Dared: The Early Years of the CIA.* New York: Simon & Schuster, 1995.

Trento, Joseph J. *The Secret History of the CIA.* Roseville, CA: Prima/Forum Publishing, 2001.

Bibliography

Treverton, Gregory F. *Covert Action: The CIA and American Intervention in the Postwar World.* London: I.B. Tauris & Co. Ltd., 1987.

Turner, Stansfield. *Secrecy and Democracy.* Boston: Houghton Mifflin, 1985.

———. *Terrorism and Democracy.* Boston: Houghton Mifflin, 1985.

Twentieth Century Fund. *The Need to Know: The Report of the Twentieth Century Fund Task Force on Covert Action and American Democracy.* New York: Twentieth Century Fund Press, 1992.

Walsh, Lawrence E. *Firewall: The Iran-Contra Conspiracy and Cover-Up.* New York: W.W. Norton, 1997.

Warner, Michael, ed. *Central Intelligence: Origin and Evolution.* Washington, DC: Central Intelligence Agency, 2001. The Web version, which is full-length (and used for this work) may be accessed at www.odci.gov/csi/pub.html.

———. *The CIA Under Harry Truman.* Washington, DC: Central Intelligence Agency, 1994.

Warner, Roger. *Shooting the Moon: The Story of America's War in Laos.* South Royal, VT: Steerforth Press, 1996.

Weber, Ralph E., ed. *Spymasters: Ten CIA Officers in Their Own Words.* Wilmington, DE: Scholarly Resources Books, 1999.

Weigley, Russell F. *The American Way of War.* New York: MacMillan, 1973.

West, Nigel. *The Third Secret: The CIA, Solidarity and the KGB's Plot to Kill the Pope.* London: HarperCollins, 2001.

Wicker, Tom. *One of Us: Richard Nixon and the American Dream.* New York: Random House, 1991.

Wise, David, and Thomas B. Ross. *The Espionage Establishment.* New York: Random House, 1967.

Woodward, Bob. *VEIL: The Secret Wars of the CIA, 1981–1987.* New York: Simon and Schuster, 1987.

Yergin, Daniel. *Shattered Peace.* Boston: Houghton Mifflin, 1977.

JOURNAL ARTICLES

Anderson, Elizabeth E. "The Security Dilemma and Covert Action: The Truman Years," 11 *International Journal of Intelligence and Counterintelligence* 4 (Winter 1998–1999): 403–27.

Aspin, Les. "Covert Action: Questions to Consider," 6 *First Principles* (May 1981): 9–11.

Barrett, David M. "Congress, The CIA, and Guatemala," 45 *Studies In Intelligence* 10 (Winter–Spring 2001, Unclassified Edition): 23–30.

Barry, James A. "Managing Covert Political Action: Guideposts From

Bibliography

Just War Theory," 36 *Studies In Intelligence* 5 (Fall 1992, Unclassified Edition): 19–30.

Berkowitz, Bruce D., and Allen E. Goodman. "The Logic of Covert Action," *National Interest* 51 (Spring 1998): 38–46.

Bernstein, Carl. "The Holy Alliance," *Time* 24 February 1992, 28.

Bittman, Ladislav. "The Use of Disinformation by Democracies," 4 *International Journal of Intelligence and Counterintelligence* 2 (Summer 1990): 243–61.

Bloomfield, Lincoln P., Jr. "The Legitimacy of Covert Action: Sorting Out the Moral Responsibilities," 4 *International Journal of Intelligence and Counterintelligence* 4 (Winter 1990): 525–37.

Bruemmer, Russell J., and Marshall H. Silverberg. "The Impact of the Iran-Contra Matter on Congressional Oversight of the CIA," 11 *Houston Journal of International Law* 1 (Fall 1988): 219–43.

Bukovsky, Vladimir. "Secrets of the Central Committee," *Commentary* (October 1996) at www.commentarymagazine.com/9610/bukovsky.html (accessed 28 December 2000).

Chomeau, John B. "Covert Action's Proper Role in US Policy," 2 *International Journal of Intelligence and Counterintelligence* 3 (Fall 1988): 407–13.

Cinquegrana, America R. "Dancing in the Dark: Accepting the Invitation to Struggle in the Context of 'Covert Action,' the Iran-Contra Affair and the Intelligence Oversight Process," 11 *Houston Journal of International Law* 1 (Fall 1988): 177–209.

Cline, Ray S. "Covert Action as a Presidential Prerogative," 12 *Harvard Journal for Law and Public Policy* 2 (Spring 1989): 357–70.

Cogan, Charles G. "Covert Action and Congressional Oversight: A Deontology," 16 *Studies in Conflict and Terrorism* 2 (April 1993): 87–97.

Cohen, William S. "Congressional Oversight of Covert Actions," 2 *International Journal of Intelligence and Counterintelligence* 2 (Summer 1988): 115–62.

Colby, William E. "The CIA's Covert Action," *The Center Magazine* (March–April 1975): 71–80.

Collins, J. Foster, and B. Hugh Tover. "Sukarno's Apologists Write Again," 9 *International Journal of Intelligence and Counterintelligence* 3 (Fall 1996): 337–57.

Damrosch, Lori Fisler. "Covert Operations," 84 *American Journal of International Law* (October 1989): 795–805.

Earl, Robert L. "A Matter of Principle," *US Naval Institute Proceedings* (February 1983): 30–36.

Fein, Bruce E. "The Constitution and Covert Action," 11 *Houston Journal of International Law* 1 (Fall 1988): 53–68.

Bibliography

Gasiorowski, Mark J. "The 1953 Coup D'Etat in Iran," *International Journal of Middle East Studies* 19 (1987): 261–86.

———. "The Qarani Affair and Iranian Politics," *International Journal of Middle East Studies* 25 (1993): 626–44.

Gavin, Francis J. "Politics, Power, and US Policy in Iran, 1950–1953," *Journal of Cold War Studies* 1 (Winter 1999): 56–89.

Godson, Roy, and James J. Wirtz. "Strategic Denial and Deception," 13 *International Journal of Intelligence and Counterintelligence* 4 (Winter 2000): 425–37.

Goodman, Allan E. "Does Covert Action Have a Future?" 18 *Parameters: The Journal of the US Army War College* (June 1988): 74–88.

Gorst, Anthony, and W. Scot Lucas. "The Other Collusion: Operation Straggle and Anglo-American Intervention in Syria, 1955–56," 4 *Intelligence and National Security* 3 (July 1989): 576–95.

Gustafson, Kristian C. "CIA Machinations in Chile in 1970: Reexamining the Record," 47 *Studies In Intelligence* 3 (2003, Unclassified Edition): 35–50.

Gunter, Michael M. "The Iraqi Opposition and the Failure of US Intelligence," 12 *International Journal of Intelligence and Counterintelligence* 2 (Summer 1999): 135–67.

Halperin, Morton H. "Decision-Making for Covert Operations," *Society* (March–April 1975): 45–51.

———. "Prohibiting Covert Operations," 12 *First Principles* 2 (April 1987).

Hitchens, Christopher. "Unlawful, Unelected, and Unchecked," 283 *Harpers* 1967 (October 1991): 59–64.

Holland, Max. "The Power of Disinformation: The Lie That Linked CIA to the Kennedy Assassination," 45 *Studies In Intelligence* 11 (Fall–Winter 2001, Unclassified Edition): 5–17.

Horton, John. "Reflections on Covert Action and its Anxieties," 4 *International Journal of Intelligence and Counterintelligence* 1 (Spring 1990): 77–90.

Hulnick, Arthur S. "United States Covert Action: Does It Have a Future?" 9 *International Journal of Intelligence and Counterintelligence* (Summer 1996): 145–54

Isenberg, David. "The Pitfalls of US Covert Operations," *Policy Analysis*, 118 (7 April 1989).

Johnson, Loch. "Covert Action and Accountability: Decision-Making for America's Secret Foreign Policy," 33 *International Studies Quarterly* (March 1989): 81–109.

———. "On Drawing a Bright Line for Covert Operations," 86 *American Journal of International Law* 2 (October 1989): 284–309.

Bibliography

Knott, Stephen F. "The Great Republican Transformation in Oversight," 13 *International Journal of Intelligence and Counterintelligence* 1 (Spring 2000): 49–63.

Laqueur, Walter. "The Future of Intelligence," 35 *Society* 2 (January 1988): 301–10.

Love, Richard A. "The Cyberthreat Continuum," *Beyond Sovereignty: Issues for a Global Agenda*. New York: Worth Publishers, 1999.

Manget, Fred F. "Presidential Powers and Foreign Intelligence Operations," 5 *International Journal of Intelligence and Counterintelligence* 2 (Summer 1991): 131–53.

O'Brien, Kevin A. "Interfering With Civil Society: CIA and KGB Covert Political Action during the Cold War," 8 *International Journal of Intelligence and Counterintelligence* 4 (Winter 1995): 431–56.

Onate, Benjamin F. "What Did Truman Say About CIA," *Studies In Intelligence,* Fall 1973 (unclassified article in an otherwise classified edition; unclassified article is in the possession of this author).

Peake, Hayden B. "Harry S Truman on CIA Covert Operations," 25 *Studies In Intelligence* 1 (Spring 1980): 31–41, and 97.

Perry, David L. "Repugnant Philosophy: Ethics, Espionage, and Covert Action," *Journal of Conflict Studies* (Spring 1995), at www.home.earthlink.net/~davidlperry/covert.htm (accessed on 28 December 2000).

Pforzheimer, Walter. "Remarks of Dr. Walter Pforzheimer," 11 *Houston Journal of International Law* 1 (Fall 1988): 143–48.

Pike, John. "The CIA Budget," Federation of American Scientists, at www.fas.org/irp/cia/ciabud.htm (accessed 7 August 2002).

Rindskopf, Elizabeth. "Intelligence Oversight in a Democracy," 11 *Houston Journal of International Law* 1 (Fall 1988): 21–30.

Ritchie, James. "Covert Propaganda in the Cold War," University of Wales Aberystwqyth: http://users.aber.ac.uk/scty34/50/coldprop.htm (accessed 4 July 2002).

Rivkin, David B., Jr. "Intelligence Oversight and Congress: Practical and Constitutional Considerations," 11 *Houston Journal of International Law* 1 (Fall 1988): 31–46.

Sayle, Edward F. "The Déjà Vu of American Secret Diplomacy," 2 *International Journal of Intelligence and Counterintelligence* 3 (Fall 1998): 399–406.

Shulsky, Abram N. "The Iran-Contra Affair and the Intelligence Oversight Process," 11 *Houston Journal of International Law* 1 (Fall 1988): 245–54.

Silver, Daniel B. "The Uses and Abuses of Intelligence Oversight," 11 *Houston Journal of International Law* 1 (Fall 1988): 7–20.

Simmons, Robert Ruhl. "Intelligence Policy and Performance in Reagan's First Term: A Good Record or Bad?" 4 *International Journal of Intelligence and Counterintelligence* 1 (Spring 1990): 1–22.

Snider, L. Britt. "Remarks of L. Britt Snider," 11 *Houston Journal of International Law* 1 (Fall 1988): 47–52.

Stafford, Thomas T. "Hidden in Plain Sight: Searching for the CIA's 'New Missions.'" 13 *International Journal of Intelligence and Counterintelligence* 2 (Summer 2000): 144–59.

Stern, Gary. "Covert Action and the Bush Administration," 15 *First Principles* 1 (February 1990): 4–5.

Strong, J. Thompson. "Covert Activities and Intelligence Operations: Congressional and Executive Roles Defined," 1 *International Journal of Intelligence and Counterintelligence* 2 (Summer 1986): 63–72.

Tenet, George J. "The CIA and the Security Challenges of the New Century," 13 *International Journal of Intelligence and Counterintelligence* 2 (Summer 2000): 133–44.

Treverton, Gregory F. "Covert Action: From 'Covert' to Overt," *Daedalus* 116 (Spring 1987).

Turner, Robert F. "Coercive Covert Action and the Law," 20 *Yale Journal of International Law* 2 (Summer 1995): 427–49.

———. "The Constitution and the Iran-Contra Affair: Was Congress the Real Lawbreaker?" 11 *Houston Journal of International Law* 1 (Fall 1988): 83–127.

Tuttle, Andrew C. "Secrecy, Covert Action, and Counterespionage: Intelligence Challenges for the 1990s," 12 *Harvard Journal for Law and Public Policy* 2 (Spring 1989): 523–40.

Warner, Michael. "Origins of the Congress for Cultural Freedom, 1949–50," *Studies In Intelligence* (1996, Unclassified Edition). The Web version, which is full-length (and used for this work) may be accessed at www.odci.gov/csi/studies/95unclass/Warner.html.

Weiss, Guy W. "The Farewell Dossier," *Studies In Intelligence* (1996, Unclassified Edition), located at www.odci.gov/csi/studies/96unclass/farewell.htm (accessed on 11 August 2002).

Willard, Richard K. "Law and the National Security Decision-Making Process in the Reagan Administration," 11 *Houston Journal of International Law* 1 (Fall 1988): 129–42.

NEWSPAPER / NEWSMAGAZINE ARTICLES

Adams, James. "All the Presidents' Methods," (London) *Sunday Times*, Overseas News, 9 February 1997, 1.

Bibliography

———. "Clinton Considers Covert Operations Against Haiti," (London) *Sunday Times*, Overseas News, 3 July 1994, 1.

Andrew, Christopher. "Focus Espionage: Apply the Test of Shame as It Has Its Uses, but Much of America's Covert Action Has Been Immoral and Counter-Productive," (London) *Sunday Telegraph*, 22 October 1995, 32.

Arkin, William M. "The Secret War: Frustrated by Intelligence Failures, the Defense Department Is Dramatically Expanding Its 'Black World' of Covert Action," *Los Angeles Times*, 27 October 2002. Accessed on the World Wide Web on 23 November 2002 at http://pqasb.pqarchiver.com/latimes/doc/224237991.html.

Associated Press. "Reagan Gave CIA Agents Wide Powers; Anti-Terrorism Orders Called License to Kill," *San Diego Union-Tribune*, 5 October 1988, A1.

———. "US Grab for Noriega Was Scrapped; Plan Dropped as Coup Fizzled, Officials Say," *San Diego Union-Tribune*, 9 October 1989, A1.

Baker, Russell W. "CIA: Out of Control," *The Village Voice*, 10 September 1991.

Bamford, James. "CIA Gets Billing Again in Nicaragua, as Covert Action Becomes the Norm," *Los Angles Times*, 5 October 1986, part 5, 1.

Barber, Lionel. "White House Puts the Blame on Congress," *The Financial Times* (London), Sect. 1, 3.

Bearden, Milt. "Lessons From Afghanistan," *New York Times*, 2 March 1998, A17.

Berkowitz, Bruce D. "Operation Backfire: Covert Action Against Milosevic Is Neither Secret nor Smart," *Washington Post*, 18 July 1999, B01.

Blum, William, and David N. Gibbs (trs.). "Les Révélations d'un Ancien Conseilleur de Carter," *Le Nouvel Observateur*, 15–21 January 1998 (located on www.gened.arizona.edu/gibbs/brerzinski_interview.htm, accessed 18 March 2002).

Brauchli, Christopher. "Best Kept Secrets Found in Newspapers," *Tampa Tribune*, 24 February 1996, 15.

Carver, George A. "Covert Action: It's Necessary but It Must Be Used Precisely," *San Diego Union-Tribune*, 16 August 1987, C-1.

DeWine, Michael. "Views of the Strike Against Libya," *New York Times*, 23 April 1986, A23.

Dobbs, Michael. "US Advice Guided Milosevic Opposition," *Washington Post*, 11 December 2000, A1.

Editorial. "Covert Action in Nicaragua?" *Christian Science Monitor*, 11 March 1982, 24.

———. "Change the CIA: End the Covert Action Role," *USA Today*, 18 September 1991, 10A.

Bibliography

————. "Let's Outlaw Covert Action Before It Destroys US, *New York Times*, 12 October 1989, A22.

————. "No Pentagon Propaganda," *USA Today*, 18 December 2002, A12.

————. "Restricting the President on Covert Action is Too Dangerous," *Washington Post*, 3 September 1988, A25.

Gerstenzang, James. "Reagan Reportedly Authorizes New Action," *Los Angeles Times*, 27 July 1988, Part 1, 5.

Getler, Michael. "Hill Panel Protests CIA Covert Plan; CIA Plan Draws Written Protest From Hill Panel," *Washington Post*, 25 July 1981, A1.

Godson, Roy. "Focus—Espionage: Dirty Tricks, Inc," (London) *Sunday Telegraph*, 22 October 1995, 32.

Goodman, Alan E. "Covert Action Is Overdue for a Cost-Benefit Analysis," *Los Angeles Times*, 21 October 1986, Metro 5.

Goodman, Melvin A. "CIA Covert Actions—An Overt Failure," *Christian Science Monitor*, 1 November 1996, 18.

Gordon, Michael. "Bush and Senators Meet on Coup that Failed," *New York Times*, 12 October 1989, A12.

Grier, Peter. "US Is Beefing Up Its Covert Activities," *Christian Science Monitor*, 19 March 1985, 20.

Hoagland, Jim. "The Costs of Covert Action," *Washington Post*, 19 October 1989, A27.

Hoffman, David, and John M. Goshko. "Administration Sought Funds Last Spring for Covert Action," *Washington Post*, 11 October 1989, A1.

Horrock, Nicholas M. "Senate Intelligence Panel Calls for a Law to Curb Covert Action as Implement of Foreign Policy," *New York Times*, 27 April 1976 (www.nytimes.com/library/national/042276realcia.html; accessed 4 July 2002).

Houston, Lawrence R. "Hillenkoetter's Lawful Resort to Covert Action," *New York Times*, 26 July 1982, A14.

Ignatius, David. "Innocence Abroad: The New World of Spyless Coups," *Washington Post*, 22 September 1991, C1.

Kennedy, William V. "A History of Covert Activities Backfiring," *Toronto Star*, 27 August 1987.

————. "Let's Outlaw CIA-Style Covert Action Before it Destroys US," *New York Times*, 27 June 1990, A22.

Lardner, George, Jr. "History of U.S-Greek Ties Blocked: CIA Opposes Disclosure of Proposed Covert Actions in '60s," *Washington Post*, 17 August 2001, A21.

————. "House Rejects an Effort to Cut Off Funds for Angola Rebels;

Bibliography

Bush Administration Is Urged to Drop Secrecy Surrounding CIA's Biggest Covert Aid Programs," *Washington Post*, 18 October, A30.

———. "Restrictions Approved on Covert Action; Bush Signs Revision of CIA Oversight," *Washington Post*, 16 August 1991, A22.

———. "Tighter Rein on Covert Action Urged," *Washington Post*, 5 May 1992, A23.

Leahy, Patrick J. "CIA, Covert Action, and Congressional Oversight," *Christian Science Monitor*, 31 March 1988, 13.

Lefever, Ernest W. "Don't Reject Covert Action," *USA Today*, 18 September 1991, 10A.

Loeb, Vernon. "Whatever America's Role Was in Chile That Fateful Day in 1973, Retired CIA Spy Jack Devine Knows the Truth," *Washington Post*, 17 September 2000, F1.

Los Angeles Times. "Bush Approved Covert Action by CIA to Halt Spread of Arms; Secret Finding Noted Change in Threat to US," reprinted in the *Washington Post*, 21 June 1992, A20.

Mathias, Charles McC., and Patrick J. Leahy. "Covert Aid to Angola?" *Christian Science Monitor*, 14 August 1986, 14.

McCarthy, Colman. "The Consequences of Covert Tactics," *Washington Post*, 13 December 1987, F2.

McClory, Robert. "Covert Action is Up to the President—not Congress," *Christian Science Monitor*, 1 June 1983, 23.

McManus, Doyle, and Robin Wright. "Covert Action Fails to Oust Haiti's Rulers," *Los Angles Times*, 16 September 1994, A8.

Nelson, Jack, and Ronald J. Ostrow. "CIA Reported Got OK to Spirit Suspects to US," *Los Angeles Times*, 21 February 1987, Part 1, 1.

Newsom, David, D. "Aiding Guerrillas Cannot Be Covert," *Christian Science Monitor*, 14 September 1987, 14.

———. "When Covert Action is Successful," *Christian Science Monitor*, 28 April 1983, 23.

Oberdorfer, Dan. "A Carefully Covert Plan to Oust Hussein," *Washington Post* (National Weekly Edition, 25–31 January 1993), 19.

Omang, Joanne. "Reagan Defends U.S. Right to Use Cover Activity," *Washington Post*, 20 October 1983, A1.

———, and Walter Pincus, "Security Experts Differ on Effects of CIA's Mining," *Washington Post* 21 April, 1984, A1.

Pallister, David. "US 'Abandoned Kurds to Iraq': An Inglorious Episode in American Relations With Baghdad," *The Guardian*, 26 October 1990 (accessed via Lexis-Nexis on 15 August 2002).

Phillips, David Atlee. "The CIA, Covert and Overt, Always Survives Its Critics," *Los Angeles Times*, 18 October 1987, Part 5, 3.

Bibliography

Pincus, Walter. "CIA Had a Hit List of 58 Guatemalans, in 1950s," *Washington Post*, 24 May 1997, A-4.

———. "CIA Proffers More Cloak, Less Dagger," *The Guardian* (London) 16 September 1997, 13.

———. "CIA Turns to Boutique Operations, Covert Action Against Terrorism, Drugs, Arms," *Washington Post*, 14 September 1997, A-06.

———. "Relaxed CIA Covert Action Rules Urged: Blue-Ribbon Panel Wants More 'Risk-Taking' Within Limits of the Law," *Washington Post*, 30 January 1996, A-13.

Risen, James. "Covert Plan Said to take Aim at Milosevic's Hold on Power," *New York Times*, 18 June 1999, 1.

———. "Documents Reveal CIA Guatemala Assassination Plots," *New York Times*, 24 May 1997, A11.

———. "Gingrich Wants Funds for Covert Action in Iran," *New York Times*, 10 December 1995, 1.

San Diego Union-Tribune. "Reagan Gave CIA Agents Wide Powers," 5 October 1988, A-1.

———. "U.S. Grab for Noriega was Scrapped," 9 October 1989, A-1.

Schorr, Daniel. "Fifty Years—Too Many?—For the CIA," *Christian Science Monitor*, 15 August 1997.

———. "How Kissinger, Nixon, and the Shah Rallied—Then Shrugged Off—An Uprising," *Washington Post*, 7 April 1991, D3.

———. "The Sad History of Covert Action Has Bred Caution," *Christian Science Monitor*, 25 October 1989, 19.

Shanker, Thom, and Eric Schmitt. "Pentagon Proposes Propaganda Push in Allied Nations," *New York Times*, 16 December 2002, A1.

Shogan, Robert. "Sizing Up the CIA in Cold War's Wake," *Los Angeles Times*, 19 March 1994, A-21.

Smith, R. Jeffery. "Critics 'Wrong,' CIA Chief Says; Deutch Defends Agency's Efforts to Combat International Terrorism. *Washington Post*, 6 September 1996, A21.

———. "Expansion of Covert Action Eyed." *Washington Post*, 13 September 1995, A7.

———, and Thomas W. Lippman. "White House Agrees to Bill Allowing Covert Action Against Iran," *Washington Post*, 22 December 1995, A27.

Southerland, Daniel. "CIA Running 'Lots' of Covert Action, but Not Subversion," *Christian Science Monitor*, 28 February 1980, 4.

Stone, I.F. "Loophole for Rogue Operations; Toothless Safeguards Allow Covert Action by Outsiders," *Los Angeles Times*, 30 August 1987, Part 5, 5.

Bibliography

Sullivan, Dan. "Review: The Cultural Cold War." www.startribune.com/stories/385/23182.html (accessed 18 December 2002).

Thomas, Evan. "Shadow Struggle," *Newsweek*, 14 October 2002, 29–31.

Turner, Stansfield. "CIA Covert Action at What Price?" *Christian Science Monitor*, 31 May 1984, 14.

Walcott, John, et al. "Covert Action: Reagan Ruling to Let CIA Kidnap Terrorists Overseas is Disclosed," *Wall Street Journal*, 20 February 1987, Section 1, 1.

Washington Post. "'There Never Was a Formal NSC Meeting,' on Iran Initiative: Vice President Bush's Response to Mary McGrory's Questions," *Washington Post*, 14 January 1988, A7.

Weiner, Tim. "CIA Spent Millions to Support Japanese Right in 50s and 60s," *New York Times*, 9 October 1994 (www.nytimes.com/library/national/100994real-cia.html).

Wicker, Tom. "'Covert' Means Fiasco," *New York Times*, 10 October 1989, A29.

———. "Not Covert, Not Smart, Not Right," *New York Times*, 2 August 1988, A19.

———. "The Price of Secrecy," *New York Times*, 10 September 1987, A31.

———. "The Trouble With Covert Action," *St. Petersburg Times*, 14A.

———. "Covert Action in Iraq: Call in the CIA and Cross Your Fingers," *New York Times*, 15 September 1996, Section 4, 3.

———. "US Plans to Oust Iran's Government Is an Open Secret," *New York Times*, 26 January 1996, A1.

Wise, David. "Another CIA Disaster," *New York Times*, 13 September 1996, A35.

———. "CIA Should Forget Covert Actions," *Cleveland Plain Dealer*, 16 September 1996, 9B.

Woodward, Bob. "Carlucci Launched CIA Operation in Yemen That Collapsed," *Washington Post*, 4 December 1986, A1.

———. "CIA Anti-Qaddafi Plan Backed; Reagan Authorizes Covert Operation to Undermine Libyan Regime," *Washington Post*, 3 November 1985, A1.

———. "U.S. Covert Influence Still Sought in Iran," *Washington Post*, 23 November 1986, A1.

———, and Vernon Loeb. "CIA's Covert War on Bin Ladin: Agency Has Had Green Light Since 1998, but Terrorist Proves Elusive," *Washington Post*, 14 September 2001, A1.

Wright, Robin. "Any Effort to Oust Iraqi President a Tall Order," *Los Angeles Times*, 2 March 1998, A-1.

———, and John M. Broder, "US Secretly Aids Anti-Terror Units," *Los Angeles Times*, 2 July 1989, A-1.

INDEX

Index

Index

Ford, 178; Johnson, 165;
Kennedy, 151–52, 153;
Nixon, 167–68, 172; presidents' opinion of truth of, 26–
27; Reagan, 193, 204,
253n32; and restrictions on
using DoD, 61; through
Presidential Findings, 93–94,
110–11, 178; Truman, 119,
120–21, 126, 128–30; truth
of, found by Church Committee, 3, 25–26
covert action, programs: as
alternative to military actions,
19–20, 23, 60, 149; bad press
about, xix, 226n8, 231n23;
under Bush, George H.W.,
216; under Carter, 185–92;
under Clinton, 51–54, 64–68,
218–19; compromise of, 40,
57, 65, 95, 98, 110, 127,
143–44, 175, 253n30; as
defense against Soviet Union,
41–42, 232–33n35; and
domestic media, 13–14; under
Eisenhower, 131–49; financing of, 14–15, 94–95; under
Ford, 178–81; and foreign
policy initiatives, 49–50, 51–
54, 56–57, 79, 102–3, 111; as
instrument of statecraft, 1–2,
19–22, 38, 47; under
Johnson, 159–65; under
Kennedy, 151–59; measure of
success of, 4–7; under Nixon,
167–77; peacetime versus
wartime, 60–61, 68; under
Reagan, 197–211; under
Reagan, amount of, 26, 131,
193, 241n22; summary of
post–World War II programs,

xviii–xix, 226n9; technologies
for, 66, 236n14; against
terrorism, 11–12, 87–89,
207–9, 214, 219–20, 238–
39nn28–29; during Truman
era, 113–29; during World
War II, 59, 79, 80, 132. See
also costs of covert actions;
myths of covert action by
CIA; paramilitary operations;
pitfalls of covert action;
political action programs;
under countries; under
presidents
Covert Action Planning Group
(CAPG), 104
Covert Action Policy Approval
and Coordination Procedures
(NSDD-159), 101, 196
Crisis Pre-Planning Group, 197
Cuba: Bay of Pigs operation, 25,
49, 98, 99, 140, 144, 152,
154–55, 159; and Eisenhower,
146–47; and El Salvador, 203;
involvement in Angola, 178–
80; and Kennedy, 154–56;
and Yemen, 189
Cuban missile crisis, 7
Cutler, Robert, 136
cyberterrorism, 86–89

Deaver, Michael, 203
deception operations, 71–72, 79–
81; faulty equipment to
hostile governments, 200–
201, 219–20; by Soviet
Union, 81, 238n18; during
World War II, 59, 79, 80,
237n17
"Deep Throat," 11
Defense Intelligence Agency, 68

Index

Department of Defense (DoD): congressional oversight of, 30; differences with Department of State during Eisenhower administration, 133; expense of operations, 63, 64; Iran hostage rescue operation as action of, 45; lack of authority to undertake covert action, 61, 67, 122; part played in approval and review of covert action, 135–36, 159, 168, 177, 184, 187, 215, 217; part played in covert action, 54, 60; reasons not assigned covert action missions, 59–62, 68. *See also* Central Intelligence Agency (CIA) advantages over Department of Defense (DoD) in covert action

Department of State. *See* State Department

Deputies Committee (DC), 215

Desert One. *See* Iranian hostage rescue operation

Deutch, John, 59, 64–67, 69, 235n11

Diem, Ngo Dinh, 43–44

Directorate of Operations (DO), xxi, xxiii, 67, 100, 105, 172, 186

"dirty tricks," covert action as, 38

disinformation programs, xvii, 77–79, 198

Dominican Republic, 147, 157–58, 160

Dornan, "B-1 Bob," 204

Double Cross operation, 80

Drug Enforcement Agency (DEA), 11, 106

Dulles, Allen, 121, 136, 145, 146, 148, 152, 154–55

Dulles, John Foster, 131, 138, 145

Eagle Claw operation. *See* Iranian hostage rescue operation

Egypt, 149

Eisenhower, Dwight D., xviii, 26, 131–49; in Africa, 145–46; and assassination plans, 132, 145–48, 246–47n34, 247n38; and covert action as alternative to war, 20, 149; and covert action programs set in place during Truman's time, 128–29; and Cuba, 146–47; and Dominican Republic, 147; and Guatemala, 133, 134, 138–40; and Indonesia, 83, 141–44, 146, 149; and Iran, 137–38, 140; and Japan, 140–41; and Middle East, 148–49; myth of not being in control of foreign policy, 131; security organization under, 134–37; and Tibet, 144–45; understanding of covert action, 48, 132

El Salvador, covert action in, 190–91, 203

Erskine, Graves B., 136

Ethiopia, 191

European labor unions, assistance to, xviii–xix, 5, 114, 120, 122

Executive Orders: EO 11905 (Ford banning assassinations), 43, 177–78, 208; EO 12036, 184; EO 12333 (1981), 40, 67, 69; EO 12333 (1981), tenets of covert action in, 13–15, 195–96. *See also* National Security Council Documents

Index

Iranian hostage rescue operation, 45, 98–99, 184, 207, 235n4

Iraq, 7, 84; covert action during Nixon administration, 173; deception operation during 1991 war in, 79; and Kurdish rebellion, 173, 174–77; support for during Reagan administration, 57

Isenberg, David, 154–55

Israel, and Iran, 16–17, 175

Italian Communist Party (PCI), 83, 116, 117, 120, 158, 159–60

Italy: CIA counter-program to communists in, 6, 20, 42, 83, 117–20, 158–60, 238nn20–21; covert political actions in, 6, 83, 115–20, 159–65, 238nn20–21; fears of Communist takeover in after World War II, 115–20

Jagan, Chedi, 157

Jandal, Shafik, 203

Japan: and Aum Shinrikyo, 86–87; covert political actions in, 6, 83, 140–41

Japanese Liberal Democratic Party, 140–41

Jefferson, Thomas, 28, 31

John Paul II, 188, 201

Johnson, Loch K., 72, 82, 185

Johnson, Lyndon B., 26, 53, 159–65; and British Guyana, 160; and Chile, 21, 156, 160, 165, 229n20; and Dominican Republic, 160; and Indonesia, 160; and Japan, 140; security organization under, 159

Johnson, U. Alexis, 83, 141, 156, 163–64, 238n20

journals, use of for "gray" propaganda, 76–77

Karabell, Zachary, 137

Kasten, Robert, 167

Kennan, George F., 113, 115, 116, 118, 121

Kennedy, John F., xviii, 151–59; assassination of, myth of CIA involvement in, xvii, 78; and assassination plans for foreign leaders, 147–48, 155–56, 233n40, 248n12; and Bay of Pigs operation, 25, 49, 98, 99, 140, 144, 152, 154–55, 159; and British Guyana, 157; and Chile, 21, 156–57, 248–49n14; congressional oversight of covert action, reduction of by, 98, 152; costs of covert actions during administration of, 34; and Cuba, other covert action programs in, 155–56; and Cuban missile crisis, 7; and direct leadership of covert action, 151–53; and Dominican Republic, 157–58; and Eisenhower covert action programs, 149; and Italy, 158; and Japan, 83, 140; and Laos, 20–21; security organization under, 151–53, 169; and South Vietnam coup, 43–44, 233n40; and Tibet, 158

Kennedy, Robert F., 49, 152, 169

KGB (Komitet Gozudarstevennoye Bezopasnosti), 127; disinformation programs against United States, xvii,

Index

77–78, 198, 225n5; Trust,
The, deception program, 81,
238n18
Khmer Rouge (KR), 210
Kissinger, Henry A., 44, 167–77,
248n8; and Angolan civil war,
179–80; and positions held in
Nixon administration, 168;
understanding of covert
action, 48
Komitet Gozudarstevennoye
Bezopasnosti (KGB). See KGB
(Komitet Gozudarstevennoye
Bezopasnosti)
Kurds, 48, 173, 174–77

Lake, Anthony, 48, 52
Lansdale, Edward, 128
Laos, 20–21, 62, 85, 156, 238n23
Lebanon, 148; terrorist acts in
against U.S., 207–8,
254nn41–42
legal aspects of covert action, 13–
17, 60–61, 122, 123; dissent
about legality of, 16; illegality
of, 18–19; illegality of under
international law, 19, 31–32,
230–31n18; undemocratic,
19, 23
legal scrutiny of covert actions,
35–36, 105, 111, 196
Lethal Finding, 110
Liberal Democratic Party, Japan,
83
Libya, 209
Love, Richard A., 87
Lovett, Robert, 121
Lowenthal, Mark, 5, 60
Lumumba, Patrice, 43, 145–46,
148, 245n4, 246–47n34
Lymnitzer, Lyman, 152

Madison, James, 31
Magsaysay, Ramón, 128
Mao Tse-Dong, 143
Marshall, George C., 115, 121
Marshall Plan, 50, 119, 121
Masjumi Party, Indonesia, 141
McCarthyism, 125
McCone, John, 152
McNamara, Robert S., 151
Meese, Edwin, 203
Memoranda of Notification
(MON), 93, 104. See also
Presidential Findings
Meyer, Cord, 179
Millis, John, 59
Mitchell, John, 169–70
MI-6. See British Secret Intelli-
gence Service (BSIS)
Mondale, Walter, 183, 190
Monroe, James, 23, 31
Morrison, James, 143
Mossadegh, Mohammad, 6, 127,
137, 140
Most Favored Nation status, 199
MPLA (Popular Movement for
the Liberation of Angola),
179–80
Mujahedin, 42, 189, 206
Murphy, Walter F., 91
myths of covert action by CIA,
23–45, 221, 230n6; assassination of John F. Kennedy, xvii,
78; assassinations of foreign
leaders, xvi, 42–45, 78, 157–
58, 173, 198, 233n40; CIA
exists only to run covert
action programs, 32–34,
231n19; CIA independent of
president's control ("rogue
elephant"), xvi–xvii, 3–4, 24–
28, 34–37, 100, 110–11, 151,

Index

Index

Index